London's Disused Railway Stations
The East End

J. E. Connor

Capital Transport

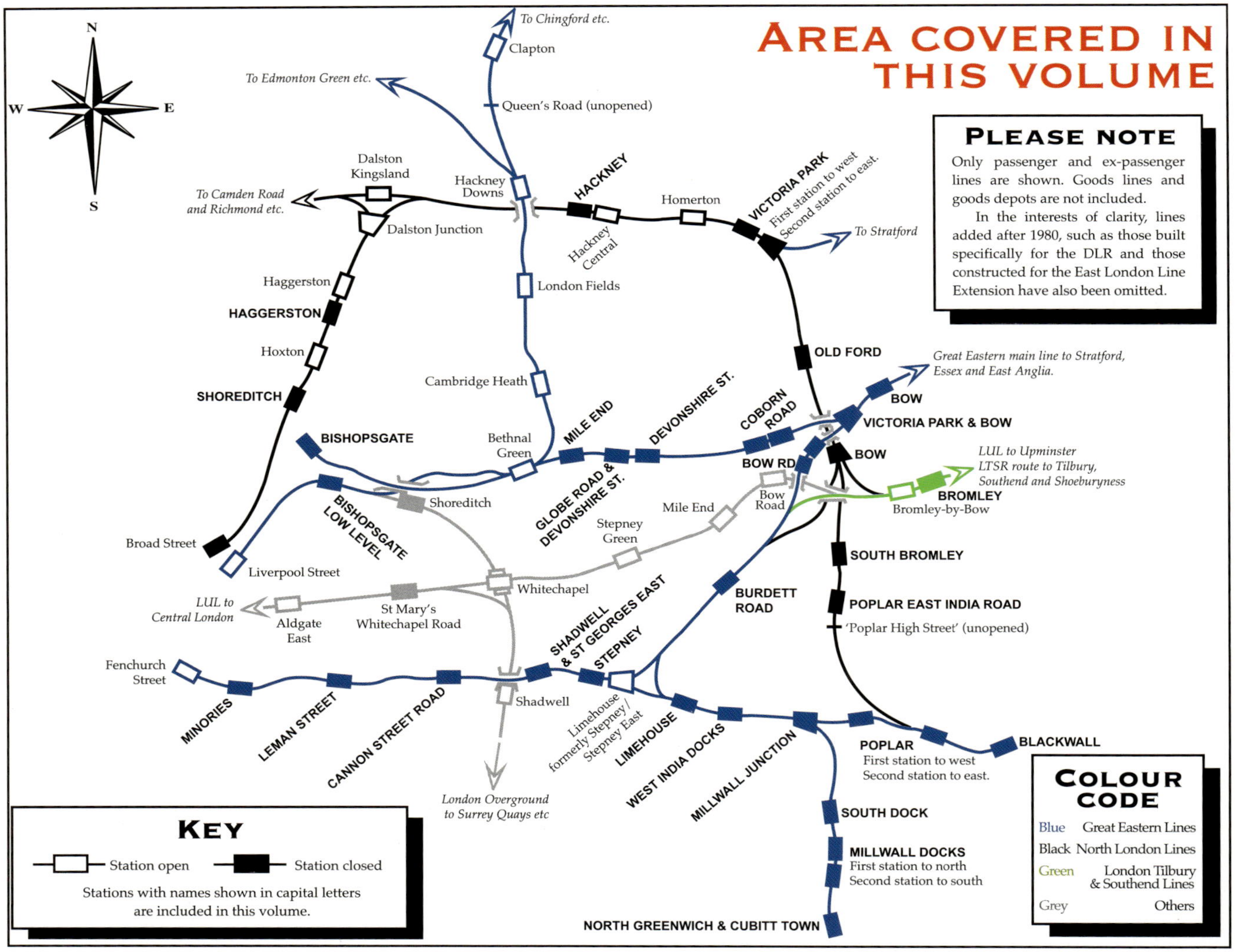

PHOTO CREDITS

I Baker: 157, 165, 173 (bottom).
T. Baker: 68 (top right).
B. Blackwell: 66 (top left)
Britain From Above: 30, 55, 172.
British Rail: 8, 13 (top), 17 (bottom).
R Carpenter: Railway Photographs: 132(both).
H.C. Casserley: 42 (all), 43 (top), 147 (both).
R.A.P. Cogger: 90 (top and middle), 98 (bottom), 146 (bottom).
L. Collings: 66 (top right), 99 (both), 100 (top left), 134.
J.E. Connor: 9 (bottom), 14 (bottom), 15 (bottom), 19 (all), 20 (both), 21 (both), 28, 29 (bottom), 32, 44 (all), 57 (both), 58 (all), 59 (both), 60 (all), 66 (bottom), 67 (all), 68 (top left and bottom), 70 (both), 71, 76 (bottom), 77 (top left and bottom), 78, 85 (bottom), 92 (both), 93 (both), 101 (both), 102 (both), 126 (bottom), 127 (both), 128 (both), 129 (all), 135 (both), 136 (top two), 139 (right), 149 (both), 150 (both), 151 (both), 152 (top), 153 (both), 159 (all), 160, 162 (bottom), 163, 164 (both), 166, 168 (both), 171 (all), 173 (top), 175, 176.
J.E. Connor collection: 9 (top), 13 (bottom), 33, 38 (all), 46, 54, 56, 62, 65 (right), 77 (top right), 79, 81, 85 (top), 88 (both), 100 (top right), 103, 104, 105, 116, 118 (top and bottom), 119, 120, 121 (bottom), 122, 123 (bottom), 130, 136 (bottom), 137, 139 (top left), 148 (bottom), 174.
E.A. Course: 148 (top).
A.W. Croughton: 145 (both), 146 (top).
J. Downing collection: 156.
R A Gillham: 65 (left bottom).
Great Eastern Railway: 53 (top), 74, 75, 76 (top), 121 (top), 155.
Hackney Archives: 162 (top).
Illustrated London News: 6.
A. A. Jackson: 29, 90 (bottom), 91 (top), 126 (top).
A. A. Jackson collection: 170.
D. Lawrence: 26.
Lens of Sutton Association: 48, 117, 118 (middle), 124 (both), 125 (both).
Locomotive & General Railway Photographs: 113 (both), 114.
London Metropolitan Archives: 25, 143 (top).
London & North Eastern Railway: 15 (top), 16 (both), 17 (top), 31, 39, 40 (both), 41 (both),
43 (bottom), 86, 143 (bottom), 144 (both).
K. A. C. R. Nunn: 14 (top), 50, 51 (both), 108, 110 (top), 111 (top), 123 (top).
J. S. Phillips: 91 (bottom).
J. S. Phillips collection: 97 (both).
T. R. Powel: 89, 98 (top), 111 (bottom), 112 (both).
Tower Hamlets Local History Library: 34, 37, 53 (bottom), 65 (top left), 110 (bottom), 133 (both).
B. Ward: 4.

Contents

Published by Capital Transport Publishing
www.capitaltransport.com

Printed by Parksons Graphics

Title page: The former North London Railway station at Shoreditch looking north from the old up No 1 Lines platform in 1968.

Introduction

In this book, I will be looking at the various passenger stations within the inner East End of London which have fallen into disuse. Their reasons for closing have varied, but they have all now slipped into history.

When I first became interested in the subject back in the mid-1960s, there were lots of abandoned stations in Greater London, and it seemed very unlikely that any of these would be revived. However, the 1980s saw the start of a national trend whereby some stations which had been closed for many years were rebuilt and brought back into use by British Rail. Of these, Homerton, Hackney and Kingsland were on the North London Line and new platforms were erected on the sites of their predecessors. Because of this, I do not feel that these stations can be described as being closed, because they are now very much in use again, albeit completely rebuilt. The exceptions to this rule are stations which are now served by Light Rail, namely Shadwell & St George's East and Poplar East India Road and these have both been included.

There were also two stations within the area which were constructed, or partially constructed, but never opened. The earliest of these was located on the North London line and stood on the south side of Poplar High Street. It was built between May and July 1851 but, being unfinished when inspected by the Board of Trade, it was not sanctioned to open. The work was later completed, but there were other problems, not concerning the station itself, and when the line linking Bow with Poplar was opened, it was used by coal and goods trains only. Passenger services were eventually introduced in 1866, but these served the new station at Poplar East India Road and the original remained unused. It was still standing eleven years later, as in December 1877 the North London Railway decided to convert it into living accommodation for the foreman of the company's hydraulic works, which stood nearby. As it remained unopened, the station does not seem to have been positively identified on any maps, although a building which seems to be a likely contender, is shown on the First Edition 1:2500 Ordnance Survey, but had gone by 1894.

There is no mystery regarding the other unopened station however. It was located on the Great Eastern Railway between Hackney Downs and Clapton and was to be named Queen's Road or "Queensdown Road". According to H V Borley, work started in 1875 and was abandoned twenty years later. Its two platforms were positioned on the north side of Downs Road, immediately north of Hackney Downs tunnel, but it is thought that no buildings were ever erected, so these remained empty. The only exception was a signal box, which stood at the London end of the up platform, close to the tunnel mouth. The platforms remained, overgrown and minus their coping, for many years, but eventually disappeared around 1965.

To me, the inner East End covers the present London Boroughs of Tower Hamlets and Hackney, so these are the districts which I have featured. I know that the term "East End" is often used these days to describe anywhere in east London, including places which were part of Essex until the formation of the GLC in the 1960s, but here I am concentrating on the areas immediately east of the City.

The stations included were on lines once owned by the Eastern Counties, Great Eastern, London & Blackwall, London Tilbury & Southend and North London Railways.

It would be impossible to give detailed histories of each company within the available space, but suffice to say that the Eastern Counties became part of the Great Eastern Railway in 1862 and until 1844 had a non-standard track gauge of 5ft.

Another line with the same gauge was the rather quirky London & Blackwall, which opened in 1840 but, because of possible fire risks employed cable haulage until 1849. The reason for this being that parts of the route adjoined docks, and the sparks emitted by steam locomotives could easily have ignited the sailing ships moored nearby.

Eventually changes were made to improve safety and locomotives took over from the stationary winding engines in 1849, when the track gauge was narrowed slightly to the standard four-feet eight and a half inches.

The London & Blackwall, which was once nicknamed "The Fourpenny Rope" because of its mode of traction and price of a second class ticket, therefore became a conventional railway and was leased to the Great Eastern in 1866.

Part of the LBR network was the equally quirky Millwall Extension Railway, which operated a passenger service between Millwall Jct on the Blackwall line and a station at the southern tip of the Isle of Dogs, which was named North Greenwich. Again it passed through dock areas and the fear of lineside fires was taken so seriously that horses were used as motive power for most of the route until 1880. Locomotives were then introduced throughout, but as the line was subjected to severe weight restrictions, these had to be very small.

From the branch terminus, passengers could join a ferry, which took them across the Thames to Greenwich itself, although the ferries were later withdrawn following the opening of the nearby foot tunnel.

The London Tilbury & Southend Railway also features in the book, but only because one of its stations, Bromley was resited from one side of the road to the other. Although I have avoided stations which have since been revived, I have included resitings as the original locations have indeed fallen into disuse.

The North London started operation in 1850, when a passenger service was introduced between Islington and Fenchurch Street on the London & Blackwall. The line had been promoted to link the London & Birmingham Railway (soon to become part of the London & North Western Railway) with the docks around Poplar and it was intended primarily for goods traffic. It was originally known as the East & West India Docks & Birmingham Junction Railway, but changed its name to the more appropriate "North London Railway" in 1853.

The NLR was a very successful undertaking and its booming traffic soon outgrew the facilities available at Fenchurch Street. It therefore built a new line into its own City terminus at Broad Street and brought it into use in 1865.

At the time of writing, a series of books providing detailed histories of all NLR stations, both open and closed, is currently being prepared by the North London Railway Historical Society and will be published in due course.

The North London was worked by the London & North Western Railway from 1909 and was absorbed by the larger company in 1922. A year later, the LNWR became part of the London Midland & Scottish Railway, along with the London Tilbury & Southend, which had been taken over by the Midland Railway in 1912.

The 'Railway Grouping' of 1923 also brought an end to the independent existence of the GER, which became part of the London & North Eastern Railway. Both the LMSR and the LNER continued to function until 1948 when the country's network of lines was nationalised and became part of British Railways.

J. E. Connor, Colchester, August 2018

Brush Type 2 A1A-A1A No D5507 is seen emerging from Hackney Downs tunnel and passing the unopened platforms of Queen's Road station, whilst electrification work was under way. The signal box is visible on the left, adjoining the tunnel mouth.

Bishopsgate (Terminus)

Opened as Shoreditch (Eastern Counties Railway): 1st July 1840.
Renamed Bishopsgate (Eastern Counties Railway): 27th July 1846.
Closed (Great Eastern Railway): 1st November 1875.
Site subsequently used to accommodate goods depot which opened 1st January 1881.
Goods depot closed after fire damage (British Railways Eastern Region): 5th December 1964.

Bishopsgate station was opened as 'Shoreditch' by the Eastern Counties Railway in 1840 and stood on viaduct to the east of Shoreditch High Street. Prior to its completion ECR trains ran to and from a temporary terminus at Devonshire Street, Mile End and although this was subsequently used as a through station, it closed soon after. *(See page 33)*

Along with the viaduct, Shoreditch terminus was designed by the engineer, John Braithwaite, but it was hampered from the outset by being constructed on a fairly restricted site with little room for expansion. The station comprised a pair of platforms, with one designated for departures and the other for arrivals.

The station was provided with four tracks, but only the outer roads were served by platforms, as the others were used to accommodate empty carriages. There was no pointwork beneath the overall roof, but the tracks were linked at either end by turnplates.

In September 1840, the Northern & Eastern Railway was opened between Broxbourne and Stratford and came to an arrangement with the ECR so that they could use Shoreditch as their London terminus. This brought additional strain on the station's limited capacity and within a short while it became apparent that its facilities were fast becoming inadequate. The advent of the line serving North Woolwich resulted in yet more traffic, so a further departure platform and booking office were added on the north side of the site in 1847. These were beyond the limits of the original train shed. Various other changes took place around the same time, including the widening of the 1840 departure platform and lengthening of the overall roof.

In 1862, both the ECR and the N&ER were absorbed by the newly formed Great Eastern Railway, then, two years later, Parliamentary authority was received to construct a line which would branch off near Bethnal Green and descend into a replacement terminus at Liverpool Street.

In the opposite direction, new routes were being built to link Bethnal Green with Walthamstow and Enfield and, until Liverpool Street was ready, these would place more pressure on Bishopsgate. To accommodate the anticipated extra traffic, additional platform accommodation was squeezed into the 1847 extension,

The interior of the station, as depicted in the *Illustrated London News* of 21st December 1850. Above the platforms rose an overall roof, which was fabricated from corrugated iron and constructed in three sections. That in the centre was the widest, with a span of 36ft, whilst those on either side each had a span of 20ft 6ins. The roof was badly damaged in a storm on the night of 26th/27th December 1852 and had to be replaced.

north of the site, and brought into use in 1872. This part of Bishopsgate was referred to as the "Woolwich station" or the "North station".

Whilst these were being constructed, work on the Liverpool Street extension continued and on 2nd February 1874, it became possible to open part of the new station. Understandably this could not handle all the traffic from the outset, so some trains continued to use Bishopsgate until 1st November 1875. From this date Liverpool Street became fully operational and the old terminus was closed.

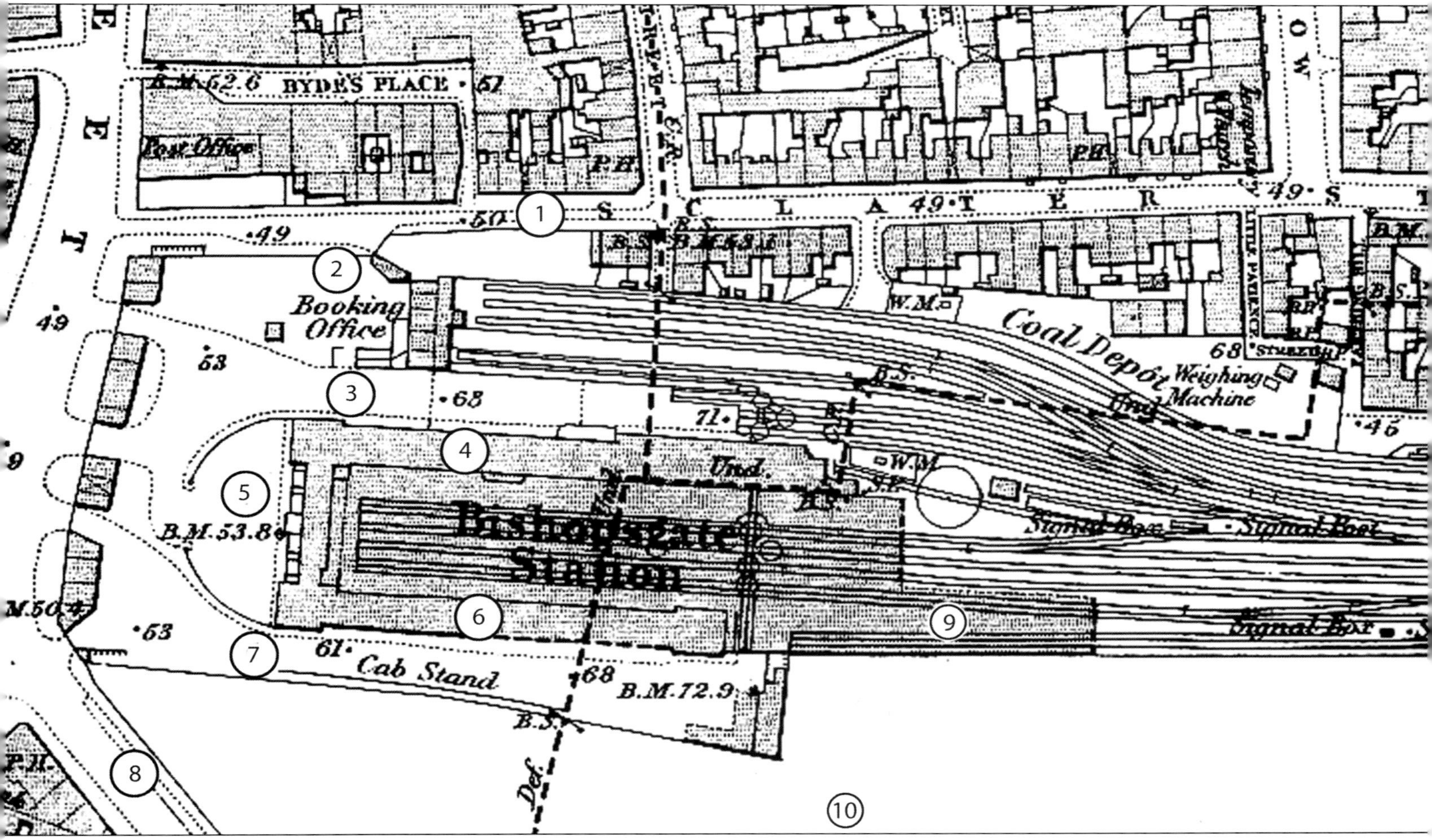

Enlarged Extract from the 1st Edition 1:2500 Ordnance Survey map, showing the location of Bishopsgate terminus and its layout in 1872.

1. Sclater Street.
2. The 'Woolwich' or 'North Station'.
3. The departure side approach road / carriageway.
4. 1840 station departure platform.
5. 1840 station entrance to offices.
6. 1840 station arrival platform.
7. 1840 station arrivals side approach road / carriageway.
8. Commercial Street.
9. Additional arrival platform, converted from a former ticket platform and brought into use in 1847. The viaduct was widened in 1853 so this platform could be enlarged and provided with a bay as seen here.
10. Site cleared for Liverpool Street extension works.

A little to the east of the station, the up line split to provide an extra track to serve two ticket platforms, although these do not appear here. Incoming trains would stop at one of these before arriving at the terminus itself, so that inspectors could check and collect tickets from the passengers. The furthest platform was located east of Vine Street, whilst the closest stood east of Wheler Street. This ceased to serve its original purpose in 1844 and three years later was converted into the additional arrival platform, which is shown as No 9 on the OS map extract reproduced above. North of Sclater Street lay the notorious slum district known as 'The Old Nichol', which was infamous as a hive of criminality and gave the area a bad reputation. This deterred some passengers from using the station as they felt unsafe and was serious enough for the ECR company minutes to record that some of the men employed on construction had to be provided with *"firearms and ammunition."* The 'Old Nichol' inspired the Arthur Morrison book *'A Child of the Jago'* and was described in 1846 as *"a sort of receptacle for pickpockets, housebreakers and prostitutes..."*

Above: The exterior of Bishopsgate station, viewed from Shoreditch High Street around 1865, showing the frontage which was designed by the architect Sancton Wood. Public access was by means of the two stairways or the sloping approaches on either side.

Left: Second class half ticket from Bishopsgate to Lea Bridge issued on 23rd May 1863.

Although regular passenger trains ceased to serve Bishopsgate terminus after 1st November 1875, it has been stated that a few relief workings used the station after closure. After this the station was demolished and its site redeveloped as a goods depot. This opened on 1st January 1881 and was subsequently enlarged. It remained in use until December 1964, when it was gutted in a disastrous fire which resulted in two deaths. The buildings were demolished, leaving just the viaduct and some of the accommodation at street level. A section around the forecourt was listed in 1979 and the 1840 viaduct between Wheler Street and Brick Lane was listed in 2002. Another section was removed however and its site has been returned to railway use, accommodating the current London Overground station at Shoreditch High Street. Part of the old viaduct can be seen to the left of the new station entrance in the photograph which is reproduced here.

Bishopsgate (Low Level)

Opened (Great Eastern Railway): 4th November 1872.
Closed (Great Eastern Railway): 22nd May 1916.
Often referred to as 'Bishopsgate (Low Level)', although this name does not seem to have appeared on tickets.

When the Great Eastern Railway constructed its extension to Liverpool Street, it was decided to include a new station at Bishopsgate to cater for passengers who had previously used the old terminus.

The extension diverged from the existing formation at Tapp Street, Bethnal Green, then descended on a gradient of 1 in 70 and continued beneath the original lines, until it was below street level. The new Bishopsgate station was located at the foot of this incline.

Building the extension was a major task and it would clearly be a while before Liverpool Street was ready. Therefore, it was decided to open the low level platforms at Bishopsgate as soon as possible and use the station as a temporary terminus.

Much of the permanent way remained to be completed, but a pair of tracks on the north side of the formation were pressed into use and passenger services to and from the new station commenced on 4th November 1872.

Bishopsgate, or 'Bishopsgate (Low Level)' as it was often called, comprised a side platform and an island and these were protected by a glazed overall roof. This was supported on either side by the retaining walls and was located both east and west of the Commercial Street bridge. Adjoining the western end of the roof was a hipped roof building, which spanned above the tracks and contained the booking office. Passenger access to this was by means of two pathways which stretched along both sides of the line and linked Commercial Street with Norton Folgate.

A secondary booking office was subsequently erected near the main building on the north side of the station courtyard and, although details of this are scant, it is understood to have been used primarily to issue excursion tickets. The station also had a refreshment room, which was operated by the firm of Spiers and Pond, but little seems to be recorded about this and it is not known how long it was in use.

Initially Bishopsgate (Low Level) was served by trains using the new routes to Enfield and Walthamstow only, whilst other services continued to use the old terminus above.

After just over a year, the GER announced that Liverpool Street station was ready for opening and trains were extended into the City on 2nd February 1874.

Bishopsgate station was now fully functional, but its platforms only served the two Local lines and the Down Main. Soon after Liverpool Street opened, the GER began to consider erecting a platform to serve the Up Main, but lack of space made this difficult. However, eventually, it was decided that one should be provided, but built beyond the country end of the existing premises, east of the Wheler Street bridge. The plans for this were quickly approved and the new platform was opened on 8th May 1875.

Sited as it was, there was no possibility of providing an overall roof as at the main part of the station, so a ridge and furrow canopy was erected, similar to those employed on the Enfield and Walthamstow new lines. At its western end it was connected by stairway to Quaker Street and some of the GER minute books referred to the latest addition as "*the Quaker Street platform*".

The years that followed brought further changes, including the rebuilding of the "excursion" booking office, which by September 1882 was described as being "*worn out and in need of replacing by a permanent structure in keeping with the general character of the building*". With no known photographs it is difficult to assess what the work entailed, although the builder's estimate was £120.

The next development at the station was rather more significant and resulted in the addition of two more platforms.

For some time it had been planned to enlarge Liverpool Street and space was made within the basement of Bishopsgate goods depot for the provision of an extra pair of tracks. The formation remained dormant for a decade, but they were eventually laid and brought into use on 5th April 1891.

The two new Bishopsgate platforms were located east of Commercial Street and therefore required their own entrance. This was provided by adapting three existing arches on the north side of Commercial Street and fitting one of them out as a booking hall. This was known appropriately as the 'Commercial Street Office' and was indicated on tickets issued there by the initials 'C.S.O'.

As the nineteenth century drew to a close, the condition of the old overall roof began to be a cause of concern and the company decided to have it removed. It was taken down around 1902 but the company minutes regarding the new awnings are confusing and the contract appeared to be awarded to three different firms. Whether something was subsequently changed and not recorded is not known, but the replacement canopies on the down local and island platforms were of different designs, so they may have been erected independently of each other.

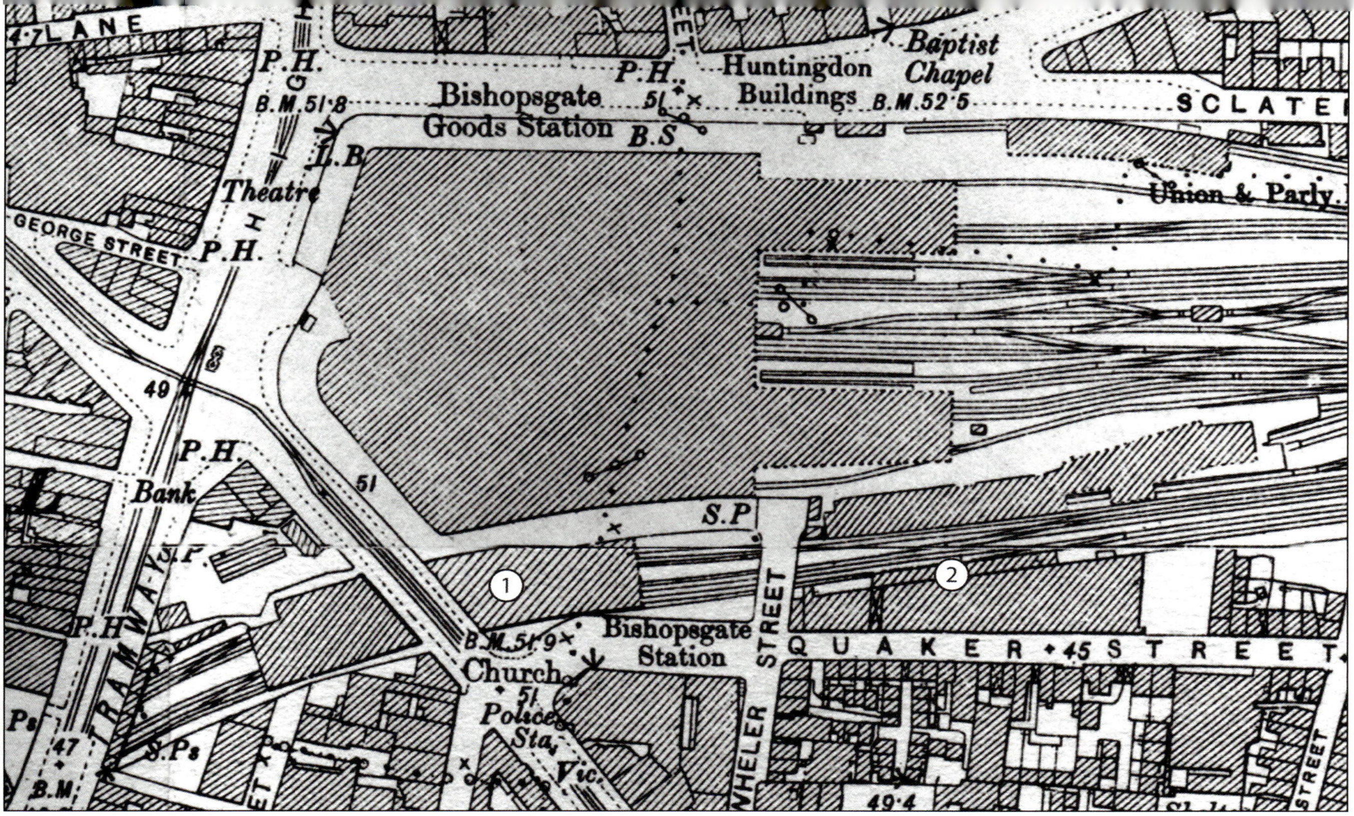

In fact, the canopy on the island is a bit of a mystery, as it employed a style last used by the GER in 1885 and was not of the type generally being erected in the early twentieth century. The ridge and furrow design was similar to that fitted to the 'Quaker Street platform', but it seems unlikely that there was a deliberate effort at matching the style, particularly as the awning protecting the Down Local side was of a different type.

No photographs have surfaced of the two 1891 platforms, which is perhaps not surprising as they were located within 'tunnel' under the goods depot, although daylight entered behind the up side. With the constant passage of trains, all steam hauled of course, the station was invariably engulfed in smoke and visibility was so bad that it was reputedly difficult at times to see one platform from the other.

Smoky or not, Bishopsgate suffered from the effects of tramway and 'bus competition as the twentieth century progressed and eventually, in May 1916, it was among a group of GER stations to be closed as a wartime economy measure. A number of the others subsequently reopened after hostilities ceased, but Bishopsgate fell into permanent disuse and work began on its demolition. Nevertheless some of its features, both obvious and obscure, have survived and can still be seen today.

Above: Enlarged extract from the 1:2500 Ordnance Survey map surveyed in 1893-4 showing Bishopsgate Low Level station, together with the large goods depot which occupied the site of the former ECR terminus.

1. The original Bishopsgate Low Level of 1872, with its platforms largely protected by an overall roof, positioned either side of the Commercial Street bridge.

2. The Up Through line platform of 1875. The stairway connection with the north side of Quaker Street can be seen a little to the left of the circled number 2.

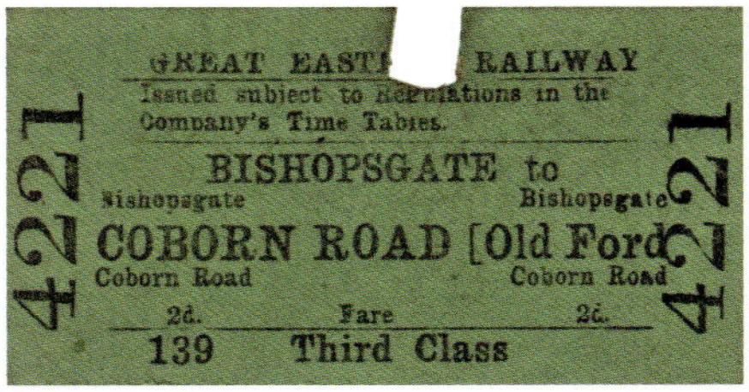

Right: GER tickets from Bishopsgate station.
(Top) Third class single to Coborn Road, issued from the main office on 5th March 1906.
(Bottom) Third class single to Liverpool Street, issued at the Commercial Street Office on 29th April 1904.

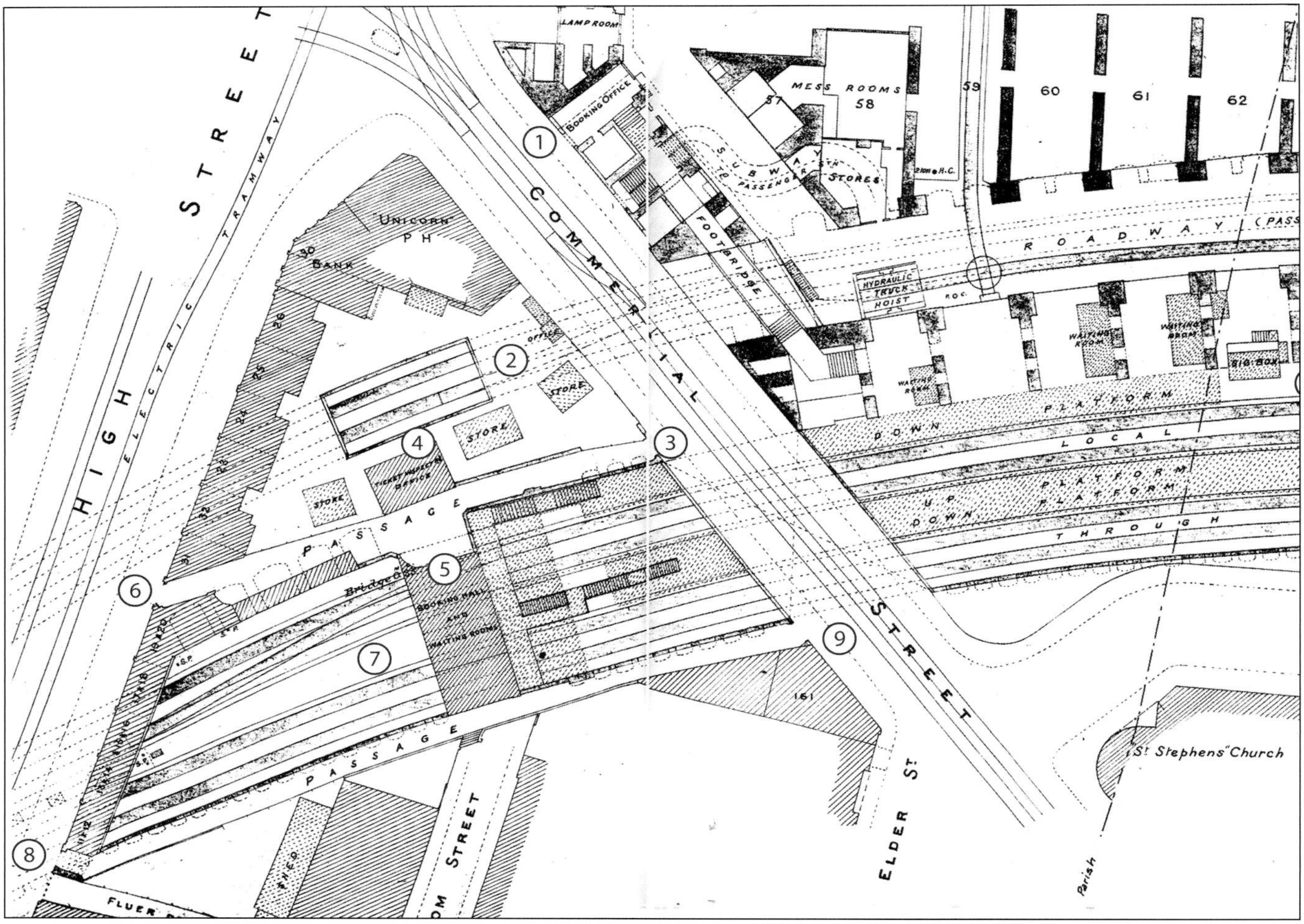

A Great Eastern Railway plan of Bishopsgate Low Level, dating from around 1910, showing the layout after the 1872 overall roof had been removed and replaced by conventional awnings.

1. Entrance to the 'Commercial Street Office' of 1891.
2. The new Suburban Lines of 1891 within 'tunnel' beneath Bishopsgate goods depot.
3. Commercial Street entrance to north side footway link with main booking office and Shoreditch High Street.
4. 'Ticket Inspector's Office'. It is understood that this was subsequently used as a parcels office.
5. The station building, accommodating both booking hall and waiting room, with galleried footbridge to rear.
6. Shoreditch High Street entrance to north side footway link with main booking office and Commercial Street.
7. Tracks linking Bishopsgate with Liverpool Street, opened 1874.
8. Shoreditch High Street entrance to south side footway link with main booking office and Commercial Street.
9. Commercial Street entrance to south side footway link with main booking office and Shoreditch High Street.

Above: The original part of Bishopsgate station, as it appeared after the overall roof had been removed around 1902-3. Unfortunately, the Commercial Street bridge is hiding the booking office building and associated gallery.

Right: The Up Through Line platform of 1875, looking east on an unknown date. From right to left the tracks are Up Through, Down Through, Up Local and Down Local. The two Suburban Lines of 1891 are within the basement of the goods depot on the left and therefore hidden. The ridge and furrow canopy was typical of its period.

Above: The 1.45pm train from Liverpool Street to Gallions passes the Up Through Line platform at Bishopsgate behind M15 Class 2-4-2T No 577 on 9th May 1912. The view includes what appears to be a station nameboard fixed to the retaining wall on the left, along with the eastern end of the canopy. Just ahead of this, although largely lost in the general murk, is a small gents' urinal and its attendant sign set at a right angle. This urinal was a later addition and was the only 'building' on the platform. To the right, behind the train, rises part of Bishopsgate goods depot.

Left: Access to and from the Up Through platform was by way of an obscure doorway on the north side of Quaker Street. This view, taken in the early 1970s, shows that although the opening had been partially bricked-up after closure in 1916, a pair of doors were fitted for staff use and emergencies. The platform seems to have been intended for alighting only, as no booking office was provided and its siting ruled out the possibility of a physical connection with the main station. The building to the left was a school, dating from the 1870s, whilst that to the right is a stable block erected by the GER in 1887 to accommodate up to 189 horses, employed around Bishopsgate goods depot. The former station doorway still survives at the time of writing, although the upper section with its iron lamp bracket has sadly long-gone. The school building was demolished soon after the photograph was taken, but the Quaker Street stables remain standing and in 2015 were used as business premises.

Opposite top: The 1907 gateway was recorded in this February 1939 photograph, which included the contemporary shops to its left and some earlier shops to its right. These dated from 1874 and were demolished soon after the view was taken.

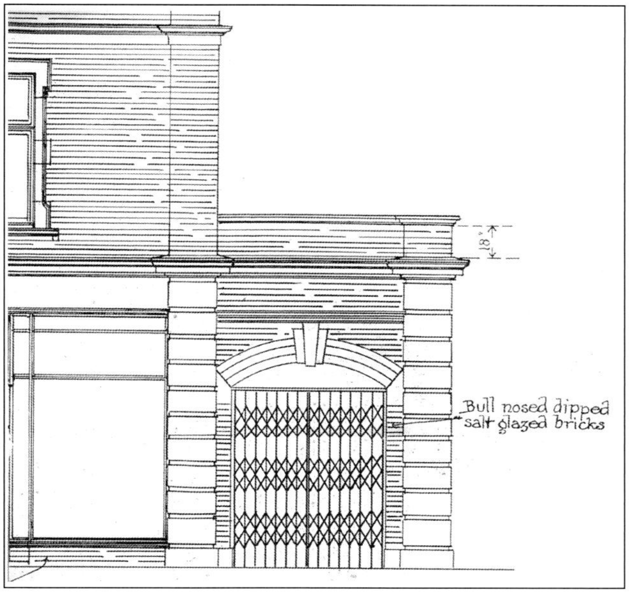

Above: Norton Folgate/Shoreditch High Street entrance to the northern passageway, leading to the main Booking Office, is seen in this February 1939 photograph, sandwiched between two groups of shops. Those nearest the camera, dated from 1874 and were demolished soon after the view was taken.

Right: This view, dating from the 1980s, shows the entrance gateway leading from Commercial Street to the southern footway. At this time the footway itself stretched for a short distance westward but was then blocked off. From their styling, it appears that the pillars on either side were erected in the 1870s and were therefore almost certainly original.

Two views taken from the former Down Local platform in June 1936. That at the top includes the Commercial Street bridge which still displayed evidence of the original overall roof, whilst the break in the retaining wall on the right indicates the site of the old booking office. On the other side of the bridge stands Bishopsgate South signal box, which dated from 1882. The lower photograph was taken from the eastern end and looks towards the bridge carrying Wheler Street, with the 'Quaker Street platform' of 1875 visible beyond. It is known that some of the arches backing onto the Down Local platform were fitted out as waiting rooms and this may have been the case with the pair on the left.

Above: The western end of the station site in 1939, showing the rear of the 1874 Shoreditch High Street shops, which were then undergoing demolition. At the top of the retaining wall on the right are the remains of the north side access footway, which was subsequently adapted to serve the BR Norton Folgate telephone exchange. The site of the Down Local platform, which had been demolished in 1938, also lies to the right. The erstwhile island platform had gone completely by this time, having lost its awning by 1925.

Below: The bulk of Bishopsgate goods depot overlooks the Commercial Street bridge, which still shows evidence of the old overall roof. The photo is undated, but was taken after the erection of overhead wires above the tracks below.

Left: A photograph from the 1950s showing part of the 1891 'Commercial Street Office' accommodation within the arches beneath the goods depot approach road, although sadly, the former entrance is out of shot to the left. The bricked up arch near centre had served as the station exit.

Below: Plan showing the layout of the 'Commercial Street Office':
1. Entrance.
2. Possibly parcels office, but unconfirmed.
3. Exit.
4. Landing at base of entrance and exit stairs and at top of stairs serving down side subway.
5. Subway serving down platform.
6. Footbridge linking landing with up platform.

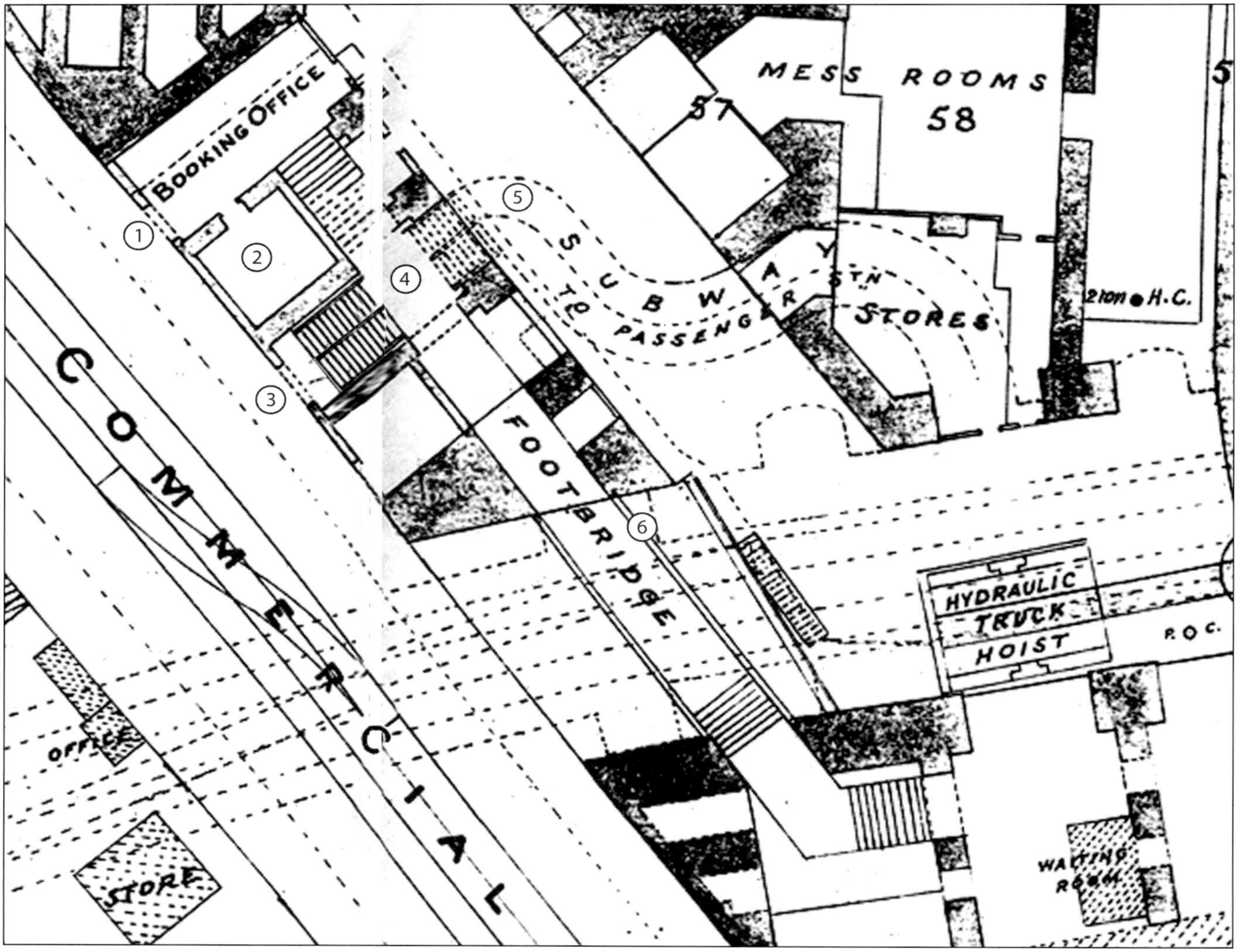

The remains of the 1891 'Commercial Street Office' in 2001.

Top: View from the landing, looking towards the former entrance stairs. The foot of the exit stairs is just visible near the centre.

Middle: The exit stairs viewed from the landing.

Bottom: The bricked-up archway, which once led to the passenger footbridge.

Above and below: The snaking subway, lined in white glazed bricks, which provided access to the erstwhile down Suburban platform.

Left: A view looking down the Quaker Street stairs in the 1980s. The corbels on either side indicate that it was once roofed. The stairs were subsequently renewed so that they could be used in an emergency and continued to survive in 2015.

Below: The old Up Through Line 'Quaker Street' platform of 1875, long since devoid of its awning and small gents' urinal, was put to good use in 2012, when the retaining wall arches were provided with displays to promote the Olympic Games, which were being held at Stratford. Above the top of the retaining wall stand the former Quaker Street Stables. Other traces of the station continue to survive, but these are less obvious. The 1872 gate pillars remain standing on the west side of Commercial Street, together with a short section of the southern footway which they served. A fragment of glazed brick wall on the east side of Shoreditch High Street marks where the 1907 entrance once stood, whilst down below a protruding section of retaining wall and areas of rendering show where the booking office 'bridge' had been. Parts of the 1891 Suburban platforms also remain and these can be glimpsed from passing trains.

Mile End

Opened (Eastern Counties Railway): c. June 1841.
Closed (Great Eastern Railway): 24th May 1872.

Mile End station was opened by the Eastern Counties Railway around June 1841 and was located on the west side of what is now Cambridge Heath Road. It comprised two narrow platforms and had a signal box on its up side. Parts of the structures were acquired second hand from the earlier station at Devonshire Street.

Little seems to have been recorded of the station in its early days, but it is known that in August 1850, the ECR Engineering and Traffic Committees agreed that the up platform should be extended by 50 feet and provided with an additional lamp. It was estimated that the work would cost £27 and the contract was awarded to the firm of Messrs. Piper, who subsequently completed it £4 within budget.

In September of the same year, Mile End station was reported to be in a *"dirty disreputable state"* and the stationmaster received a caution from company management.

Mile End was positioned on a busy stretch of line and delays sometimes resulted when trains stood at the platform longer than their allotted time. This was particularly the case when visibility was poor, so in January 1856, the Traffic and Locomotive Committee minutes recorded that *"Authority* (was to be) *asked for all up trains to pass through without stopping when fog is dense and notice of this* (was) *to be placed in the published timetable."*

Despite this it seems that delays continued to take place at the station, even in better weather conditions. One of the causes was deemed to be the loading and off-loading of parcels, so in March 1857, the Locomotive, Traffic and Permanent Way Committee announced that the practice would cease. Although seen as a problem, parcels traffic at Mile End appears to have been fairly light, so it probably caused little local aggravation when it was transferred to Bishopsgate instead.

Such minor operating difficulties aside, the station seems to have been well used and in May 1857 it was reported that the booking office required enlargement. The subject was still under discussion four months later, but it is not known whether the changes were actually made.

Some of the trains which called there appear to have been too long for the platforms, as in April 1858, the Engineering and Traffic Committees stated that a handrail was required on the parapet of the bridge immediately to its east. One was also thought to be needed near the foot of the stairs and, at the same time, it was decided to add ramps to the platform ends.

Whether these alterations were carried out is uncertain however, as in June 1861, the same committee recorded that the London ends of both platforms were to be *"stepped down"* and that the bridge parapet still needed a handrail.

During the spring of the previous year, a gate had been added to the top of one of the stairs *"to assist ticket collection"*. Such changes imply that the station continued to be busy, but it seems that the local authorities thought that it would be more convenient if resited to the east. A suggestion was made by the Clerk of Mile End Old Town that it should be relocated to Devonshire Street, presumably on or near the site of the original temporary terminus, but the company dismissed this as *"not acceptable"*.

Although in an excellent position, adjoining a main road, the station at Mile End was cramped and far from ideal. In 1912, the *Great Eastern Railway Magazine* published a letter from a member of staff which described the facilities: *"In course of my duties I had to go from the Mile End station which was an ugly wooden building, a short platform about 12ft. wide, no covering, and for waiting room a square box not much larger than a huge packing case, so that on wet days when an extra amount of passengers were present it was no unusual thing to get damp while waiting for the train. It seems strange to compare that station with the elaborate ones now, viz., Globe Road and Coborn Road."*

Enlargement of the Great Eastern suburban network finally put an end to the station, when, on 24th May 1872, it was replaced by Bethnal Green on a new site to the west. Apart from the seemingly inadequate facilities at Mile End, the change was necessary to fit in with the new route linking Bethnal Green with Hackney Downs and Stoke Newington, which opened three days later.

Mile End station, along with its signal box was presumably demolished soon after closure and any surviving remnants would have disappeared when the viaduct was later widened.

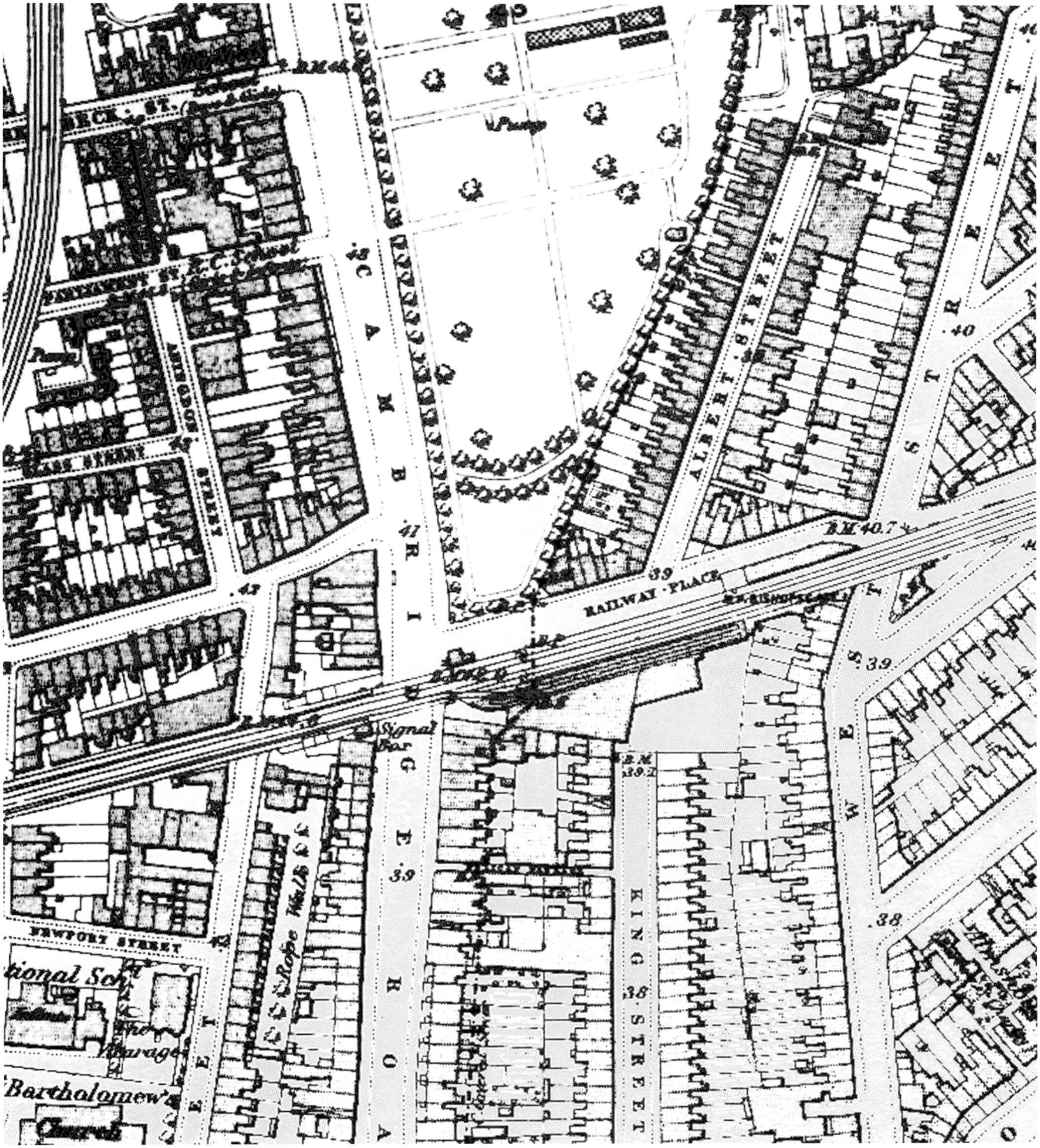

Extract from the First Edition 1:2500 Ordnance Survey map of 1872, showing the two platforms of Mile End station west of Cambridge Road, along with the signal box, which was located on the up side. The station is not shown with a name as it had already been closed and replaced by Bethnal Green Junction when the survey was made.

Globe Road & Devonshire Street

Opened (Great Eastern Railway): 1st July 1884.
Closed (Great Eastern Railway): 22nd May 1916.

When the route west of Bow Junction was being quadrupled, the Great Eastern Railway decided to construct a new station between Bethnal Green and Coborn Road. It was to have platforms on the Local lines only and entrances at both ends.

The widening of this stretch was carried out on the north side of the formation and the tracks and platforms were accommodated on viaduct. Construction of the station started in the second half of 1883 and was completed by the following June. Shortly before opening it was visited by the Board of Trade inspector, Major C.S. Hutchinson, and was described in his report as being of *"a very elaborate character"*.

The new tracks were brought into use on 29th June 1884 and the station followed on 1st July. The original lines on the south side became the Through lines and had no platforms.

The entrance at the London end was located on the east side of Globe Road, south of the line and was separated from the pavement by a pair of large cast iron gates. These were hung from substantial pillars, built of white stock bricks on a blue-brick plinth. The adjoining walls were of similar construction and were topped by a stone sill with a succession of iron railings. Above the gates, a globular gas lamp was suspended from a curved cast iron plate, which displayed the station's name in raised lettering.

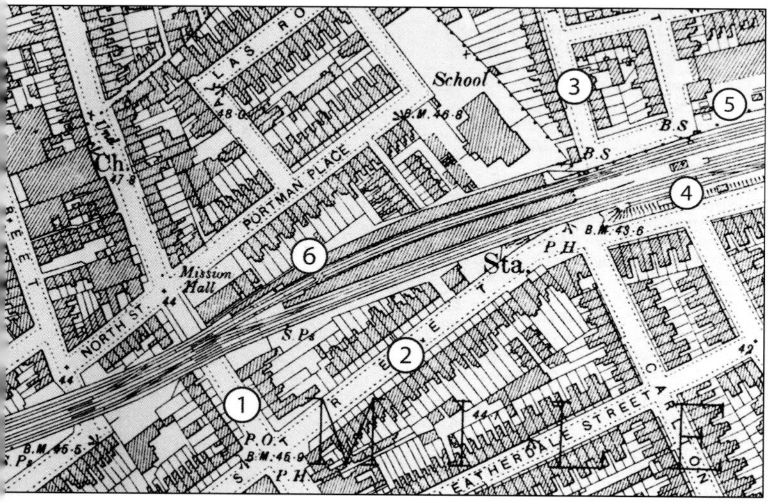

From here, passengers entered the booking hall, which was constructed within an arch and had a glazed wooden frontage. This was protected from the elements by a canopy which stretched the full width of the arch and carried "Globe Road and Devonshire Street Station" in gilt block lettering.

Up above, the platforms were covered by ridge-and-furrow awnings with sawtooth valancing, similar to those erected on the Bethnal Green - Lower Edmonton and Walthamstow lines which had opened in the previous decade. The awnings were supported by cast iron columns and brick rear walls, with terracotta coping, whilst wooden buildings on both sides provided the usual facilities.

The Devonshire Street entrance was similar to that at the opposite end, although the woodwork below the frontage glazing may have been slightly different. Again, a canopy displaying the station's name protected it and again, it was accessed by means of gates leading from the pavement. These were located on the north side of Devonshire Street and were similar to those already described, except that there were two pairs instead of one. Both the arches were dressed externally in a render of Portland cement and were provided with rusticated quoins by way of embellishment.

An additional gateway led from the west side of Morpeth Street onto a pathway, then beneath the viaduct to reach the Devonshire Street booking hall. This entrance followed a similar pattern as that in Globe Road, with a large cast-iron name sign and gas lamp.

The station had two signal boxes, with that named 'Globe Road' being located above the tracks towards the London end. The other box, known as Devonshire Street, stood a little to the east of the up platform and was constructed on infill between the new viaduct and the original formation.

In March 1894, it was agreed to close the Globe Road box and transfer its duties to Devonshire Street.

Apart from the loss of its western signal box, the station remained little altered for the rest of its existence and the only time it seems to have appeared in company minutes was when repairs or redecoration was needed.

There can be little doubt that the station was well used in its early days, but its fortunes were subsequently eroded by other forms of transport.

Extract from the 1:2500 Ordnance Survey map revised in 1893-4, showing the station and its immediate environment.
1. Globe Road. 2. Devonshire Street. 3. Morpeth Street. 4. Devonshire Street signal box 1884-1948, latterly known as Devonshire Street West.
5. Entrance to Devonshire Street goods depot. 6. Globe Road signal box (above tracks).

A view of the gates (far right) on the west side of Morpeth Street, looking beneath the bridge towards Devonshire Street at an unknown date. This is the only photograph known to exist which shows the station prior to closure. Globe Road & Devonshire Street was designed by the architect Edwin Wendover, who was also responsible for Coborn Road and various other GER stations, including March in Cambridgeshire.

With the opening of the Whitechapel & Bow Railway in June 1902, came a new station, named Stepney Green, which was located to the south, at the junction of Mile End Road and Globe Road. This may not have resulted in a drastic decline, but when the route was electrified in 1905, many who had previously used Globe Road & Devonshire Street were possibly wooed away by the fast and convenient Underground service. Three years later, electric tramcars were introduced to Mile End Road, although for a while these were operated by means of a troublesome experimental stud-contact system. Within a year it proved necessary to commence replacing this with standard equipment and, when work was completed, trams began to operate a regular service between Aldgate and Stratford.

The number of passengers using Globe Road & Devonshire Street fell sufficiently for it to be included in the list of GER closures brought about by the First World War and all trains ceased to call from 22nd May 1916. It remained intact for some years however and it is understood that there was talk of it reopening. However, in the spring of 1938, the platforms and their attendant buildings were demolished, leaving little at track level.

Down below, the former western entrance continued to display its cast-iron name sign until late 1964, when it was removed. Whether it was taken down for scrap or acquired by a collector is not known. Above the arch which once accommodated the Devonshire Street booking office, the legend 'Great Eastern Railway' still appeared in sunken lettering on a rendered cement panel, but although this survived for much longer, it eventually disappeared. Apart from a solitary pillar, nothing remains of the gates which led off Devonshire Street, or Bancroft Road as it later became, but the widening of the viaduct, which once accommodated the down platform, is still visible from Morpeth Street. The site of this can also be seen from a passing train, whilst a gap between what are now the Up Main and Down Electric lines indicate where the other platform once stood. The former gates on the east side of Globe Road also survive, but their original purpose has long-since been forgotten.

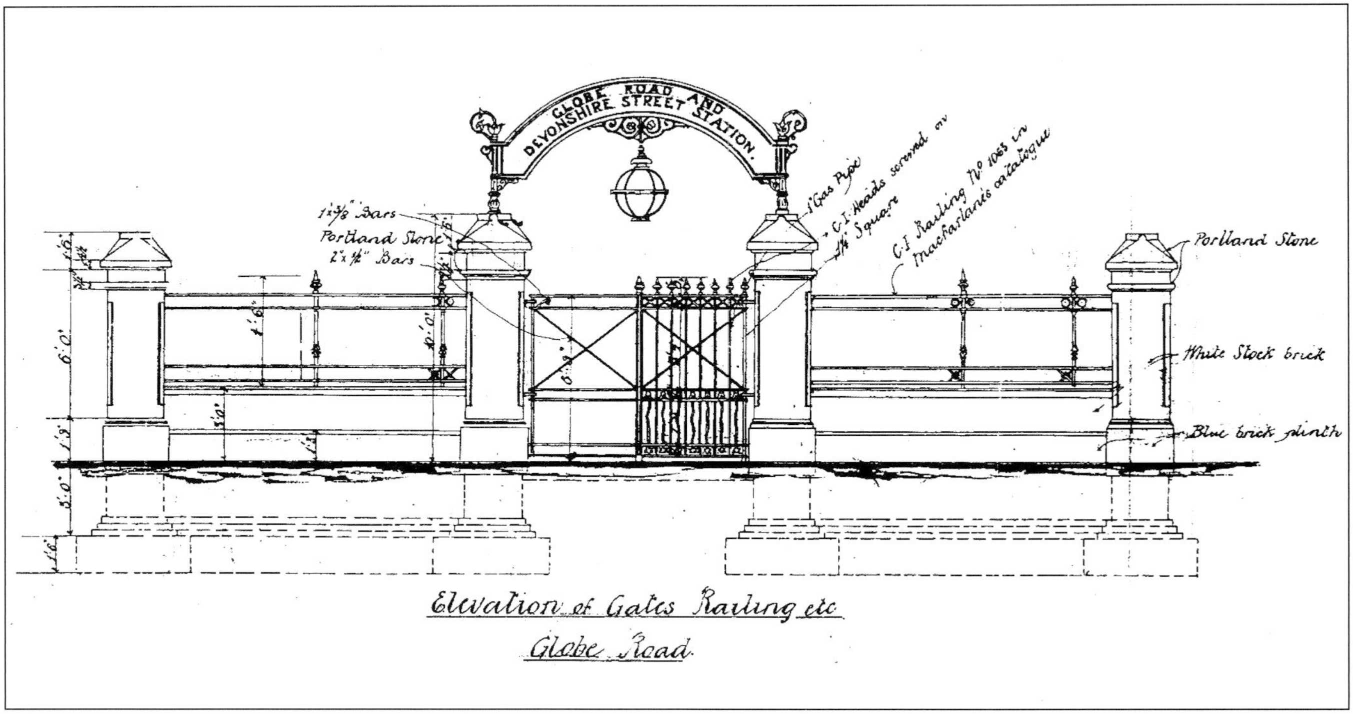
GLOBE ROAD AND DEVONSHIRE STREET STATION
Portland Stone
Portland Stone
White Stock brick
Blue brick plinth
Elevation of Gates Railing etc
Globe Road

GLOBE ROAD AND DEVONSHIRE STREET STATION
ACTON Ld
ENGINEERING Co
154.
GLOBE Rd
E.1
WOODWORKING MACHINERY

Opposite page (top): GER drawing of 1884 showing the station gates and name sign on the east side of Globe Road.

Opposite (bottom): The gateway as it appeared in the early 1960s, complete with cast iron name sign, almost fifty years after closure.

Above: Another 1884 GER drawing, this time showing the frontage of the booking office constructed within an existing viaduct arch to serve the Globe Road entrance. The brickwork was rendered in a coat of 1 inch thick Portland cement then decorated with rusticated quoins of the same material. The parapet was similarly rendered and displayed the company name in incised lettering. The canopy above the entrance had a depth of 8 feet and was supported on cast iron brackets. The rusticated quoins and gilded canopy name doubtlessly added to the *"elaborate character"* referred to by the Board of Trade inspecting officer Major C.S. Hutchinson in his report of 1884.

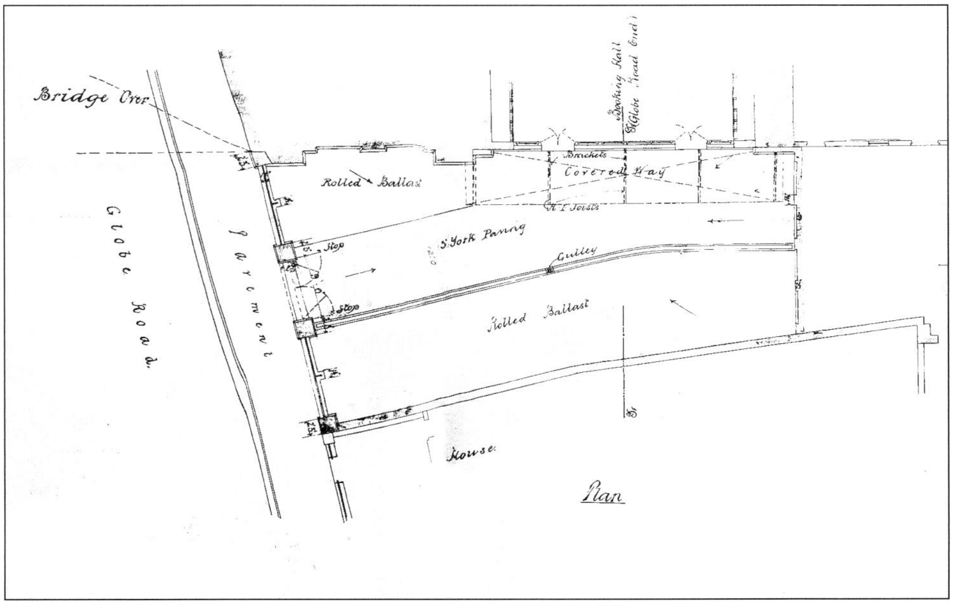

Above: The layout of the Globe Road entrance, showing the gates leading to the booking hall, the canopy of which is shown as "Covered Way".
Surviving tickets from the station generally show the issuing point simply as 'Globe Road & Devonshire Street', although some of them included a bracketed "G'Rd" or "D.St", presumably to indicate which office they originated from.

Above: The office at the east end of the station was located on the north side of Devonshire Street (now Bancroft Road), west of the junction with Morpeth Street. The glazed wooden screen was similar to that at the Globe Road office, although it differed slightly in detailing. This photograph, taken in 1975, shows the former station arch, still with its Portland cement rendering, but minus its decorative rusticated quoins.

Below: The layout of the Devonshire Street entrance in 1884, taken from a drawing signed by John Wilson, who served the GER as Chief Engineer from 1883 until his retirement in 1910.

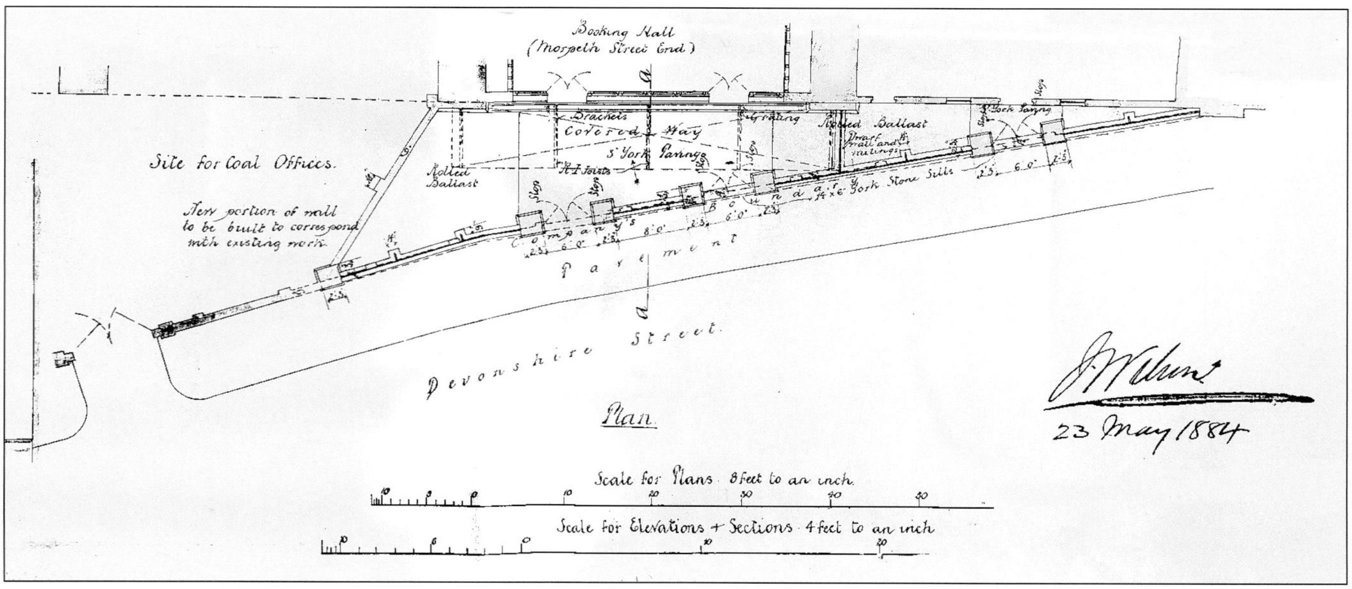

Above: The former Devonshire Street booking office arch, looking east towards the bridge over Morpeth Street. On the left can be seen a surviving 1884 gate pillar, recognisable by its distinctive Portland stone capping. What appear to be bricked-up windows near Morpeth Street were possibly designed as 'blind' and may have just been an architectural feature.

Right: The former station gates on the west side of Morpeth Street in 1975, with the site of the down platform indicated by a widening of the viaduct on the right. Having passed through the gates, passengers walked along a footpath similar to that serving the Globe Road entrance, then entered the Devonshire Street booking office from the rear.

Above: A 1931 aerial view of the station looking south-east, showing the generous canopies which sheltered the platforms virtually from end to end. The covered stairways serving the Globe Road entrance are shown on the right, but those leading to and from Devonshire Street surfaced beneath the canopies and therefore are not visible.

Below: A general plan of the station, with the Globe Road stairs on the left and the Devonshire Street stairs to the right. The Devonshire Street entrance is below these, whilst the Morpeth Street gates with their attendant footpath appear above. As can be seen, the platforms were slightly staggered. There is a possibility that the awnings were removed earlier and some of the canopy columns were re-used at Highams Park during alterations in 1934.

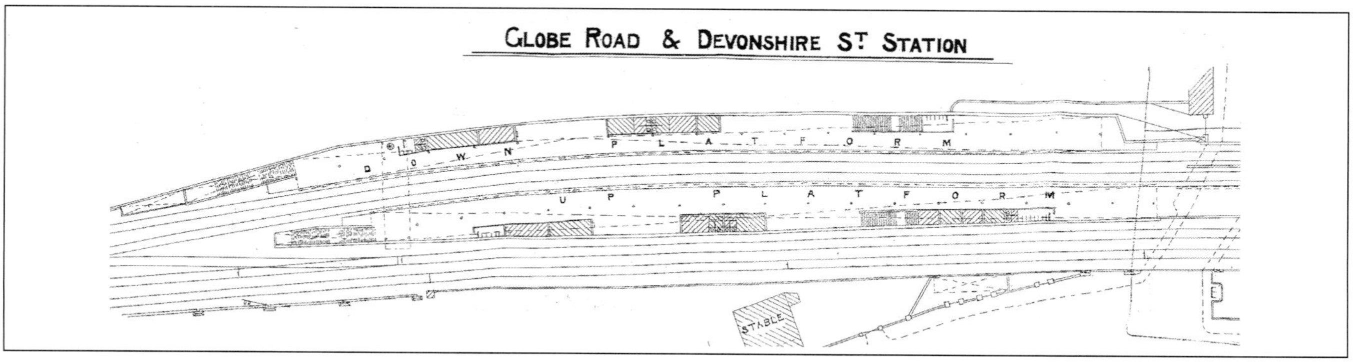

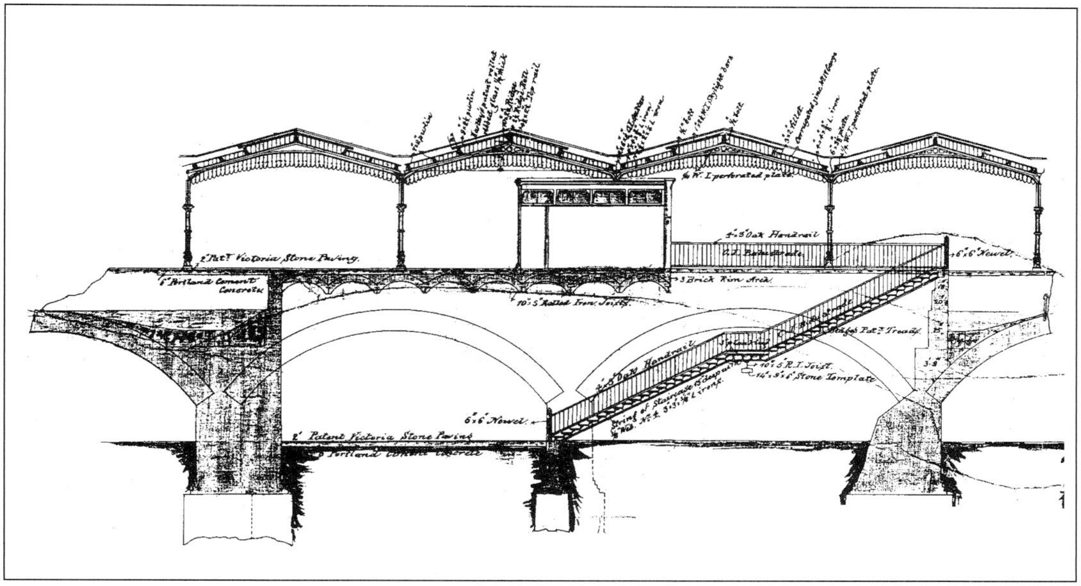

Right: A GER drawing of 1884 showing the ridge and furrow awnings carried by the station, and the layout of the stairway serving the Devonshire Street entrance.

Below: The platforms and attendant buildings were demolished in March 1938, when bridge renewal was taking place in the locality. This view, taken at the time, looks east and includes the up side covered stairway and an adjoining section of platform rear wall.

This view shows the former Globe Road entrance gates as they appeared in the 1990s. They remain standing at the time of writing and are the most obvious of the few surviving relics of the station. Traces remain around the site of the Morpeth Street entrance and this is the best spot to view the widened viaduct which once accommodated the down platform. Up above, the site of this platform continues to be visible from passing trains, together with what is thought to be the capped Devonshire Street end stairway.

A SELECTION OF TICKETS. *Top left:* Third Class single to Liverpool Street issued on 24th June 1902. *Top centre:* Third Class single to Bishopsgate issued on 3rd March 1891. *Top right:* Third Class single to Coborn Road issued on 19th September 1886. *Bottom left:* Third Class return issued on 26th April 1916. Given the date and immaculate condition of the ticket it seems likely that this was purchased by a collector as a souvenir shortly before closure. The 'D'St' under the station's name is thought to imply that it originated from the Devonshire Street office. *Bottom centre:* Third Class single to Stratford possibly issued on 2nd February 1891, although the actual year is faint and unclear. *Bottom right:* Third Class single to Chigwell or Grange Hill, unissued.

Devonshire Street, Mile End

Opened (Eastern Counties Railway): 20th June 1839.
Closed (Eastern Counties Railway): c. May 1841

Not to be confused with the later Globe Road & Devonshire Street station, this was the original London terminus of the Eastern Counties Railway and was only intended as a temporary measure.

The Eastern Counties Railway Guide, printed by G. Mansell of 3 King Street, Borough in 1838, makes this quite clear. It described the line as starting at Shoreditch, and continuing on viaduct to near the *"exceedingly oblique"* bridge at Devonshire Street. The piece then continues and states that *"A temporary depot is formed at the termination of the viaduct, with arrival and departure sheds"*, but apart from an illustration, nothing more is mentioned in the text.

Devonshire Street, Mile End lost its importance when services were extended to Shoreditch in July 1840 and, although it remained in use for a short while after this date, it closed some time between April and June 1841.

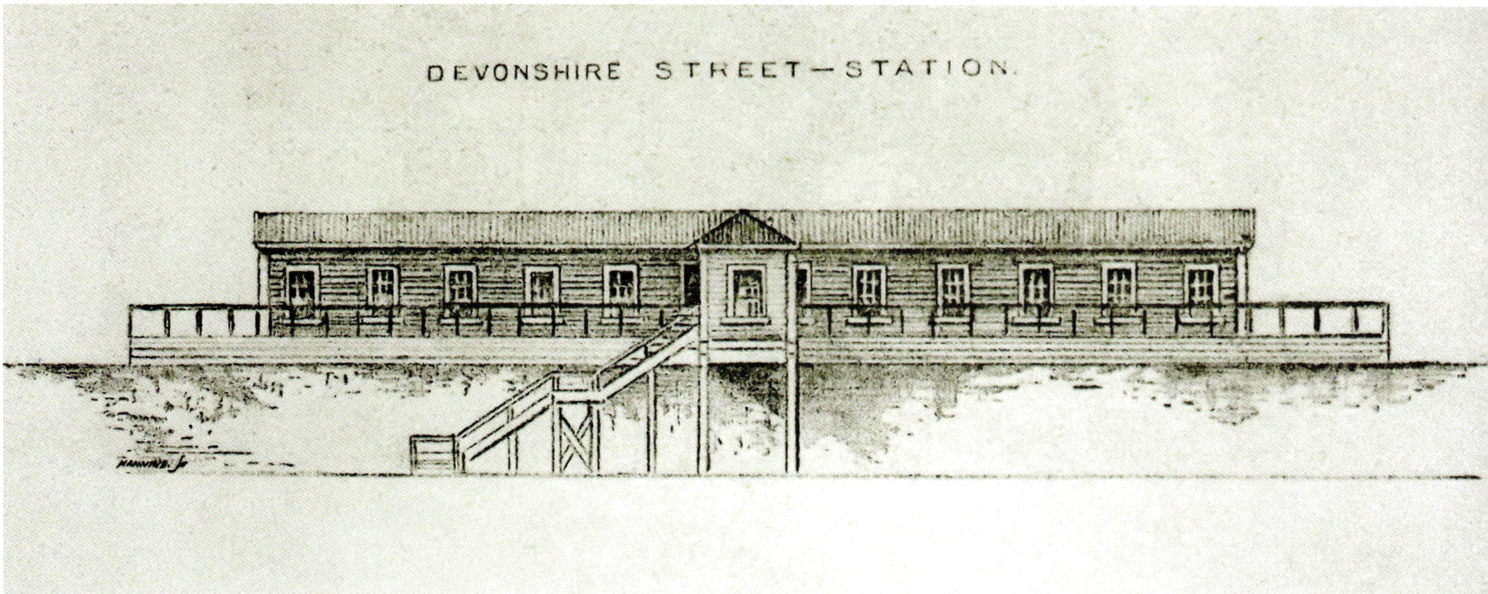

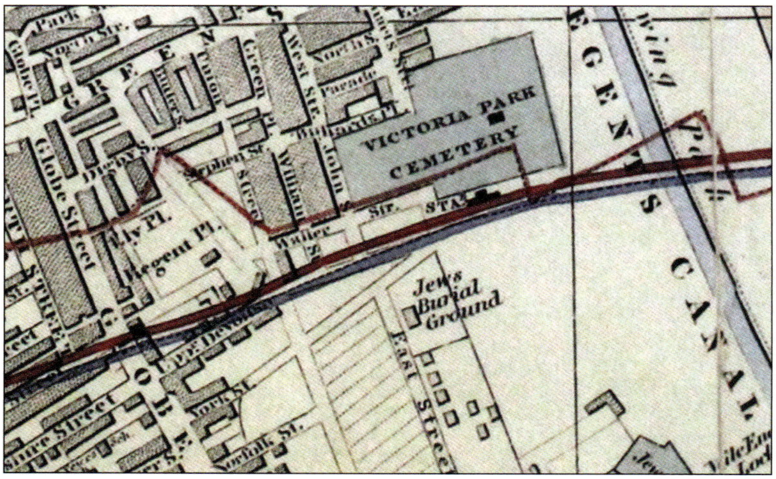

The only known illustration of Devonshire Street station appeared in the Eastern Counties Railway Guide of 1838 and is reproduced above. It was located on the east side of Walter Street, close to the southern boundary of Victoria Park Cemetery and was accessed by means of external stairs. According to the ECR Management minutes of April and May 1841, parts of it were re-used in the construction of the new station at Mile End. However, something must have survived after this as the minutes of April 1845 stated that the remains were to be dismantled and moved to Colchester where they would be incorporated into a goods depot. Devonshire Street station had been dismantled prior to the advent of the Ordnance Survey and is only known to have appeared on editions of Cross' and Kelly's maps. The 1847 Cross map is shown on the right and has been included out of interest. However it is believed that the station was actually sited a little further to the west, close to the southern end of John Street. Part of Walter Street still exists and Victoria Park Cemetery is now Meath Gardens.

Coborn Road (Old Ford)

Opened as Old Ford (Great Eastern Railway): 1st February 1865.
Renamed Coborn Road (Old Ford) (Great Eastern Railway): 1st March 1879.
Resited to west (Great Eastern Railway): 2nd December 1883.
Temporarily closed (Great Eastern Railway): 22nd May 1916 - 5th May 1919.
Closed (London & North Eastern Railway): 8th December 1946.
Station sometimes referred to as 'Coborn Road for Old Ford', which is known to have appeared on nameboards.

THE FIRST STATION

In September 1863, a group of residents from the area around Victoria Park approached the Great Eastern Railway and asked whether it would be possible to build a station at or near Grove Road. The directors promised to consider the idea, but first had to ascertain that it was indeed practical.

The plan was duly discussed and in the following March the GER Traffic Committee recorded that the *"new station at Victoria Park"* would be built *"at the Coborn Road bridge, half a mile from Bow Junction."*

Two months later, in May 1864, the company engineer suggested that Grove Road would be a more suitable site, but said that the directors should make the final decision.

This was duly made and the location at Coborn Road was chosen. The work was put out to tender and, on 4th August 1864, the company's Way & Works Committee awarded the contract to the firm of Patrick & Sons, at an agreed cost of £1,132.

Facilities at the new station, which was named Old Ford, were fairly basic, so the work was soon completed and it opened on 1st February 1865.

The entrance was on the east side of Coborn Road, with the ticket office seemingly south of the line, whilst the two platforms were located on embankment above. The buildings were located at the London end, although the extent of these as originally constructed is uncertain.

After a while however, various improvements were made, starting in May 1872, when a request was placed with the GER General Manager to erect a room for lamps and porters. This was approved the following month and the work was completed.

As built, it seems that the station was not provided with any awnings, but on 3rd November 1875, the Way & Works Committee agreed that one should be added, at a cost of £30. The actual committee minute referred to the addition of a *"covered way"*, although this was how awnings were generally described at the time.

Facilities continued to improve and, on 6th February 1877, it was agreed to erect additional up side accommodation. Three months later, on 15th May, the Way and Works Committee approved a plan to lengthen the platforms by 60ft, whilst on 5th November 1878, it was decided to provide a ladies' waiting room on the up side. At the same time, it was thought that the approaches to both platforms should be provided with covering and the combined cost of this and the new ladies' room came to £95.

Traffic continued to grow and on 23rd September 1879, it was agreed to provide a booking hall on the down side, although whether this was an additional facility or replacement for the original is unclear.

Back in 1876, Parliamentary Powers had been received to quadruple the formation between Bethnal

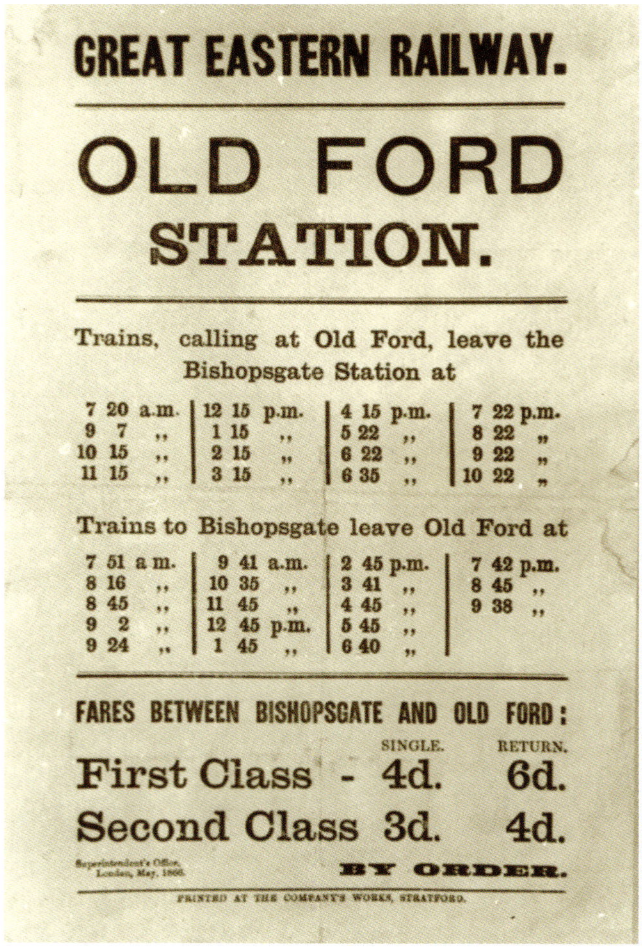

GREAT EASTERN RAILWAY.

OLD FORD STATION.

Trains, calling at Old Ford, leave the Bishopsgate Station at

7 20 a.m.	12 15 p.m.	4 15 p.m.	7 22 p.m.
9 7 ,,	1 15 ,,	5 22 ,,	8 22 ,,
10 15 ,,	2 15 ,,	6 22 ,,	9 22 ,,
11 15 ,,	3 15 ,,	6 35 ,,	10 22 ,,

Trains to Bishopsgate leave Old Ford at

7 51 a.m.	9 41 a.m.	2 45 p.m.	7 42 p.m.
8 16 ,,	10 35 ,,	3 41 ,,	8 45 ,,
8 45 ,,	11 45 ,,	4 45 ,,	9 38 ,,
9 2 ,,	12 45 p.m.	5 45 ,,	
9 24 ,,	1 45 ,,	6 40 ,,	

FARES BETWEEN BISHOPSGATE AND OLD FORD:

	SINGLE.	RETURN.
First Class -	4d.	6d.
Second Class	3d.	4d.

Superintendent's Office, London, May, 1866.

BY ORDER.

PRINTED AT THE COMPANY'S WORKS, STRATFORD.

A handbill of May 1866, showing the service between Old Ford and Bishopsgate, together with the relevant fares.

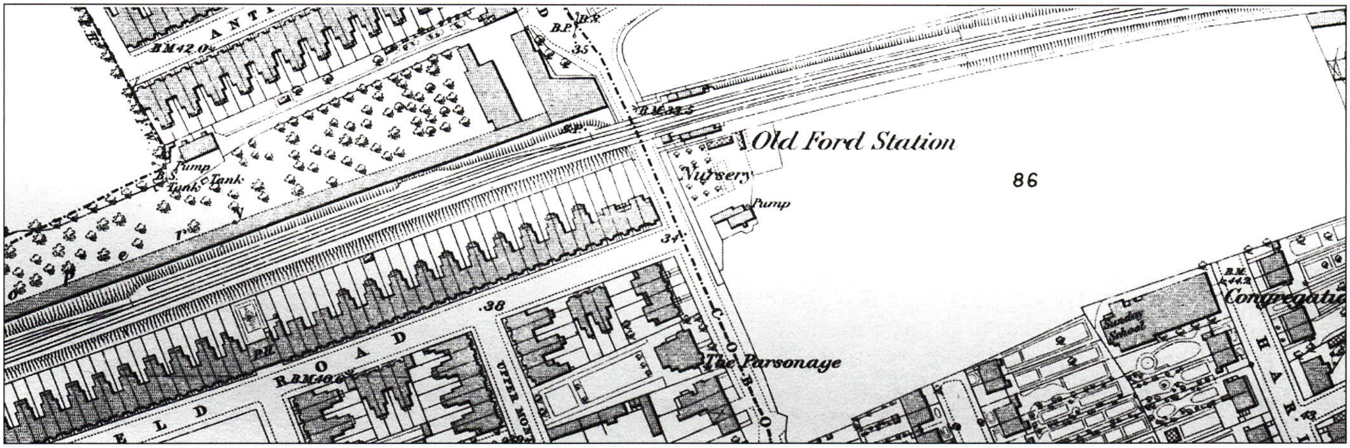

An extract from the First Edition 1:2500 Ordnance Survey map of 1870, showing Old Ford GER station at centre.

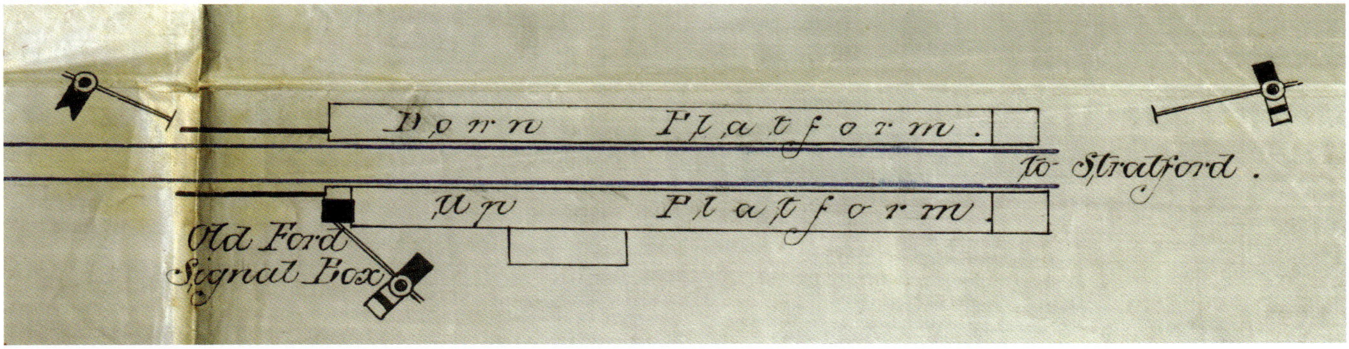

Signalling diagram of Old Ford station, produced by the GER Engineer's Office at Liverpool Street in December 1876.The signal box probably opened in 1865, but this cannot be confirmed.

A selection of tickets. *Left:* Third class single to Cambridge Heath issued 13th April 1883. *Centre:* Second class single from Leyton issued 26th June 1871. *Right:* Third class single to Clapton issued 14th July 1883.

Green and Bow Junction, and this included the stretch on which Old Ford station was located. Once the work was under way, the company decided to resite the station and provide it with entrances at both ends. With these changes impending, it was renamed 'Coborn Road' on 1st March 1879, although 'Old Ford' was retained in the title as a bracketed suffix.

At the GER Board Meeting of 18th August 1880 it was stated that the annual bookings at Coborn Road had increased to £11,000 and this did not include season tickets. It was felt that the provision of an additional entrance would improve upon this and increase the takings to £15,000.

Despite now being on borrowed time, the station received one further improvement around December 1881, when the Way & Works Committee agreed to provide ladies waiting accommodation on *"both platforms"*. Again the actual nature of the work is uncertain, but it seems likely that it was restricted to the down side, as there had been a ladies' room on the up platform since 1878.

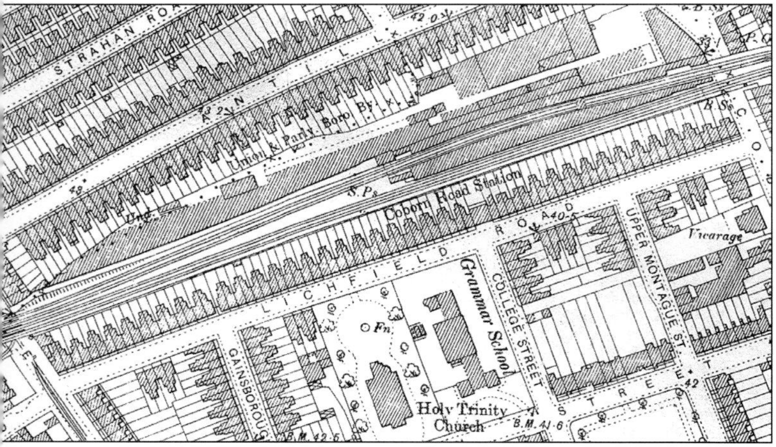

Extract of the 1894 1:2500 Ordnance Survey map showing the second Coborn Road station, with its two entrances.

THE SECOND STATION

Additional land, to the west of the existing station, was purchased for £750 at the beginning of 1880 and on 17th April 1883, the contract to build its replacement was awarded to Perry & Co, who agreed to complete the work within twenty weeks at a cost of £15,982.

The new station was brought into use on 2nd December 1883, but the quadrupling was still unfinished at the time. Therefore the platforms, which stood on the altered alignment, had to be served by diverting the existing running lines between them. This arrangement continued until June 1884, when the widening was completed and the two additional tracks were commissioned. These (the Through lines) had no platforms.

The new station was designed by architect Edwin Wendover, who was employed in the GER Engineer's Department and was also responsible for Globe Road. The main entrance took the form of a doorway on the west side of Coborn Road, to the north of the formation. From here, stairs ascended to the two platforms, which were similar in appearance to those at Globe Road, and were covered for their full length by ridge and furrow awnings. At the opposite end was another set of stairs and these served the Grove Road entrance This did not face directly onto the pavement however, and had to be accessed by means of a 250 yard long footway, which paralleled the north side of the line.

Coborn Road signal box was located towards the east end of the station and was supported by an overhead gantry above the platforms. This dated from 1884 and had a twenty lever McKenzie and Holland frame.

Tickets issued at the eastern office showed the station of origin simply as 'Coborn Road', but those from the London end included the bracketed initials "G.R.O", indicating the Grove Road Office.

The station remained more or less in original condition for the majority of its life, and very few changes were recorded in the company minute books. Among these was a £45 extension to the parcels office in the autumn of 1891 and the installation of electric lighting during the latter part of 1907.

Like many inner suburban stations it suffered from tramway competition in the early twentieth century and during the First World War, it was recommended for closure along with Bishopsgate and Globe Road. This decision was approved by the GER Board of Directors on 2nd March 1916 and the list of stations affected totalled no fewer than nineteen. The closure date for all was set for 1st May, but this was amended to 22nd May so that talks with local protest groups could take place. Some of them were subsequently reprieved, but not Coborn Road.

The Railway Magazine of May 1916 reported on the forthcoming changes and stated that *"The drastic closing on inner London stations will no doubt drive much of the traffic to and from the City to the trams; but as they already take the bulk of it... there will be little grievance on this score."*

This could not be said of Coborn Road however where there was an outcry over the proposed closure, and meetings were held in an attempt to win a reprieve. Unfortunately, this was not to be and the station closed from 22nd May as planned. According to a local newspaper report of the time *"a number of passengers presented themselves on Monday morning at the booking office, to see if the threat had actually been carried out. They found the doors closed, and later in the day men appeared and boarded up the windows also. On Tuesday preparations were made for painting out the large notices on the iron bridge "Frequent trains to the City"... The name of the station is pasted over with a placard reading Station Closed."*

Given the amount of local opposition, it is perhaps not surprising that after the hostilities ended, Coborn Road was tidied up and reopened on 5th May 1919.

The station weathered its three years of disuse very well, although it was perhaps not to everyone's taste. According to a personal recollection published in the October 2008 edition of *London Railway Record*, its interior was cavernous and dirty, with just a pair of low wattage light bulbs for illumination.

Since the grouping of 1923, the station had been part of the large London & North Eastern Railway, but the most noticeable changes involved the signage and the company's title on tickets.

Under a mid-1930s programme to improve rail transport around London, the lines linking Liverpool Street with Shenfield, and Fenchurch Street with Bow Junction, were to be electrified on the overhead system. Part of this scheme also included the alteration of Local and Through lines west of Ilford, so, when completed, the Local or "Electric" lines would be on the south side of the formation instead of the north as before. The plan also involved extending the London Passenger Transport Board Central Line from Liverpool Street to Stratford, with intermediate stations at Bethnal Green and Mile End. There had been an Underground station at Mile End since the opening of the Whitechapel & Bow Joint Railway in 1902, but it was now going to gain the importance of being an interchange. Coborn Road only had platforms on the existing Local lines and being relatively close to Mile End would become superfluous and therefore closed.

Once again, local residents complained about the impending closure and in 1939 *The East London Advertiser* carried a report entitled *"Coborn Road Station Doomed"*. It stated that the LNER had no intention of keeping it open as its closure was part of a planned scheme to greatly improve suburban services in and out of Liverpool Street.

The coming of the Second World War in September 1939 resulted in the electrification work being delayed, so Coborn Road remained open longer than anticipated.

The station seems to have survived the early days of the Blitz fairly well and although bombs fell in the vicinity, none of these were reported as damaging the buildings. One notable incident occurred on 19th March 1941, when the 9.00pm express from Liverpool Street to Ipswich became engulfed in flames as a result of enemy action. Passengers were detrained then walked to Coborn Road, where they were subsequently picked up and conveyed to Stratford. The fire was so intense that two of the coaches were left to burn out, but it seems that the station itself remained unscathed.

In the summer of the following year however, demolition men moved in and began to shorten the awnings. The work was completed by August 1942, and all that then remained were truncated sections on either side.

Devastation on a large scale came at around 4.30am on the morning of 13th July 1944, when the first 'V1' flying bomb struck the bridge over Grove Road, causing it to collapse into the street below. The action took everyone completely by surprise and the rumour quickly spread that it had been an experimental aircraft shot down by the RAF. In the confusion, "news" soon spread that the pilot had bailed out and had been captured for interrogation in Aldgate. There was no pilot of course, and this was no experimental aircraft.

The report of the damage made no reference to the station and centred on the bridge. Thanks to some magnificent work by the engineers, this was replaced by a temporary structure within thirty-six hours and restricted services were then restored.

When the war ended in 1945, the station looked in a pretty sorry state, with its canopies drastically shortened in length and sections of the rear platform walls largely removed. The London end stairways had also gone, but the date when the Grove Road Office closed has not been traced.

Work resumed on the Central Line Eastern Extension and services were extended from Liverpool Street to Stratford on 4th December 1946. Coborn Road station closed permanently, after the departure of the 1.20am Liverpool Street to Brentwood on Sunday 8th December and by May 1947, the up side had been largely demolished. The signal box remained in use for a little longer but was abolished on 6th February 1949 and soon followed the station into oblivion.

The eastern stretch of the down platform rear wall remained recognisable for many years, along with its associated stairway, but the distinctive top, which once followed the line of the ridge and furrow awning was removed in November 2005.

Down below, the main station entrance still survives, bricked-up and anonymous. At one time its historical significance was marked by a commemorative plaque, but this was removed when the rear platform wall was reduced in height and has not been reinstated.

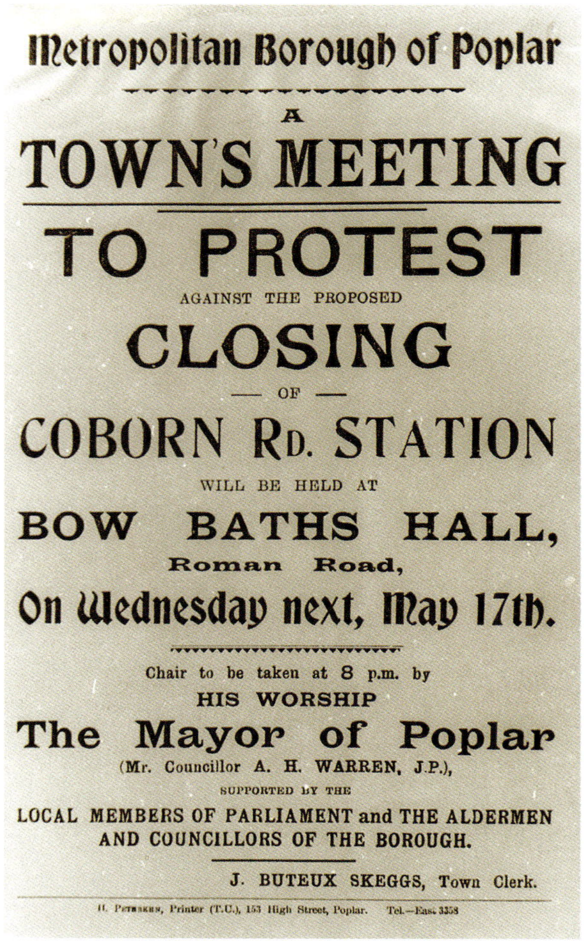

A handbill from May 1916 announcing a meeting in the Bow Baths Hall, Roman Road, to protest against the closure of Coborn Road station.

Left (top): A view from the early twentieth century, with the GER bridge above Coborn Road itself and Tredegar Road diverging on the left. The station name is just about readable on the bridge, whilst the bracket lamp and public telephone sign on the right mark its entrance.

Left (middle): Looking north along Grove Road, again in the early twentieth century, with the gates leading to the western booking office footpath visible at centre, immediately beyond the bridge abutment.

Below: A commercial postcard from around 1906, showing the station in its pre-grouping heyday, looking towards Stratford, with the 1884 signal box prominent above the awnings. The canopy valances, both here and at Globe Road, were akin to those provided on GER suburban stations around 1870-72. Part of a nameboard is just visible on the right showing 'Coborn Road' on the upper line and 'For Old Ford' beneath.

A nice general view of the station, taken from the Liverpool Street end on 19th June 1936. To the left is the name panel above the 'Grove Road' entrance, but sadly no photographs have been located which show this building in its entirety. The Through lines can be seen on the right, passing behind the up platform.

A selection of tickets *Top row left:* GER third class single to Bishopsgate or Liverpool Street, issued from the Grove Road office on 7th August 1911. *Top row centre:* GER third class single to Canning Town, issued from the Grove Road office on 12th December 1910. *Top row right:* GER third class single to Romford, issued on 7th July 1904. *Bottom row left:* Second class return issued on 14th September 1904. *Bottom row centre:* LNER platform ticket issued 23rd October 1932. *Bottom row right:* LNER third class single issued on 7th December 1946. The last train called in the small hours of the following day.

Above: Looking east from the Liverpool Street end on 3rd June 1942, whilst the awnings were being rationalised. As can be seen, the lower parts of the supporting columns had been painted white to aid visibility during the wartime 'blackout'.

Left: A photograph taken on the same date, looking from the up platform towards the western end stairways.

Right: Another view from 3rd June 1942, but this time taken from the country end. A barrage balloon can be seen in the sky above, providing a reminder of the ever-present threat of air raids.

Below: By 20th August 1942, the work of shortening the awnings and reducing the height of the rear platforms walls appears to have been completed and the station had been largely tidied up. This view was taken from the signal post, a little to the west of the down platform end.

Class N7 0-6-2T No. 9618 stands at Coborn Road on 2nd December 1946 with a Liverpool Street - Epping train. The line between Stratford and Epping subsequently became part of the London Underground system, with tube services being extended in stages between May 1947 and September 1949.

The western end of Coborn Road station on the same date, looking towards the site of the former 'Grove Road Office' stairways, which had completely disappeared by then. The wooden building on the right was the down side gents' toilet.

The eastern end of the station, showing the stairs which linked the platforms with the booking hall.

Above: Coborn Road, looking towards Liverpool Street a week before its final closure. The station was in a pretty sorry state with temporary platform lighting and a nameboard hung from the fence on the left.

Right: By 9th May 1947, the up side buildings had gone, along with the remaining awnings. Both east end stairways were still evident however, as was the gents' on the down platform.

Above (left): The former station entrance on the west side of Coborn Road, as it appeared in 1969, with the remains of a lamp evident above the bricked-up doorway.

Above (centre): Looking east along the remains of the down platform in 1973, with the site of the gents' urinal on the left. The rear wall was partially demolished in November 2005, when the upper section, which followed the line of the old ridge and furrow awning, was finally removed.

Above (right): The down side stairs, as they appeared in 1973, with the old exit onto Coborn Road visible at the bottom. Although this had been largely bricked-up, it included a door as a means of staff access.

Bow

Opened (Eastern Counties Railway): 14th September 1840.
Closed (Eastern Counties Railway): c. November / December 1840.

Undoubtedly east London's most obscure and short-lived station, Bow was opened by the Eastern Counties Railway in September 1840 and was located on the west side of Old Ford Road.

The ECR minute books made no mention of it being constructed and its existence is only recorded by the fact that it was the location of two rear-end collisions, of which the first occurred on its opening day.

It was too short-lived to appear on any maps, but from the accident reports it is understood that it comprised two platforms, and one of these accommodated a "*policeman's box*". It stood on embankment and was presumably built of wood, with stairs leading up from street level.

As well as ensuring safety at the station, the policeman on duty also had to issue tickets, so the office was presumably located within his box and not in a separate building.

Despite the absence of maps, there is no doubt about its exact position, as one of the reports states that it was "*175 yards from the Lea Bridge*", which would place it by Old Ford Road.

It does not seem to have been well used and trains calling there did so by request.

After the second accident it seems that the Eastern Counties Railway decided that it was not worth retaining the station and the Board decided on 25th November 1840 that it should be closed immediately. An exact date is not known, but the closure must have taken place within a few days of the decision being made.

The station was probably completely demolished soon after and all traces of it had disappeared by the time the First Edition Ordnance Survey map was published in the 1860s.

Bromley

Opened (London Tilbury & Southend Railway): 31st March 1858.
Resited (London Tilbury & Southend Railway): 1st March 1894.

The original station at Bromley was built by the London Tilbury & Southend Railway and opened in 1858. It was the first station beyond Gas Factory Junction, Bow on the LTSR route to Barking and stood on the east side of St Leonard's Street. It comprised two platforms, which were reached by means of stairs that descended from the booking hall, and was served by trains to and from Fenchurch Street. It was shown on the 1867 Ordnance Survey map as 'Bromley & Bow', but this name was never officially carried.

The station was badly damaged by fire on 20th December 1892 and it was decided to resite it to the opposite side of St Leonard's Street. Oddly, the new street level building was constructed on the site of its predecessor, so the new platforms had to be accessed by means of a subway under the street.

To accommodate the replacement station, the junction with the curve leading round from Bow on the North London Railway had to be moved 170yds further west.

The new station opened on 1st March 1894 and the old platforms were demolished. It is not known when they went, but no trace of them appears on the 1895 Ordnance Survey map, so they clearly disappeared around the time of the resiting.

The second station was subsequently enlarged to serve four tracks in 1905 and has undergone various changes since. It was renamed Bromley-by-Bow on 18th May 1967 and continues as such today.

Extract from the First Edition 1:2500 Ordnance Survey map of 1867 showing the original Bromley station at centre, with its two platforms and entrance building on the east side of St Leonard's Street.

Minories

Opened (London & Blackwall Railway): 6th July 1840.
Temporarily closed (London & Blackwall Railway): 15th February 1849 - 9th September 1849.
Closed (London & Blackwall Railway): 24th October 1853.

Minories station in 1840, looking east, with the winding drums in the foreground and a train at the north platform. On the extreme left can just be seen one of the Cooke & Wheatstone electro-magnetic telegraph instruments, which aided the efficient operation of the line.

The original City terminus of the London & Blackwall Railway was located to the east of Minories and comprised two low platforms beneath a wooden overall roof.

The company initially wanted to serve Houndsditch, but failed to get Parliamentary approval and eventually settled for a compromise, on the understanding that *"no rails* (would) *be laid within 200 feet of the Minories - and that no funds of the company* (would) *be applied to purchase land in the City of London."*

In 1837, another Bill was presented asking permission to built an extension to Leadenhall Street, but once again this met with opposition and had to be withdrawn. The Company therefore had no option other than to accept a terminus in Minories, although the ambition to extend further never died, and eventually a scheme to continue into Fenchurch Street met with success.

By this time work was already progressing well on the remainder of the route, with the stretch between George Street, Shadwell, and Mansell Street, being built by the firm of Robert and George Webb.

The London & Blackwall Railway was ceremonially opened on 4th July 1840 and the event was described in *The Tablet,* published seven days later: *"The visitors on Saturday were received at the entrance to the London terminus in the Minories by Alderman Humphrey, M.P.,*

Mr. Robinson, and other directors. The first train, full of company, started at twelve o'clock, and others succeeded at half-past twelve, one, half-past one, and two o'clock. The one o'clock train conveyed the Lord Mayor, the Sheriffs, and other civic functionaries... The first train performed the journey in fifteen minutes, and the other in ten minutes."

Public services commenced two days later, although only one track was initially in operation and remained as such until 3rd August that year.

Very little seems to have been recorded about the station itself, although *The Tablet* stated that its roof was only temporary, as it was intended to complete the remainder of the line into Fenchurch Street *"as soon as possible"*.

The extension duly opened on 2nd August 1841, but Minories was retained and was adapted as a through station.

The winding engine was located west of the platforms and the method of operation was described by *The Civil Engineer and Architect's Journal* of March 1848: *"The machinery at the London end, for working the railway, is situated at the Minories station. The carriages in coming towards London are disconnected from the rope, a little before they arrive at the Minories, and they perform the rest of the journey to the terminus in Fenchurch-street by their momentum. The upward inclination of the rails at this place is 1 in 150... When the down-train leaves the terminus in Fenchurch-street, it descends the incline to the Minories by its gravity, where it is stopped by the breaks* (sic), *to allow of the passengers being received at that station, and to permit the attachment of the rope..."*

The idea of using cable haulage soon proved to be more trouble than it was worth and the Company eventually decided to replace the stationary winding engines with steam locomotives. At the same time the opportunity was taken to dispense with the non-standard track gauge of 5ft, so that the line could become an integrated part of the fast growing railway network serving the capital. The LBR was re-gauged and converted to locomotive operation, with the last cable-hauled services running on 14th February 1849. Minories closed the following day and although it later re-opened, it was permanently shut from 24th October 1853.

After closure, the station was demolished, although parts of it may have been re-used in the construction of a nearby goods shed.

This was claimed to be the original station by Harold Lindsay Hopwood, writing in the May 1927 edition of the *Railway Magazine*, when he stated that *"the old Minories station... was leased to the Great Northern Railway, who converted it into the depot known as "Royal Mint Street Goods Station". The space on the ground floor formerly occupied by the stationary engines is now laid with rails, and wagons are raised to the higher level by means of a lift".*

It's a good story, but one that cannot be true. The line into Fenchurch Street passed *through* Minories station, whereas the goods shed was located to the south of the original viaduct. The depot closed in 1951 and the site of the old goods shed now accommodates part of the DLR terminus at Tower Gateway.

Cross's Map of 1844, showing the London & Blackwall Railway paralleling the north side of Rosemary Lane (later Royal Mint Street) and Cable Street. Minories station is shown as an un-named rectangle, which seems to have been accessed by way of alleys from the east side of Minories itself and the north side of Rosemary Lane. If the LBR had succeeded with its 1837 scheme, the line would have continued in a north-western direction beyond Fenchurch Street and terminated at Leadenhall Street.

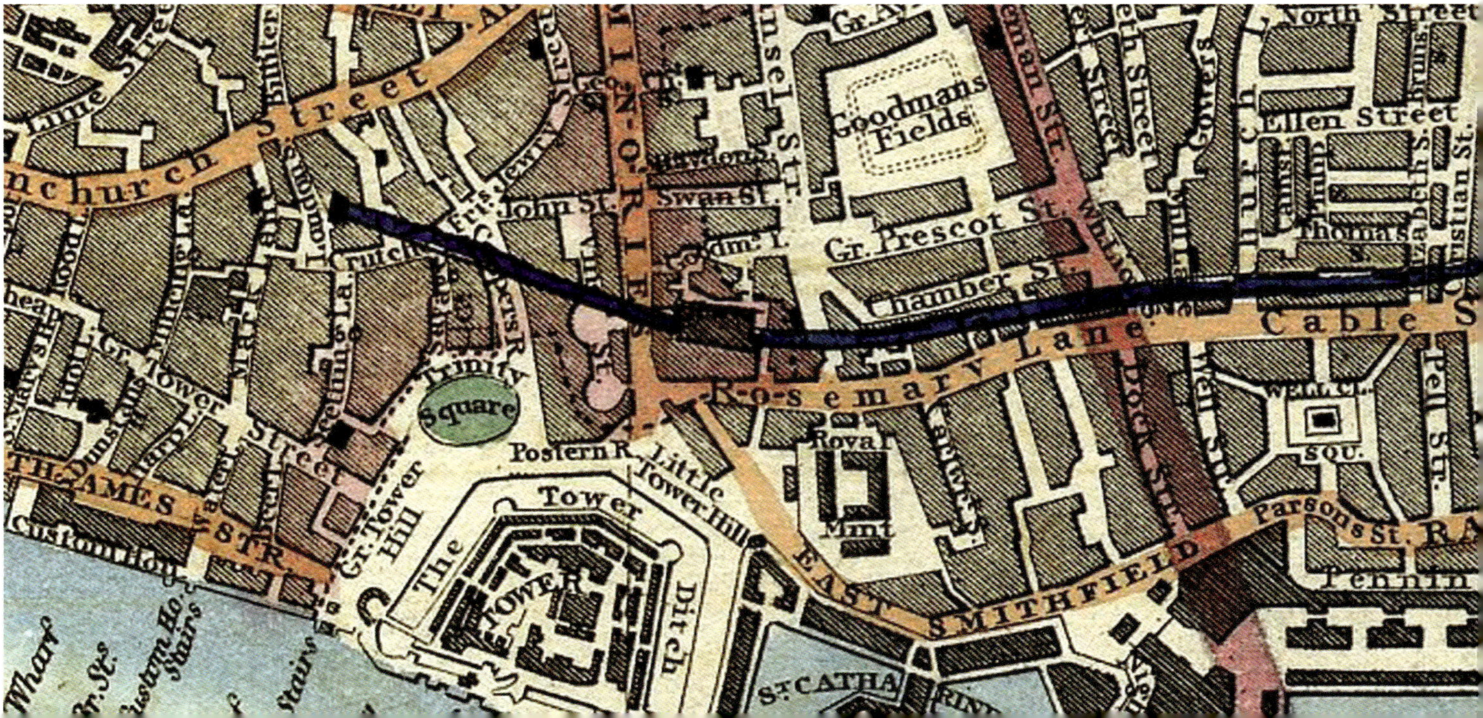

Leman Street

Opened (Great Eastern Railway): 1st June 1877.
Temporarily closed (Great Eastern Railway): 22nd May 1916 - 1st July 1919.
Closed (London & North Eastern Railway): 7th July 1941.

0-6-0T No 155 stands at Leman Street station at an unknown date with a Blackwall - Fenchurch Street train. In common with certain other locomotives of this type, she was running as a 2-4-0T with the front portion of her coupling rods removed.

In 1871, the Great Eastern Railway decided to build a new station on the London & Blackwall line. It was to be situated just 38 chains east of Fenchurch Street and would be called Leman Street.

By this time, there were three tracks on the viaduct between Fenchurch Street and Stepney, the original pair to the south of the formation, and an additional up line on the north side. Originally it seems that the GER wanted Leman Street to have platform faces to serve all three, but because of space restrictions they could only be provided on the original lines. Work commenced in the second half of 1872 and was completed by March 1873, but the Board of Trade refused to sanction the station's opening.

Passenger access was by means of a doorway, south of the formation, on the east side of Leman Street. From here, stairs led to the up platform, and passengers requiring down trains had to use a footbridge to reach the other side. The inspecting officer, Colonel Tyler felt that the steps of this bridge were too close to the up platform edge and that there was inadequate clearance between the rear of the down platform and the line which ran behind it.

The up platform was already bracketed out from the side of the viaduct, but by increasing this overhang, it proved possible to make it wider. The GER carried out the necessary work during 1874 and by January 1875 all seemed complete. Colonel Tyler returned for a second visit, but again refused to sanction opening as he remained unhappy about the down side. He was still unsure of the clearance and also stated that the down platform, which only stretched for a distance of 53 yards, needed lengthening. Once again, the GER had no option but carry out further work and accepted that the station would not be opening until all of the Board of Trade requirements had been carried out.

The various improvements obviously took time to complete, but in the May of 1877 the Great Eastern again contacted the Board of Trade and informed them that the station would be ready for a further inspection within ten days. The appointed officer, Major General Hutchinson, visited Leman Street later in the month and agreed that, at long last, all was now acceptable. Therefore, after a delay of over five years, it finally opened on 1st June 1877.

Access remained as before, with the station entrance on the east side of Leman Street, and stairs ascending to the up platform, where connection with the other side was again afforded by a footbridge. The platforms were slightly staggered and according to an engineer's drawing of May 1877, it seems that no shelter or buildings were provided for passengers travelling towards the City. Signals were worked by an existing box at London Docks Junction, which lay to the west of the station and controlled movements to and from a short goods branch. This was built to serve the London Docks Wool Warehouse and had been opened by the London & Blackwall Railway in 1864.

For many years the line serving Fenchurch Street had been very busy with both passenger and freight traffic, and in the final decade of the nineteenth century it again proved necessary to widen the formation. This enabled a fourth track to be laid on its north side and allowed vast improvements to be made at Leman Street and Shadwell. In fact, both of these stations were completely rebuilt, so that their up platforms could be accommodated on the viaduct instead of overhanging as before. The work appears to have been carried out during 1892/3, but the new arrangement was not inspected by the Board of Trade until 16th March 1896. A new signal box, 'Leman Street Junction', opened in 1895 a little to the west of the old box.

Leman Street station was rebuilt in bright red brick and, although completely new, the entrance remained more or less on its original site. The street level building faced onto the east side of Leman Street and, although

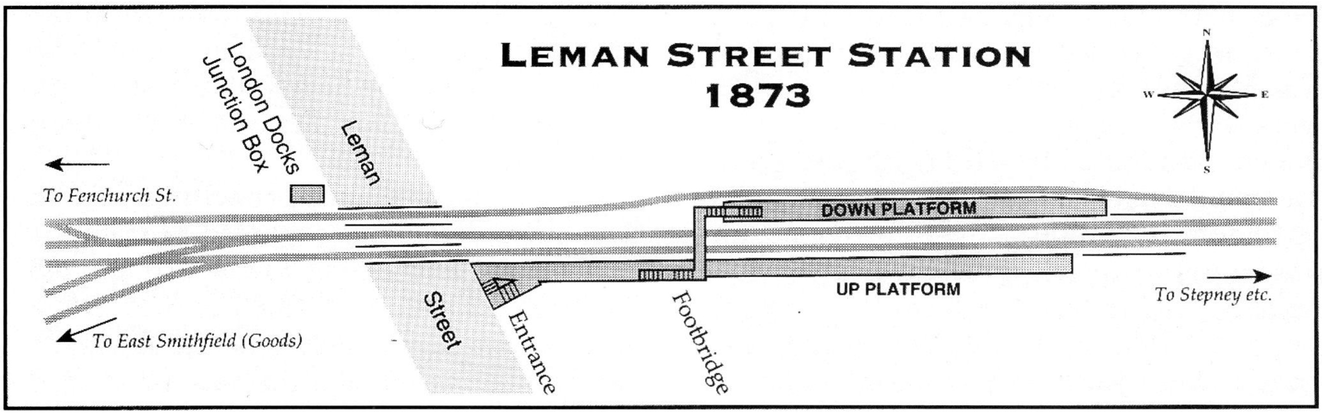

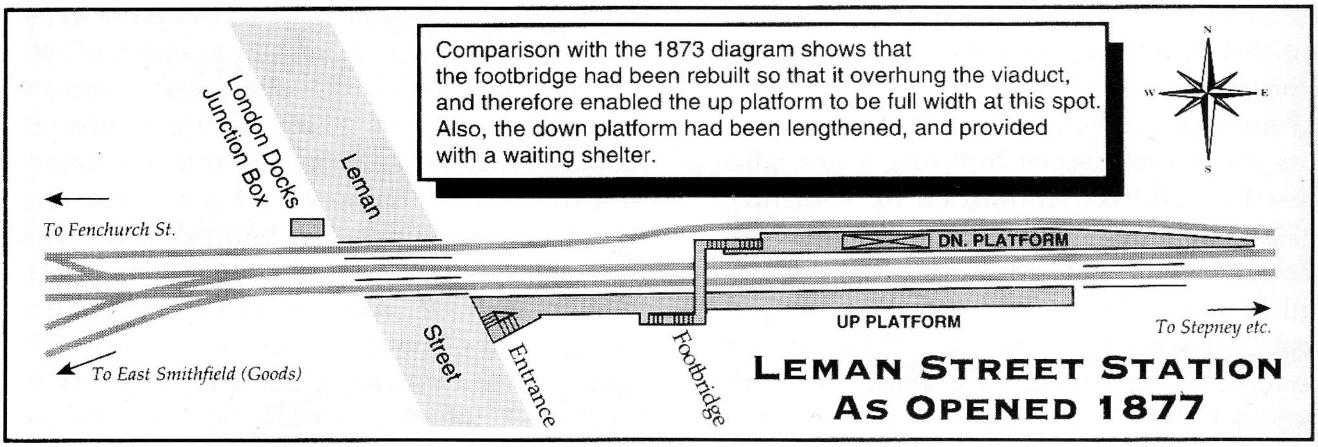

Ex-GER Class J65 0-6-0T (running as a 2-4-0T) No 7155, leaves Leman Street with the 1.40pm Fenchurch Street to Blackwall train on 28th March 1925.

Great Eastern Railway third class single to Shadwell & St Georges' East issued on 10th May 1904.

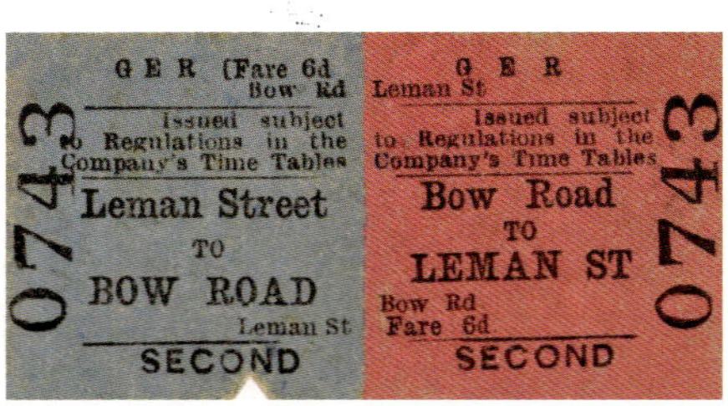

Great Eastern Railway second class return to Bow Road issued on 29th June 1900.

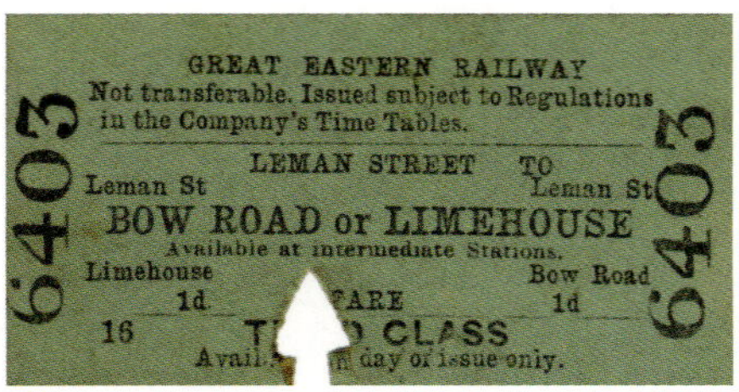

Great Eastern Railway third class single to Bow Road or Limehouse issued on 29th July 1914.

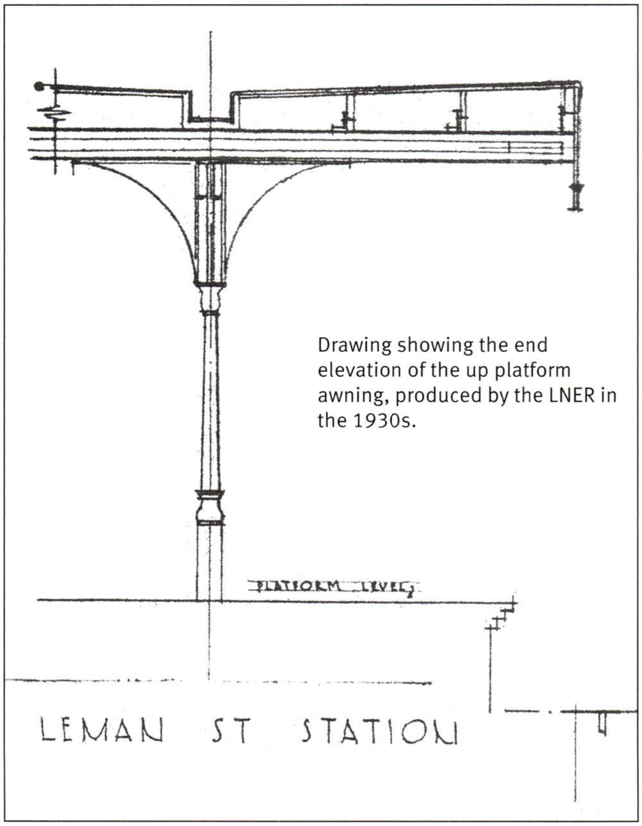

Drawing showing the end elevation of the up platform awning, produced by the LNER in the 1930s.

close to the junction with Cable Street it did not stand on the corner site as this was already occupied by a shop. To enter the station passengers would pass through a pair of heavy panelled doors and walk into the booking hall. To the right stood the ticket office, which was bow-fronted and had two issuing windows. Adjoining this was a parcels office, which had a door at its right-hand end and a pair of windows, topped with semi-circular arches, overlooking Mill Yard, which was the building's eastern extremity. To gain access to the platforms, passengers passed through the barrier gates, then either turned sharp right for up trains, or else continued straight ahead if they were travelling in the opposite direction. A passage continued beyond the down side stairway, and this served three storerooms. When built in the 1890s, the entrance to this area was open, but around the 1930s, it was partitioned off with a studwork wall, which was match lined on the public side and provided with a pair of doors. The section behind the partition wall could also be entered through a doorway under the railway bridge which, at one time, may have been used as a public exit.

Above: Ex GER Class J65 0-6-0T No 156 leaves Leman Street with the 2.30pm Blackwall to Fenchurch Street train on 28th March 1925.

Right: J65 0-6-0T No 7153 enters Leman Street with the 1.35pm train from Blackwall to Fenchurch Street on 28th March 1925. These locomotives were sometimes referred to as *'Blackwall Tanks'*, as they were associated with the line for many years.

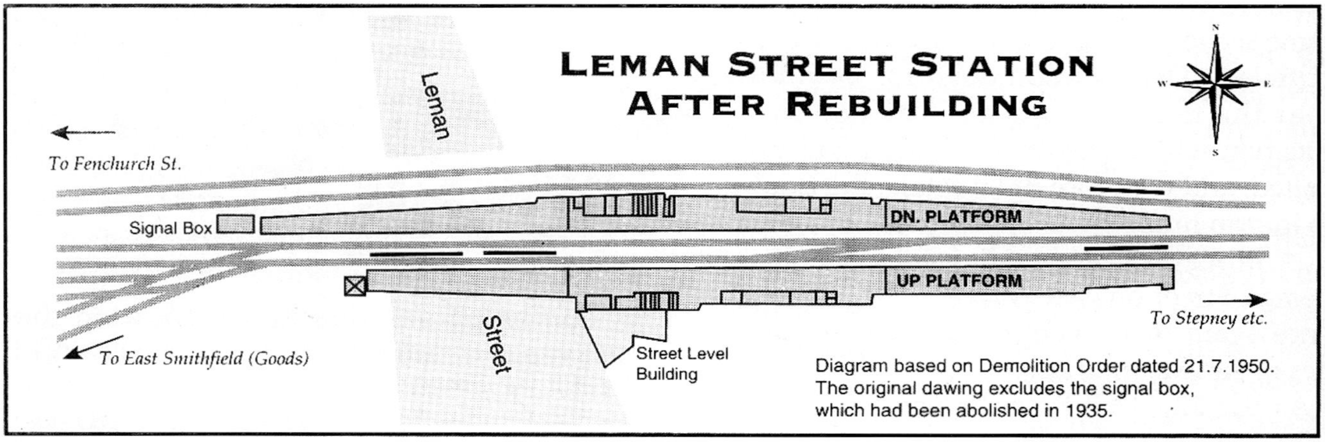

The new layout with individual stairways serving both platforms meant that there was no longer need for a footbridge, so this was removed. Up above, the appearance of the station changed completely, with wider platforms and red brick buildings, sheltering beneath generous awnings. Both platforms had a length of 450ft. The awnings seem to have shared a common length of 180ft and were provided with the style of valancing widely used by the GER in the 1890s. From west to east, the down side facilities comprised two buildings, with the first containing a gents' toilet and porter's room and the second accommodating a general waiting room and ladies' room. Between these was the rear brick wall and the stairwell which provided access to and from street level. The facilities on the opposite platform were almost a mirror reflection, although a small stationmaster's office was positioned between the porters' room and stairwell and the internal layout of the ladies' room was slightly different. Both stairways surfaced close to the west-end buildings and were protected by decorative wrought iron railings.

In the first decade of the twentieth century, Leman Street began to suffer from road transport competition and, along with a group of other lesser-used GER stations, closed on 22nd May 1916. A little earlier, a local newspaper reported the forthcoming closures and stated that the company's actions were *"due entirely to the war - the great depletion of staff owing to enlistment, and to*

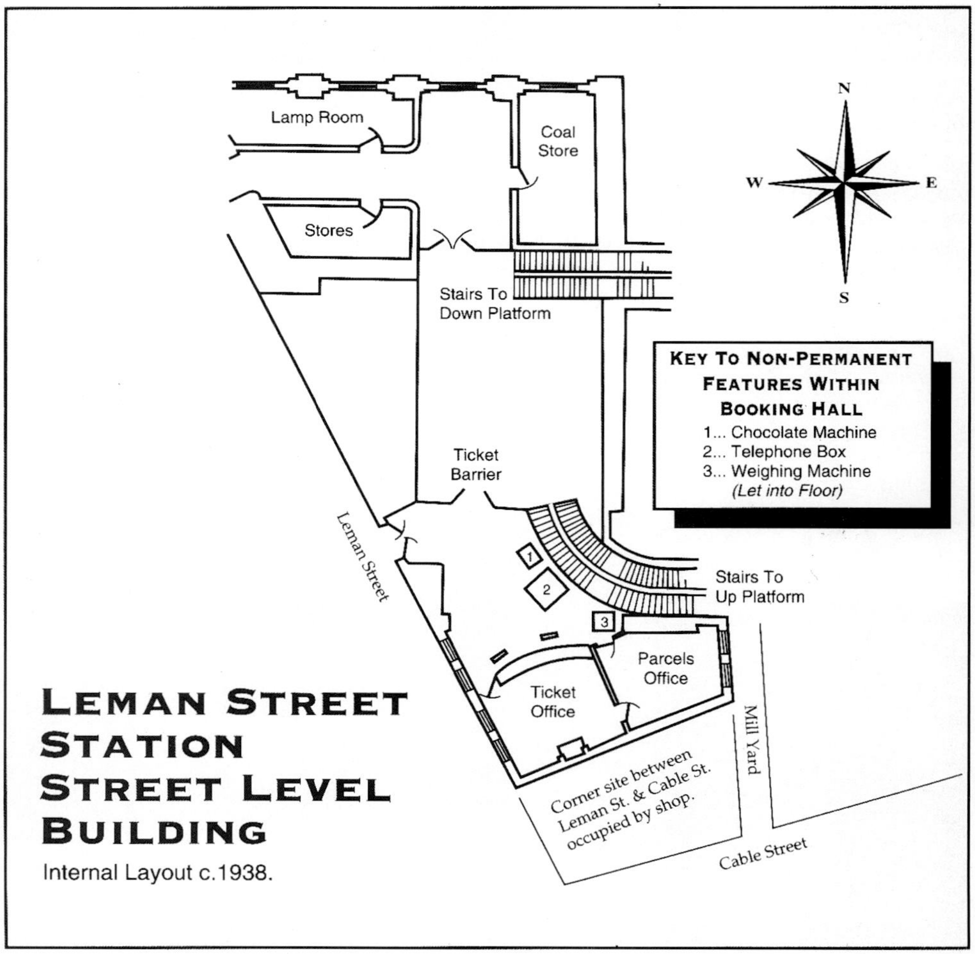

the heavy demands made by the authorities". Although the reporter felt that *"some dissatisfaction"* may arise, he continued to say that the *"closing of Leman Street in Whitechapel, and Shadwell stations should have been done a long time ago, the traffic at these stations being trifling compared with the cost of their maintenance. Besides, both districts are better served by 'buses and tramcars."*

For all this however, the closure did not prove to be permanent and Leman Street reopened on 1st July 1919. However it seems that there was little demand for it outside working hours and it lost its Sunday services in the autumn of 1920.

The signal box remained in use until it was rendered redundant by new colour light signalling, introduced between Fenchurch Street and Gas Factory Junction, Bow, in the spring of 1935.

As the years progressed it was felt that the street level accommodation was too lavish for the number of people then using the station, so a scheme was devised in the spring of 1938 whereby part of the building could be let

Above: The west end of Leman Street station, as seen from the down platform in 1922, with the signal box on the right and London Docks / East Smithfield branch diverging to the left.

Right: Looking from beneath the bridge over Leman Street towards Cable Street in the 1930s. The doorway leading into the station is to the immediate right of the LNER poster boards, whilst a little further on can be seen the four windows which illuminated the booking hall and ticket office. The building on the corner, beyond the station frontage was a grocer's shop, but whether the LMSR horse-drawn van was making a delivery is not known!

for other purposes, including a sub-post office. However, fate stepped in and the plan was abandoned.

The railways of east London suffered a great deal of damage during the Second World War and traffic was often disrupted. In September 1940, Leman Street briefly served as the City terminus for Tilbury and Southend line trains, after the tracks into Fenchurch Street had been put out of action by bombing. On 11th January 1941, an incendiary bomb penetrated the booking hall roof and damaged the ticket office, but the station remained in use. By then however, there was even less demand for it than before, as so many men had joined the armed forces and many local families had been bombed out of their homes or evacuated. Therefore, it was decided that there was little point in keeping it open any longer, so Leman Street closed from 7th July 1941 and this time the closure proved permanent. At around 3.45pm on the afternoon of 1st August 1944, the buildings on both platforms received blast damage, but, as the station was already closed, this seems to have caused little in the way of disruption.

When the war finally ended, much of inner London was left totally ruined and it took many years before the scars really started to disappear. Leman Street station stood gaunt and empty, but looked no worse than the gutted houses, shops and factories which stood nearby.

Its demolition was approved on 21st July 1950 and work started soon afterwards by removing the platform awnings and coping. However, once these had gone, it seems that little else was done until 1955-6, when more wholesale destruction took place. Eventually all that could be seen from a passing train was the derelict up platform with a row of iron railings which had once protected the stairwell. Nearby, propped up against the rear wall, lay a faded wooden board which stated *"Do Not Alight - Station Closed"*, but looking at the pathetic remains this was perhaps rather obvious. Down below, the street level building was firmly locked and had its windows bricked-up to deter vagrants.

Inside the former booking hall, light filtered through the broken roof and dappled the grimy walls. These were painted in brown to waist level and cream above, separated by a thin black line. The ticket office had long since disappeared, but no doubt some of the shattered pieces of wood which littered the floor were once part of it. On the blank wall which paralleled Cable Street was the tattered remains of an old timetable, which still displayed part of its heading *"Great Eastern Railway"* in heavy serif lettering. The stairway which led to the up platform was completely open to the sky and again showed liberal areas of brown and cream paint on its surviving plaster. The stairs themselves had been removed and the void at the top blocked by a low wall. Although the bricking-up of windows successfully deterred human intruders, it did little to stop the place attracting urban wildlife and the building latterly housed a sizeable pigeon colony.

The street level building was never leased out for non-railway purposes but remained derelict to the end. The adjoining shop, which stood at the corner of Leman Street and Cable Street, continued in use until the early 1960s. The building next to this, which backed directly

Ex-Great Northern Railway Class N2/1 0-6-2T No 4723 at Leman Street station in the 1930s with a Fenchurch Street - Ilford train. The locomotive was one of her class to be fitted with Westinghouse equipment in 1927-8 for working in Scotland. From May 1929 onwards some of these returned south and were transferred to the ex-GE section. No 4723 eventually went back to her native GN territory and had her Westinghouse equipment removed in 1939.

An aerial view of Leman Street station taken in 1949, whilst it was still intact. The sidings near the top of the photograph were part of the former London Tilbury & Southend Railway Commercial Road goods depot.

onto the station, was No 1, Cable Street. This housed a cafe and remained standing, together with the corner shop, until 1964 when they were both demolished. Their site disappeared when the road was widened slightly, but the former station building continued to stand. In 1982 there were plans to convert it into a car showroom, but these came to nothing. Two years later, work started on the construction of the Docklands Light Railway and, as the street level site was required for the new concrete viaduct, the building was finally demolished.

There are still a few vague traces of the station, although these are far from obvious. Up above, a few brick courses of the old up platform have survived and are used to partially support the DLR trackbed. These can be seen from a passing C2C train, but they are so obscure as to be easily overlooked. At street level, a bricked-up former doorway beneath the bridge is just about discernible, although it takes a keen eye to pick it out.

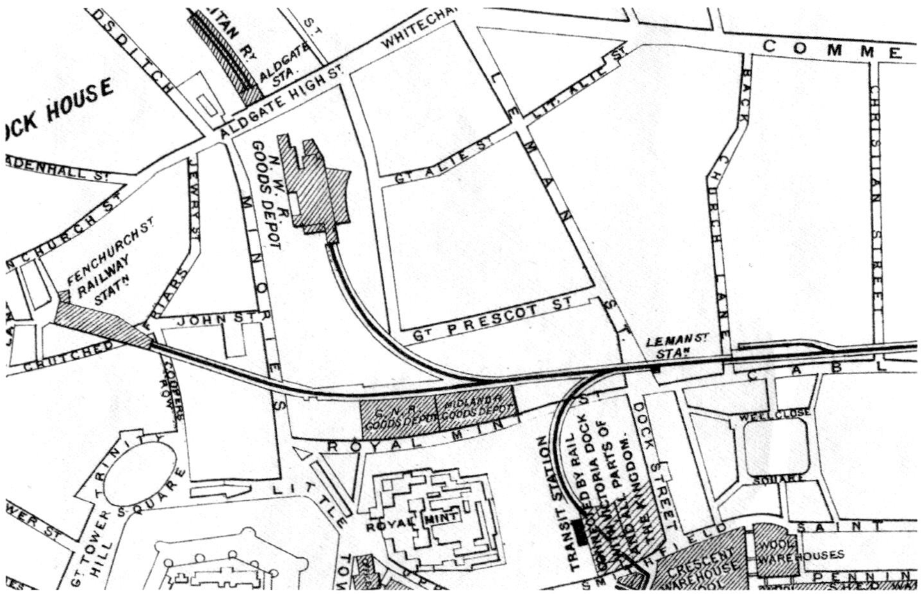

Map showing the area around Leman Street station, with various goods depots to its west. That which diverges towards the south was the GER London Docks, or East Smithfield branch, which opened in 1864 and closed in 1966. The line curving off to the north served the LNWR depot at Haydon Square, which functioned from 1853 until 1962. Close to the junction, on the south side of the Fenchurch Street line are the Midland Railway and Great Northern Railway depots at Royal Mint Street. The Midland premises dated from 1862 and were known as the 'City Goods Station'. The GNR depot was opened by the London & Blackwall Railway in 1858 as 'Minories', but was exclusively handling Great Northern traffic by early 1861. It was renamed Mint Street soon after opening and Royal Mint Street in 1870. The two depots closed in 1949 and 1951 respectively.

Above: The down platform at Leman Street seen from the Railway Correspondence and Travel Society East London Railtour on 14th April 1951. As can be seen, no time had been wasted in removing the awnings after the demolition order was approved less than a year earlier, although the buildings themselves remained standing until 1955-6. The Through lines are hidden behind the wall on the left.

Opposite (top): The former street level building at the junction of Leman Street and Cable Street, as it appeared in 1981. Widening of Cable Street resulted in the demolition of the shop which once occupied the corner site, together with the adjoining cafe.

Opposite (bottom): The former booking hall in 1981. A great deal of plaster remained on the walls adjoining the entrance door, but had disappeared from the section around the windows.

For a real r
Old Holborn
LEMAN STREET
CABLE STRE

Left: The building's interior in 1981, with the doors leading from Leman Street on the right. The two bricked-up windows closest to the camera once illuminated the booking hall, whilst the other pair looked out from the ticket office, although all traces of its wooden bow front had disappeared without trace, possibly in the mid-1950s.

Below (left): The southern face of the up side stairwell, viewed from the former booking hall in 1981. To the upper right is a well preserved section of plaster, painted in "light and dark buff", which was the colour scheme adopted in GER and early LNER days.

Below (right): The northern face of the up side stairwell, which curved on its lower section. The doorway led into Mill Yard and may have been used as an exit or used as staff access.

After the demolition of 1955/6, all that remained at track level was the up platform. Even this was not intact however, as the coping and the sections bridged over the roads at either end had been removed. All traces of the buildings had also gone, although the stairwell survived, complete with some nice wrought ironwork on the side facing the trains.

Above: The platform viewed from the Fenchurch Street end in 1969. The surviving stairwell is prominent just right of centre, whilst to the left lies the board which carried the legend "Do Not Alight - Station Closed".

Right: The former up platform looking west in 1972.

Above (left): The up side stairwell viewed from the platform in 1981.

Above (right): The up side stairway ironwork seen from the former street level building on the same day.

Left: The section of street level building looking onto Mill Yard around 1969, showing the two bricked-up parcels office windows and the "staff" doorway which lay beneath the up side stairway.

Below: A bricked-up doorway beneath the Leman Street bridge in May 2015 and understood to have been used as an exit. At the time of writing this is the most tangible relic at street level and shows signs that it was once surmounted by a lamp.

Cannon Street Road

Opened (London & Blackwall Railway): 21st August 1842.
Closed (London & Blackwall Railway): November/December 1848.

The short lived station at Cannon Street Road was opened by the London & Blackwall Railway in August 1842, a little over two years after the line was brought into use.

Before it could be built, the company had to purchase a house occupying the intended site and this appears to have slowed progress. However, on 19th July 1842, the Board of Directors instructed the engineer, Mr Wilson, that he should *"proceed without delay"*. The new station was clearly intended to be built as economically as possible, as the engineer was told to *"use his best discretion to the work"* and that he should make use of old materials recovered from elsewhere. Mr Wilson said that this would be no problem and that construction would be completed in just three weeks at an estimated cost of £100.

Mr Wilson was obviously as good as his word and the Board minutes for Tuesday 23rd August 1842 stated that *"the New Station at Cannon Street Road was opened for traffic on Sunday last"*.

From maps it appears that the platforms were located on the bridge over the road, but the means of public access is uncertain. It does not seem that the LBR erected 'staircase buildings' on either side as at their other viaduct stations, so the stairs may have been external, in the manner of Devonshire Street on the Eastern Counties Railway, or else within one of the arches.

Cannon Street Road was located fairly close to Shadwell, the next station to the east, and presumably failed to generate enough traffic to warrant it being retained. It closed towards the end of 1848, when the London & Blackwall Railway were in the early stages of converting the line to both standard gauge and locomotive haulage, instead of the cable system employed since opening in 1840.

Judging from the cost and its speedy construction, the station was probably lightly built and was therefore easily demolished. No evidence of it appears on the First Edition Ordnance Survey map, so all traces had presumably been removed by the early 1870s.

A map of the mid-1840s, showing the station at centre, on the bridge carrying the line above Cannon Street Road. The Parish Church of St George's-in-the-East, designed by Nicholas Hawksmoor, can be seen to its south, immediately above the once-notorious Ratcliff Highway.

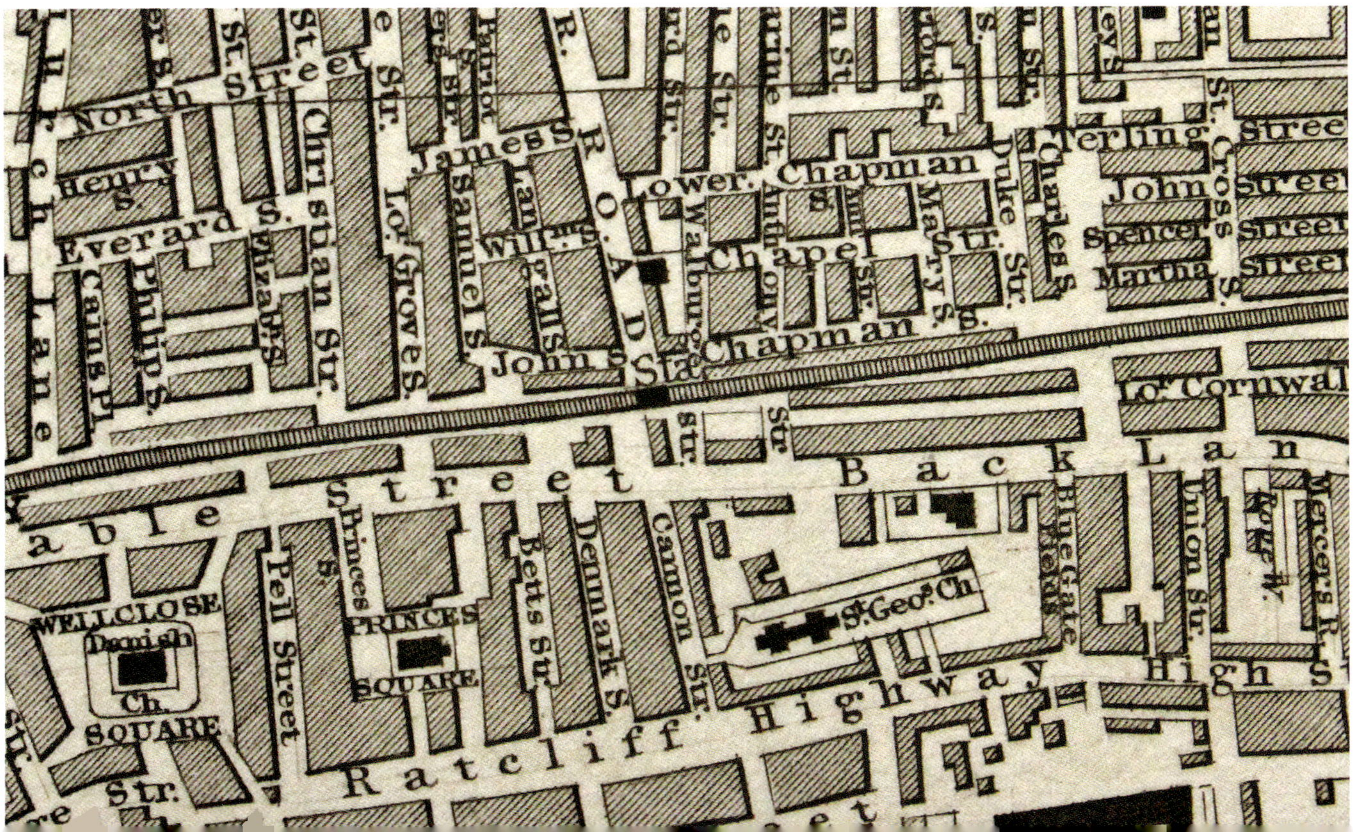

Shadwell & St George's East

Opened as Shadwell (London & Blackwall Railway): 1st October 1840.
Renamed Shadwell & St George's East (Great Eastern Railway): 1st July 1900.
Temporarily closed (Great Eastern Railway): 22nd May 1916 - 5th May 1919.
Closed (London & North Eastern Railway): 7th July 1941.

The disused station at Shadwell & St George's East looking towards Fenchurch Street on a wet, dismal day in October 1949. The awnings were removed around the summer of 1950, but the platform buildings survived until 1956.

When built, Shadwell was the only intermediate station between Minories and Stepney. It had not been part of the original scheme, but was added as an afterthought. Two months after construction commenced it seems that little if any progress had been made, so the Company decided that it should be completed as soon as possible and agreed to spend £50 on the erection of *"a temporary staircase and sheds"*.

The stations at Stepney, Limehouse and West India Docks each shared a common layout, with staircase buildings on either side of the viaduct and short platforms above, protected by overall roofs. This style does not seem to have been employed at Shadwell however, as according to early plans, its facilities are thought to have been very basic when opened on 1st October 1840. As the *"staircase and sheds"* were described as *"temporary"*, they were presumably replaced by something more substantial after opening, but further details have not been located. Its entrance was on the west side of Sutton Street.

In 1853, work started on widening the viaduct on its north side to accommodate an additional up line. By and large, this added an extra 15 feet to the width of the formation, although it was wider at Shadwell, where a new down platform was provided to replace the original.

The Great Eastern Railway leased the line from 1st January 1866 and the new management lost no time in making changes. On 20th November of that year, the GER Way and Works Committee were told that the platforms at Shadwell, along with other LBR stations, were in a bad state of repair and needed immediate attention.

Extract from the 1:2500 OS map, which was surveyed in 1870 and published five years later. It shows the staggered platforms of Shadwell station at centre, with the up side extending over the Sutton Street bridge, whilst the down side was positioned a little to the west. Although not apparent from the map, this was not an island, as it was separated by a wall or fence from the track opening in 1856, which curved around the back of it and was intended for Bow line services not calling at the station.

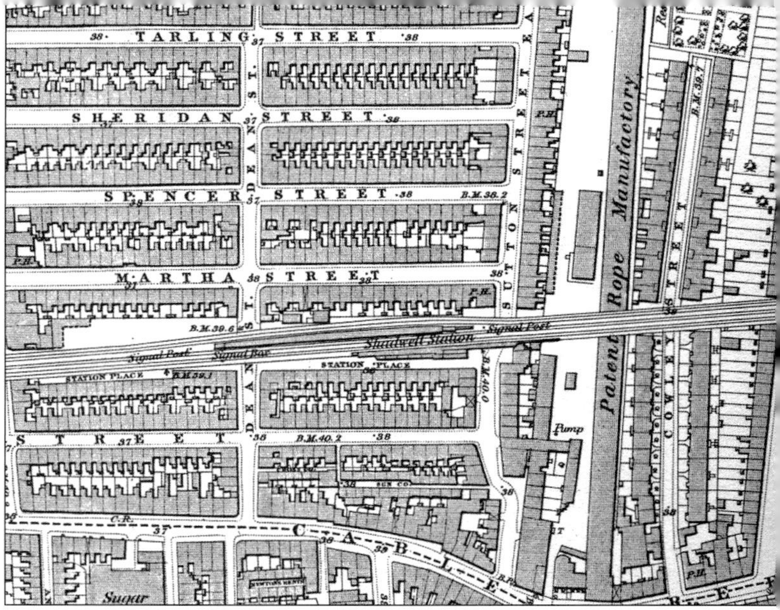

This was presumably carried out, but further complaints came in January 1870 when, as a result, it was decided to widen the up platform to 7 feet.

At this time the platforms at Shadwell were staggered, with that on the down side stretching further west and that serving the up projecting onto the bridge over Sutton Street. The layout could not have been ideal, as in November 1871 the GER were considering resiting the station to the east, but nothing came of this and in January 1875 a further £70 was authorised to improve the existing premises.

Work was then under way extending the East London Railway, from its terminus at Wapping, through Shadwell and Whitechapel to Shoreditch, where a connection would be made onto the Great Eastern. On 11th August 1875, the GER and ELR Chairmen met and discussed the possibility of providing interchange facilities at Shadwell. To achieve this it would prove necessary to acquire extra land and the scheme was put on hold until the subject had been investigated.

The East London Railway northern extension, along with the new Shadwell ELR station opened on 10th April 1876 and a covered footway linking the two was brought into use at around the same time.

Further improvements were carried out on the Great Eastern station in June 1879 when a contract was awarded to the firm of Wicks, Bangs & Co to renew the platforms at Shadwell, Stepney and Limehouse, for an inclusive figure of £2,650. A little under two years later, in February 1881, it was decided to erect new waiting rooms and the contract was awarded to the firm of J.R. Hunt, who undertook the work at a cost of £480.

After this, no additional changes seem to have taken place until the north side of the viaduct was again widened during 1892-3. Although this did not actually impinge on the station itself, the opportunity was taken to completely rebuild it in red brick, with replacement entrance doorways and improved booking hall at street level. The staircase building was very much in the style employed by the GER in the 1890s, with windows and doors topped by semi-circular arches. Red brick was also used for the buildings at platform level, which were protected by generous awnings, with canopy valancing of the type then being employed on many of the company's stations. Although the buildings themselves were of brick, it seems that timber was used for the rear screen at the western end of the up platform, presumably to reduce weight.

In the summer of 1900 it was decided to rename the station by adding a suffix to its title, thereby making it 'Shadwell & St George's East'. The exact reason for this is uncertain, but it was not to avoid confusion with its East London Railway neighbour, as this became 'Shadwell & St George's-*in-the* East' at the same time, with the only difference being a subtle variation in the wording.

Traffic at the Great Eastern station declined during the early twentieth century, after electric trams were introduced along Commercial Road, which paralleled

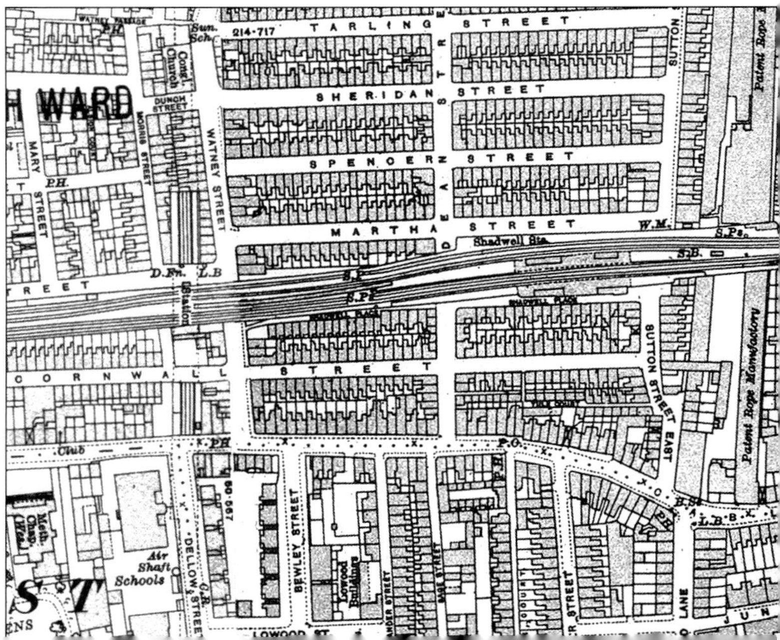

Extract from the 1:2500 OS map of 1914, showing the station after a further track was added behind the down platform in 1892-3. Once again, this by-passed Shadwell & St George's East which continued to serve the slow lines only. As part of the widening scheme the station was completely reconstructed and provided with new buildings. At the west end can be seen the covered walkways which led to the ELR station on the west side of Watney Street. The signal box east of the down platform dated from May 1895 and remained in use until 14th April 1935.

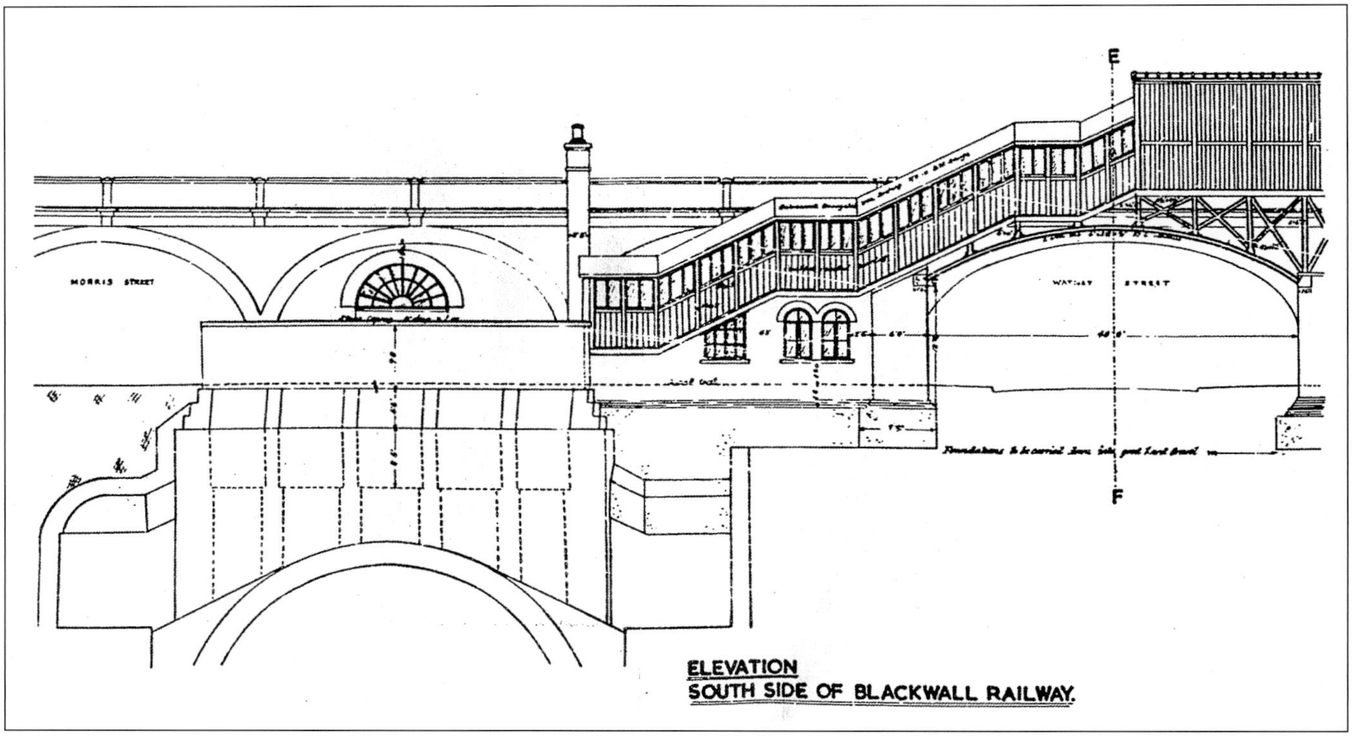

Above: Undated engineer's drawing showing the stairway linking the up platform with the East London Railway station in cutting below. The walkway serving this stretched some distance from the west end of the station and was cantilevered from the side of the viaduct.

Below: A plan of the street level accommodation dated October 1934. Passengers entered the booking hall from Shadwell Place, then climbed the stairs to the subway which led to both platforms. The stairway leading from the subway at the bottom of the diagram had been used as an exit, but was about to be sealed off by a floor to ceiling partition when the drawing was made.

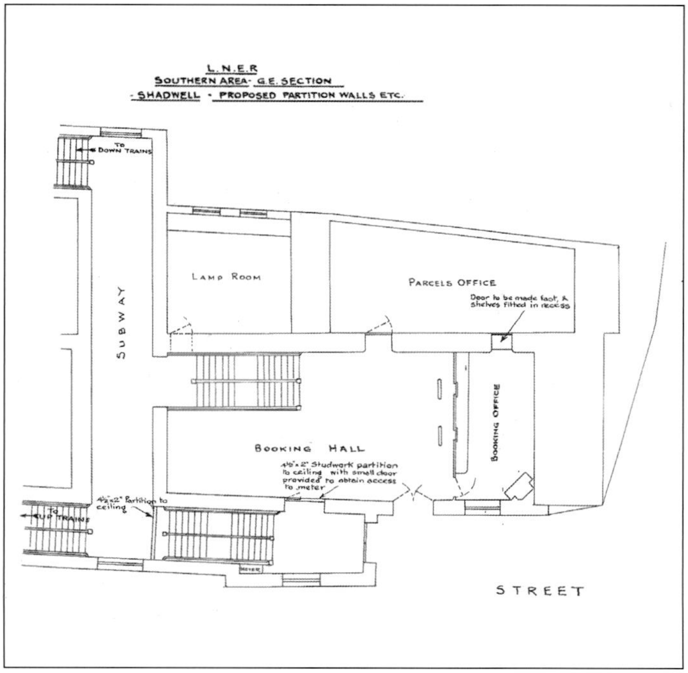

the line a short distance to the north. Therefore, it is not surprising that Shadwell & St George's East was one of the stations closed by the GER for wartime economy reasons in May 1916. On 27th of that month, five days after the closures were implemented, the *East London Advertiser* reported that *"At each of these* (affected) *the name of the station is posted over with a placard reading "Station Closed". The station staffs have not been transferred and are at present engaged in "clearing up." This is being done so thoroughly that the majority of East End people firmly believe that it is the intention of the Company not to re-open the stations."* This proved to be the case with Bishopsgate and Globe Road on the Liverpool Street line, but others in the area were subsequently brought back into use, including Shadwell, which reopened on 5th May 1919.

At the onset of the Blitz in September 1940, Shadwell received air raid damage, although this does not seem to have been too serious and services were quickly restored. Other bombing incidents in the vicinity followed, but none of these seem to have affected the station itself. On 8th March 1941 however, the arch over Sutton Street was damaged and, as this adjoined the entrance, the station had to be closed. A further raid, eleven days later on

19th March resulted in a fire and this may have been the death blow, as official closure followed on 7th July.

From the few known photographs, the station did not seem to have been too badly damaged, but patronage had been dropping off for years, so its permanent closure was perhaps inevitable.

As with Leman Street, it was partly demolished and lost its awnings in the early 1950s, but total destruction did not come until the spring of 1956, when virtually all traces at track level were obliterated. The only parts to survive were some platform fragments at the country end of the up side.

Down below, the former entrance adjoining Shadwell Place was let out for non-railway purposes, although the original 1890s doors survived for many years until being replaced by shutters fairly recently.

The present Docklands Light Railway station, opened in 1987, occupies part of the earlier site, although it consists of a single island and not two side platforms as before. Originally, the sole DLR entrance was on the east side of Watney Street, but further access has since been made at the opposite end, just a short distance from its Great Eastern predecessor, which is currently used as warehouse premises.

Views of the walkway and stairs linking the two stations at Shadwell seem to be very rare. The upper photograph looks north from behind Cornwall Street and shows the rear of the former ELR street level building with the down side walkway above. The photograph is thought to date from the 1950s, after the up side walkway had been demolished. The lower photograph shows the ex-ELR station frontage in Watney Street, with a short stretch of walkway roofing just visible above the viaduct parapet on the right. Although the station opened in 1876, the building seen here dated from 1892.

The down platform photographed in April 1951, after the awnings and platform coping had been removed. The top of the stairs leading from the booking hall and passenger subway can be seen between the two buildings.

Above left: A view from a train passing behind the station on the fast lines in late 1955.

Above right: Demolition of the platforms and buildings commenced a few months later and was well under way when this photograph was taken on 5th April 1956.

Below: the former street level accommodation as it appeared in 1965. The window and doorway on the left served the former exit stairs and lobby, whilst the other double doors led into the booking hall. The window on the right, partly obscured by the two-tone Bedford CA, illuminated the ticket office and was fitted with the original security bars.

Above left: In this view, dating from the late 1960s, the double doors serving the former exit stairs can be seen on the left whilst those leading into the booking hall appear on the right. Above them is a cast iron lamp bracket and a stout timber post which once supported a short section of wooden screen at the rear of the platform. This adjoined the east end of the buildings and was presumably taken down when the awnings were removed.

Above right: Looking east along Shadwell Place in 2015, with the window which once illuminated the passenger subway towards the top of the blue-brick wall to right of centre. The original purpose of the doorway in the foreground is uncertain, although it was presumably for staff use.

Right: The former ticket office window facing onto Shadwell Place, with its security bars still in position.

Above left: The passenger subway window, facing onto Shadwell Place.

Above right: Inside the ELR station building, a short but wide staircase led to a passageway, which in turn provided access to the two interchange stairways. Passengers wanting the up side turned left, whilst those wanting the down turned right. This view shows the bricked-up entrance to the latter.

Left: The remains of Shadwell & St George's East station, photographed from a passing train in 1969. The section at the far end was re-surfaced after general demolition in the spring of 1956 to provide weather protection to the tenants of the arches below. The ramp nearest the camera was of course added at the same time, whilst that at the far end may include some original elements but was provided with a new surface. The top of the up side stairwell was located within the section behind the catenary mast, but this, along with the stretch of platform to the right has been cut back to the width of the section in blue engineering brick, which faces onto Shadwell Place. These remains have survived the coming of the Docklands Light Railway and can easily be seen from the eastern end of the present DLR station.

Stepney

Opened (London & Blackwall Railway): 6th July 1840.
Resited to east (London & Blackwall Railway): 30th March 1857.

The first London & Blackwall Railway station at Stepney opened with the line on 6th July 1840 and comprised two platforms. It was located to the east of White Horse Street and had its entrance on the south side of Rose Lane. It was built in the style adopted for the three original LBR viaduct stations, with staircase buildings on either side and a overall roof around 67ft long above. The staircase buildings differed from those at Limehouse and West India Docks however, as they had curved frontages and were offset to the west as opposed to being symmetrical as at the other two. The booking office was located within one of the viaduct arches and a report in *The Times* on the day of opening stated that all three intermediate viaduct stations were *"Exceedingly neat externally, and fitted up internally for passengers who have to wait for the trains."* The company's architect was William Tite, so it is most likely that he was responsible for the design.

At first, only one set of rails was in operation and the second was not brought into use until 3rd August 1840. For a while, one of these tracks was used by complete trains plying between Minories and Blackwall, whilst the other served the intermediate stations. However, because of the method of operating, Stepney passengers could only travel to and from Minories until around 20th August, when a more comprehensive service was introduced. The cable-hauled trains ran back and forth along the same track all day, so neither line was referred to as up or down. This ceased in 1849 however, when locomotive working was introduced and the branch between Stepney and Bow was opened.

Before this happened, Stepney station underwent various changes, including an extension of the overall roof at its eastern end. As the locomotive-hauled trains were much longer than their cable-worked predecessors, the platforms must have been extended at the same time, but whether this was carried out at both ends is not certain. Because of the new junction, they could not have stretched any further east than the limits of the newly lengthened roof, and although wooden cantilevered extensions would have been possible at the other end, they are not shown in any plans. Down below, at street level, the staircase building on the south side of the formation was removed and replaced by one a little further to the east, built on a rectangular plan, without the previous curved frontage.

When the branch opened on 2nd April 1849, carriages for Bow would be positioned at the rear of Blackwall trains and detached at Stepney. The main train would then continue over the original route, while another locomotive would back onto the detached portion and take it through to Bow. The reverse procedure would take place in the opposite direction, so the Blackwall and Bow portions would combine at Stepney and run as a single train into Fenchurch Street. As they had not been needed during the cable-hauled period, the company had not installed any signals and a number of collisions occurred at Stepney whilst attaching and detaching. Matters improved from 9th November 1849, when separate Blackwall and Bow trains began operating to and from Fenchurch Street and the earlier practice at Stepney came to an end.

After this, the station settled down to a fairly uneventful life, although its days on the original site were numbered. Its demise was brought about when the line between Fenchurch Street and Stepney was widened between 1853 and 1857.

Apart from a short section near Fenchurch Street, which was brought into use in 1855, the new track was largely opened the following year, but even then it did not stretch as far as the station. Instead it ended at a platform a little to the west, in George Street, which was

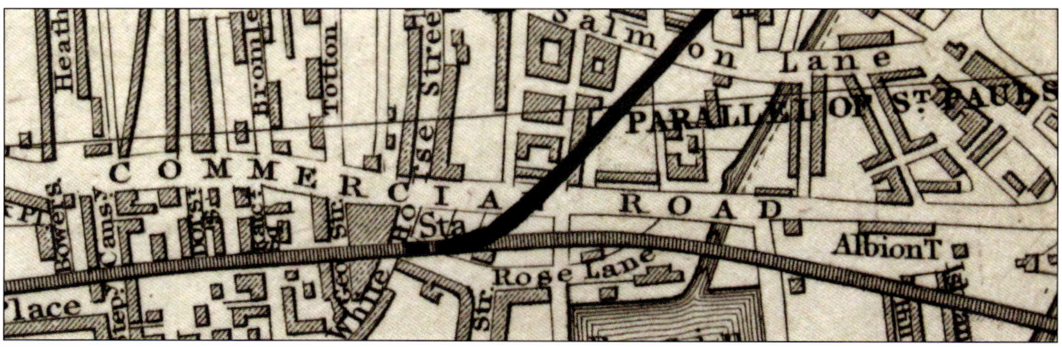

A map of the 1840s, showing Stepney station on its original site, west of the junction and with its entrance in Rose Lane. East of the station, the original route to Blackwall appears south of Commercial Road, whilst the Bow branch veers off northwards above Salmon Lane.

erected whilst work in connection with the new four-platformed premises could continue at the fork of the junction. The temporary George Street platform seems to have been used by up trains only and the original station remained open until its replacement was finally ready.

The new Stepney station, with its entrance on the south side of Commercial Road, was brought into use on 30th March 1857 and its predecessor closed. Its platforms and overall roof presumably disappeared soon after, but both staircase buildings survived until the widening of 1892-3, when that on the south side was demolished. The other survived however and remains standing at the time of writing. Not surprisingly it has undergone various changes over the years, but it is still recognisable as what it once was. The viaduct arch which housed the booking hall is now used by a firm dealing with car repairs and shows no obvious signs of its original purpose.

The replacement station of 1857 has also gone through a number of changes during its long history and its down platform has been extended westward so it is now above its predecessor's former entrance. When built however, it was much shorter and did not overlap the earlier site.

Two views of the down side staircase building of the original Stepney station taken in 2014. As can be seen, the frontage is slightly curved and had a round-arched window at street level which has been converted into a doorway. In the photograph above, the former White Horse Street, now Butcher Row, can be seen on the right, whilst Rose Lane, now Ratcliffe Lane, is on the left.
The replacement station was opened as Stepney, but was renamed Stepney East on 1st July 1923, seven months after the GER became part of the London & North Eastern Railway. As mentioned in the text, it had undergone various changes over the years. These included the loss of its two Blackwall line platforms in the mid-1930s, around a decade after passenger services were withdrawn from the branch in 1926.
When the introduction of electric services linking Fenchurch Street with Tilbury, Southend and Shoeburyness was in its early stages, the down platform was increased in length from 597ff to 657ft, and a recent further down platform extension stretches westward onto the site of the original station as seen in these photographs.
On 11th May 1987 Stepney East was renamed Limehouse and a few months later, at the end of August, public services began on the DLR, with new platforms constructed on the site of those which once served the Blackwall line.

Limehouse

Opened (London & Blackwall Railway): 6th July 1840.
Closed (London & North Eastern Railway): 4th May 1926.

The former down side stairway building at Limehouse, viewed from Three Colt Street in 1965. The facilities at street level were located within two viaduct arches, with the westernmost of these accommodating the booking hall. The double doorway seen to the right of centre is the erstwhile station entrance, whilst the round-arched window to its left had illuminated the foot of the stairs.

Limehouse station opened with the London & Blackwall Railway on 6th July 1840 and was located on the east side of Three Colt Street. It was constructed in the standard style employed by the company, with staircase buildings either side of the viaduct and a 67ft long overall roof above to protect the two short platforms. The platforms were lengthened to accommodate longer trains when locomotives replaced cable haulage in 1849, but by the autumn of 1866, less than a year after the GER began leasing the line, their condition seems to have deteriorated and they were in need of attention.

Additional exit stairs were subsequently added on the up side and the building was enlarge accordingly. These changes appear on the 1/1056 Ordnance Survey map of 1870, but the date when they were carried out is not known.

Further alterations were planned around this time, but there was concern that widened platforms would overhang adjoining properties, so on 22nd June 1870 it was decided to hold the changes in abeyance. The scheme re-emerged in September 1873, and a month later, the Way & Works Committee recorded that the work of widening and lengthening both platforms could be carried out for £822. Before the improvements could start however, it was deemed necessary to acquire additional land and this was agreed in January 1875, at a cost of £1,000. The alterations were to be paid for by the LBR, but again nothing seems to have happened, as by

February 1879, the Great Eastern were still discussing the land acquisition and asking their engineer to submit a report on the matter.

In the June of that year however, the work finally received the go-ahead and a contract was awarded to the firm of W. Bangs & Co, who agreed to make the changes, along with alterations to both Shadwell and Stepney, at an inclusive cost of £2,650.

The changes at Limehouse resulted in it being the last LBR station to lose its overall roof, which was taken down and replaced by conventional awnings during the works of 1879.

No further alterations seem to have taken place at the station until the end of the nineteenth century, when a further rebuilding was planned.

The work was put out to tender and on 27th July 1899, the contract was awarded to the south London firm of W.H. Larden & Son, at a cost of £2,383. Under this scheme, new waiting rooms and awnings were to be erected and alterations would be made to existing building. Before proceeding further, the contractor had to select bricks that were *"good, hard, sound and thoroughly burnt"* and forward samples to the Engineer at Liverpool Street for his approval. The improvements were doubtlessly thorough and covered most aspects of the station. A date when they were completed does not seem to have been recorded, but at a meeting of the GER Way & Works Committee on 5th March 1901 it was stated that the company had overspent £1,754. 4s. 11d on the project, so the changes proved more costly than anticipated.

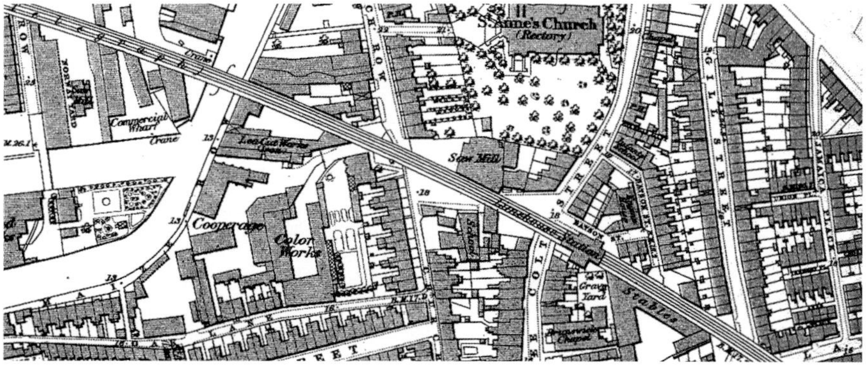

Left (upper): An extract from the 1870 1:2500 Ordnance Survey map showing Limehouse station, whilst still sporting its overall roof. The platforms must have been extended when locomotive hauled trains were introduced in 1849, but the extensions are not shown on this map.

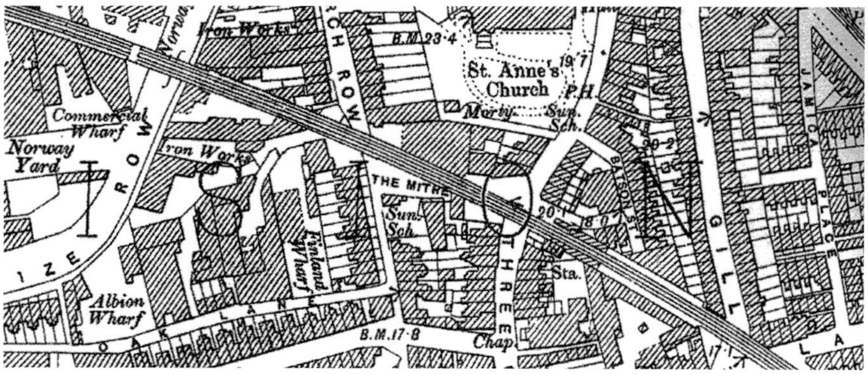

Left (middle): An extract from the 1:2500 Ordnance Survey map showing the station after the 1879 alterations, but before the rebuilding of 1899. As can be seen, the buildings and awnings were located at the western end, with the uncovered platform sections stretching eastwards beyond the canopies.

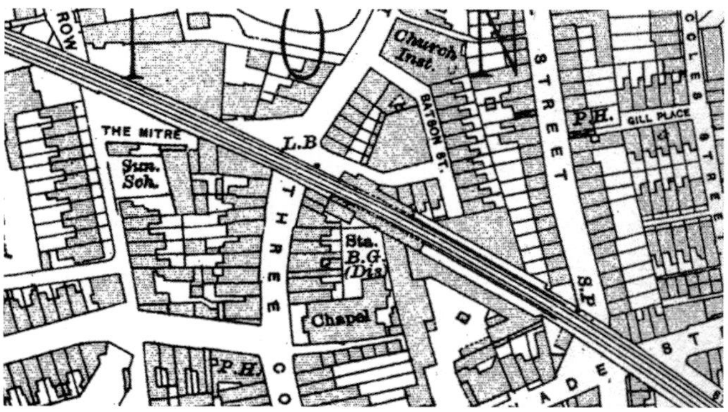

Left (bottom): Limehouse station in its final form, as shown on the 1:2500 Ordnance Survey map published in 1916. The platform buildings were still located at the London end, but the awnings were now of uneven length, with the up side being longer than the down.

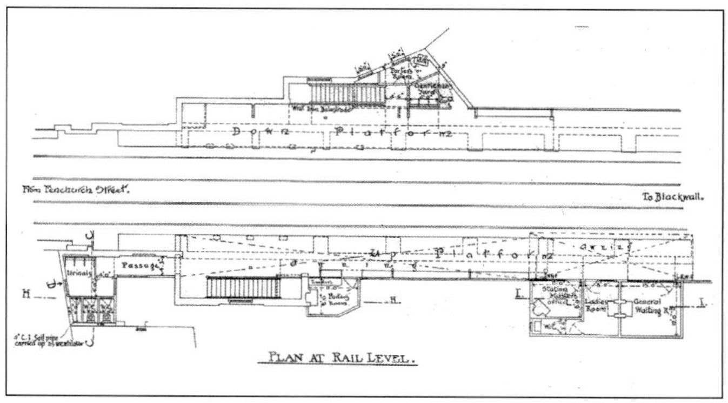

Below: Extract from an engineer's drawing of 1899 showing the layout of the up platform prior to the rebuilding. The buildings were renewed as specified in the contract: *"Take down and clear away the Porters' Room on Up platform by stairs and make good brick wall disturbed by same... Do. do. the Station Master's Room by last and do. do."*

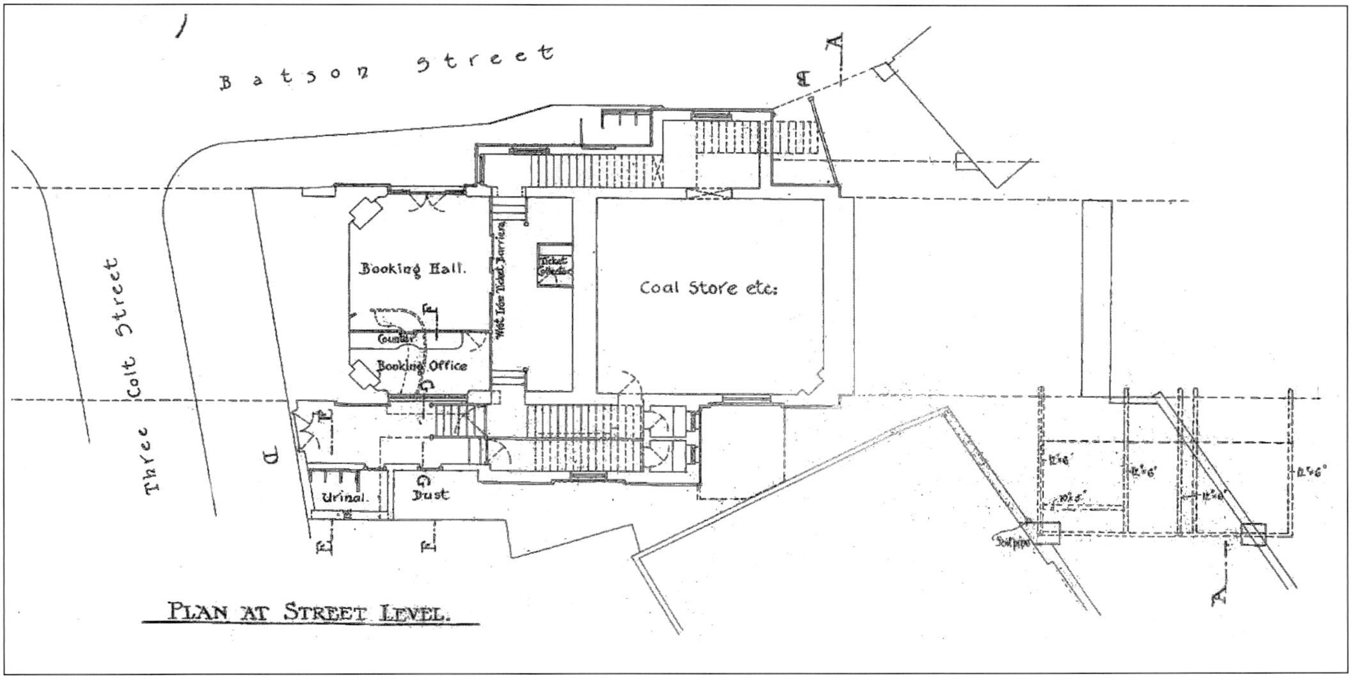

Above: An 1899 plan of the station at street level after the alterations, showing the booking hall in the arch closest to Three Colt Street and the coal store in that which adjoined to the east. The entrance was from Batson Street, whilst the other double doorway, adjoining the urinal, is thought to have been used as an exit.

Below: A plan of the platforms, after the changes of 1899, showing the station in its final form. Most of the work took place on the up side, although a few minor improvements were made to the down 'Gentlemen's yard'.

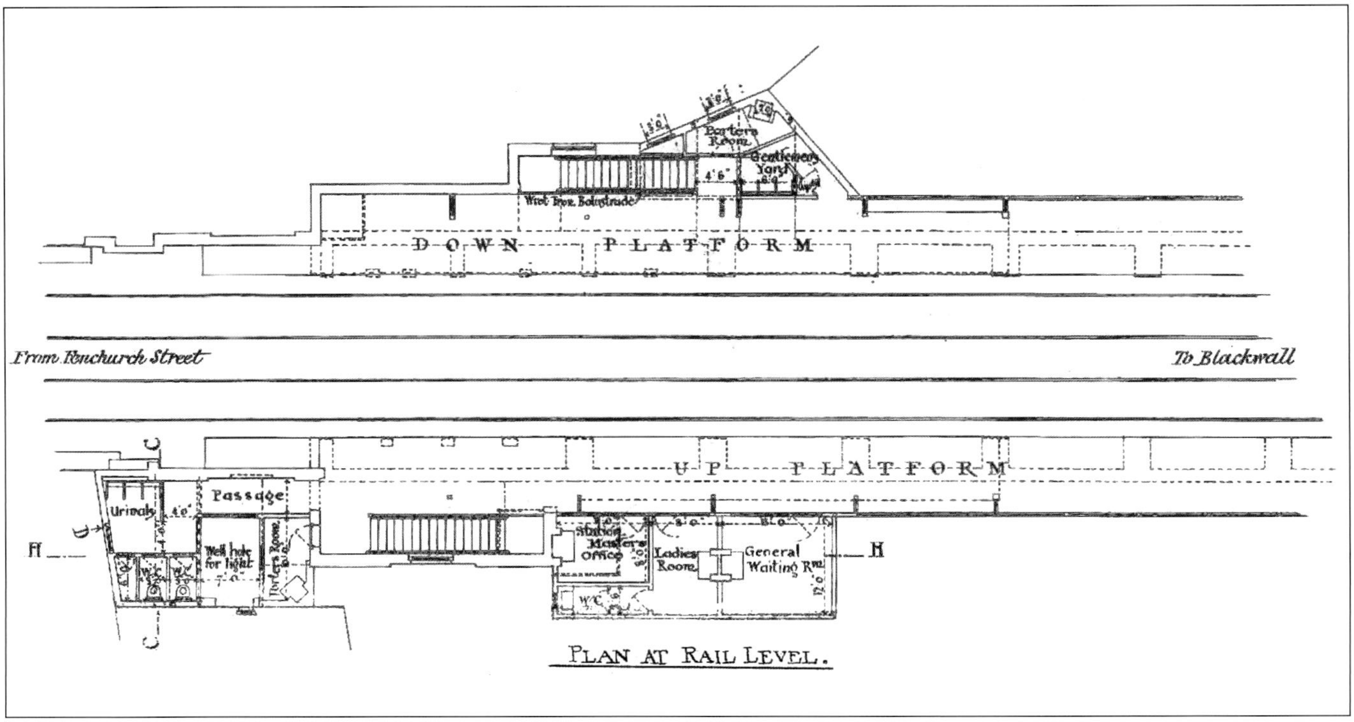

Left: Engineer's drawing from the 1899 improvements showing the ticket office screen, with the base of the down side stairway to its left.

Below: The up side buildings, photographed from the Fenchurch Street end in July 1921, with the waiting rooms on the far left and the station master's office a little closer to the camera. The stairs were renewed in 1899, along with their handrails and balusters, but the window seen on the right was original and dated from 1840. The platforms themselves were not replaced during the rebuilding, nor seemingly were the awnings, although changes were made at the London end to accommodate a new porters' room on the up side.

No more changes were destined to take place and, apart from repainting and repairs carried out in March 1912, Limehouse station remained in its 1899-1900 condition when it closed in 1926.

The wooden platforms and associated buildings were subsequently demolished, although a date for this has not been traced. However, from photographic evidence it is known that they were still standing in 1929 but had been removed by 1938, leaving just the lower parts of the two stairway buildings, which continue to survive at the time of writing.

Above: The west end of the down platform in July 1921, showing the stairs leading down to the booking hall, accompanied by another original LBR 1840 window. The selection of posters on the left is interesting, although it seems unlikely that many of the local inhabitants would have the resources to fritter away their hard-earned money on a round of seaside golf at Felixstowe at the time.

Right: A cross section of the platform buildings seen from the country end in an engineer's drawing showing the 1899 alterations.

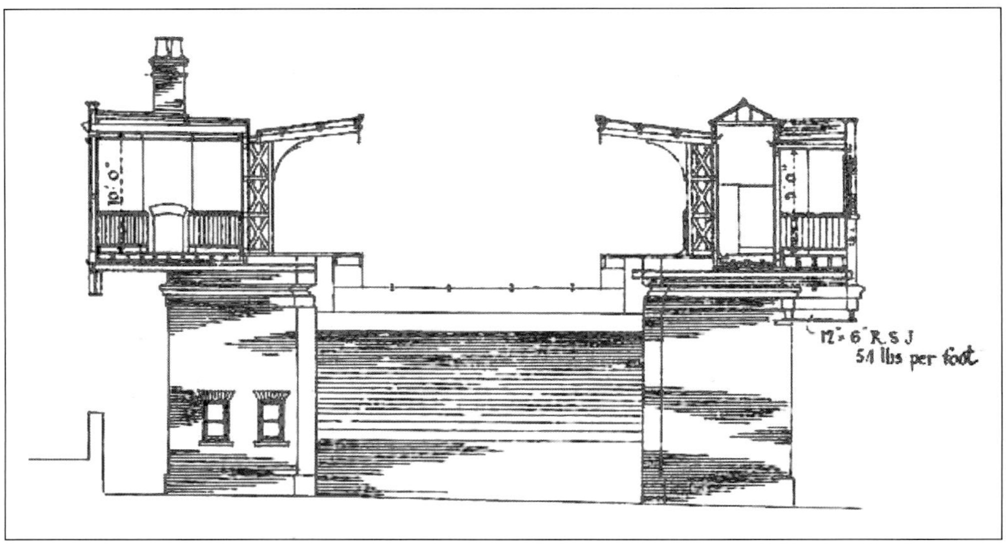

Above: The down platform seen in 1921, with the fine tower of Nicholas Hawksmoor's St Anne's Church behind.

Left: The station site in 1967, looking towards Fenchurch Street. By this time all that remained at track level were the two capped stairwells.

Below: GER third class single ticket issued on 21st September 1908.

Above: The down side staircase building (centre) in the 1980s, after the adjoining site had been cleared. The large doorway to the right was the former station entrance.

Right: The up side exit doorway in Three Colt Street, as it appeared in 1946. Inside the door, to the right, was a street level gents urinal accessed from the foot of the stairs.

Below: The up side staircase building in 1969, showing a large segmental arched window, which had been partially bricked-up sometime after the station closed.

To those familiar with the former Blackwall line during the post Second World War era, it came as a great surprise when part of it was incorporated into the Docklands Light Railway. The photograph above was taken soon after the DLR opened in 1987 and shows a train heading towards Tower Gateway. The down side staircase building of the former Limehouse station can be seen to the left, together with the top of that on the up side. These, together with the less obvious remains at Stepney, are the oldest surviving station buildings on the former GER network.

Left: An engineer's drawing from 1899, showing the eastern end of the down side staircase building, as it appeared when the station was open, with an additional storey. The part on the left, corresponds with the angled section in the photograph above, with the opening at street level subsequently fitted with two large doors. The large segmental arched window alongside has long-since been altered and partially bricked up, although its original outline can still be seen in the 1987 view.

West India Docks

Opened (London & Blackwall Railway): 6th July 1840.
Closed (London & North Eastern Railway): 4th May 1926.

West India Docks station, as it appeared soon after opening in 1840, with dock warehouses behind and an artist's impression of a cable-hauled train on the right. The company architect was William Tite and he was presumably responsible for the design. The bridge over the road is shown in its original form, with cast iron girders, which were strong enough for their intended purpose, but not to hold the weight of locomotives. The line's bridges and viaducts were largely the work of George Parker Bidder, who was appointed joint engineer for the project along with George Stephenson in 1838.

This station was located on the east side of West India Dock Road and opened with the line linking Minories with Blackwall on 6th July 1840. In common with Stepney and Limehouse, it had a staircase building on either side of the viaduct and its two short platforms were protected by an overall roof.

Not much is known of its early days, but its platforms were subsequently lengthened to handle loco-hauled trains and by November 1866, the Great Eastern Railway was expressing concern about their condition.

After this, some remedial work presumably took place, although this was not mentioned in the company minutes. Changes were in the offing however, as by the April of 1870, the GER were planning to widen the platforms and possibly make other alterations at the same time. The cost of carrying these out was estimated at £600, but this was reduced to £457 a couple of months later, on the understanding that the improved platforms were not provided with "covered ways". This was the term then used to describe awnings or canopies, so it is tempting to suggest that this was the time that the old overall roof was removed, although of course, it could have gone earlier. Be that as it may, the revised estimate obviously met with approval, as on 3rd August 1870 a contract was awarded to the firm of J. Perry & Son, who agreed to complete the job for £450.

The First Edition OS map, surveyed in 1870, shows the station with its staircase buildings and fairly short canopies, but whether the survey was made before or after J. Perry had carried out the work is not known. The

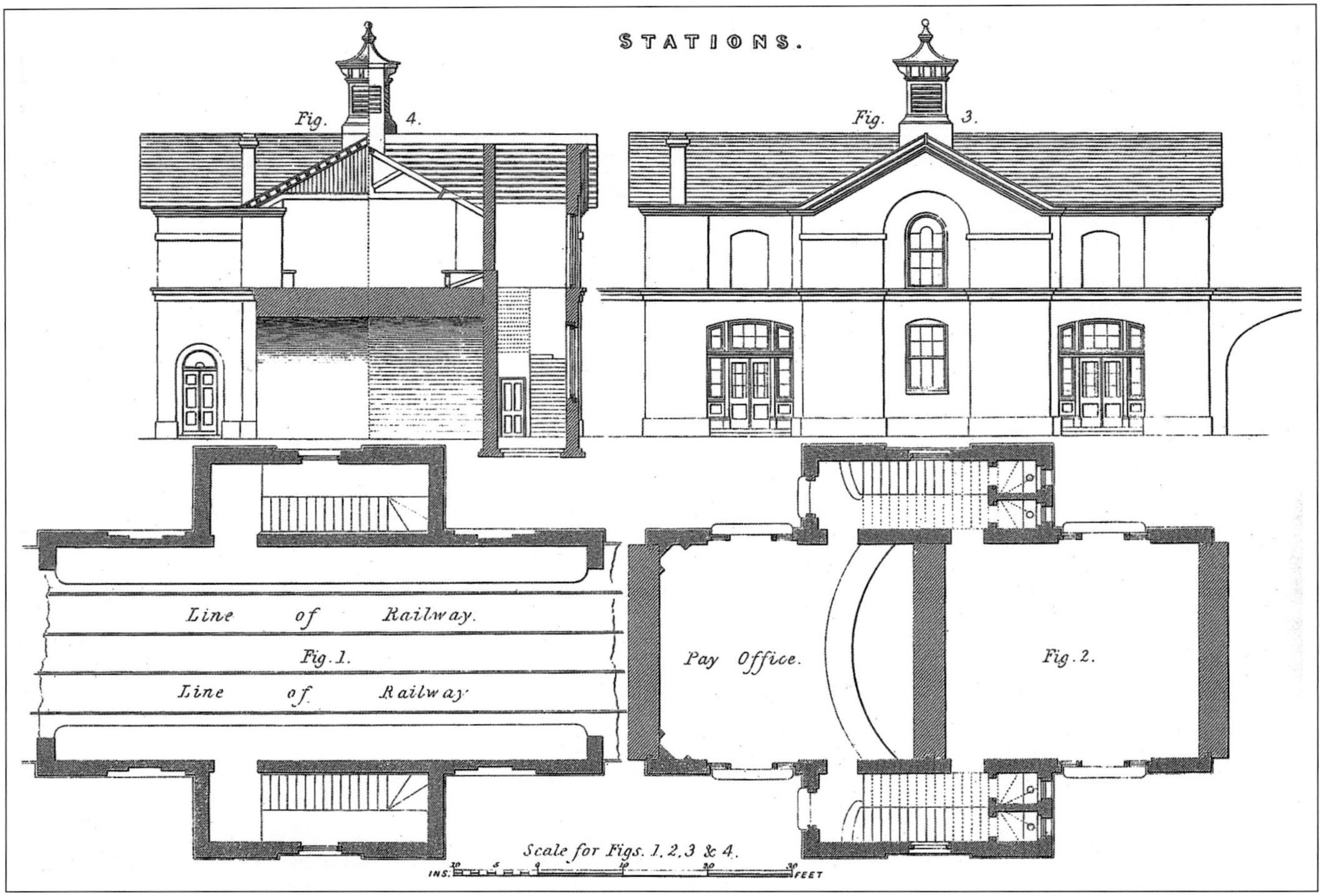

A plan and elevation of a London & Blackwall station as originally provided at Stepney, Limehouse and West India Docks. This was a general design, which could be altered as necessary to suit individual sites, so this is not thought to represent a particular location. The street level accommodation was housed within two of the viaduct arches whilst the stairs providing access to the platforms were contained within double-storey pavilions on either side of the formation. The trainshed roof shown here had a length of 67ft and was provided with an ornamental ventilator on the top. As can be seen from the track level plan, the platforms were completely covered by the roof and although these appear very short, they were only intended to serve individual cable-hauled carriages, as opposed to complete trains.

one thing that can be said with certainty however, is that by then, there was no sign of the overall roof, although one still existed at Limehouse.

In July 1872 it was decided to add a gents toilet at a cost of £40, but when similar facilities for ladies were requested a few months later, the idea was rejected. This seems very odd, but perhaps it was because further platform widening and lengthening was then under consideration and it may have been thought better to deal with this first. On 8th October 1873 it was stated that the cost of the platform work would be £120 and this presumably went ahead.

Just over a year later, the GER Way & Works Committee finally gave the go-ahead to providing a ladies waiting room at the estimated cost of £50 and was told that an attendant would be employed to take care of it.

On 13th January 1875, the same committee was advised of plans to carry out more platform work for £60, and provide a waiting room at the station for £50. As the price of the latter tallies with that of the proposed ladies room, it may well have been the same improvement, which, according to the minutes, was to be funded by the Blackwall company instead of the GER.

Some further waiting room alterations took place around the end of 1878, but as the estimated cost was just £22, they were probably not very significant.

The same cannot be said of the changes instigated as the nineteenth century drew to a close, when the station underwent a major rebuilding. The idea was discussed at the GER Way & Works Committee meeting on 3rd November 1896, but no work took place until the contract was awarded to Messrs. J. Mowlem of Grosvenor Works, Millbank in January 1899 at an estimated cost of £1,300.

The work was extensive and included new buildings and an additional entrance. Therefore it is perhaps not surprising that the estimate proved considerably less than the final price, which in March 1901 was recorded as £4,876.15.7d.

From then on the station seems to have remained unaltered until closure, although according to the Way & Works Committee minutes, some repair work and repainting took place in 1912.

It was the first station on the Blackwall branch to be demolished and its platforms are thought to have disappeared, along with their attendant buildings, around the end of 1931. A survey of the line carried out by the LNER in March 1932 showed no sign of the platforms and also stated that the passenger subway beneath the tracks was then being filled-in. The two staircase buildings probably went about the same time and no views of them are known to exist. In fact, photographs of West India Docks station seem to be virtually nonexistent, although, of course, the odd view might lie unidentified or hidden away in a private collection somewhere.

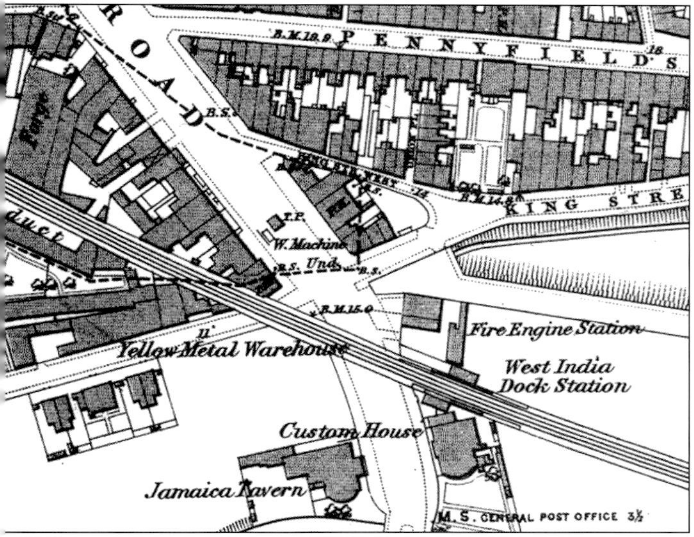

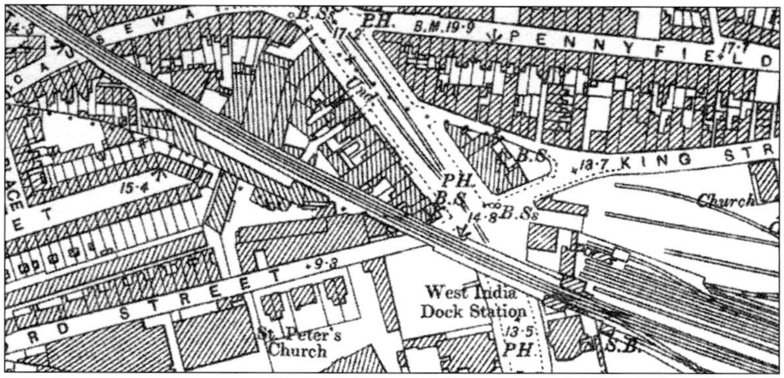

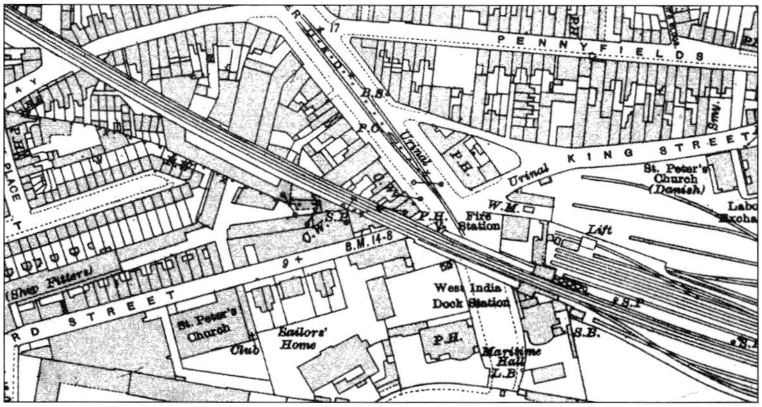

Above (left): Extract from the 1:2500 OS map surveyed in 1870, showing the station after the train shed roof had been removed. The platforms had been extended in both directions since opening, but the up was shorter than the down at its western end, and stopped just before the bridge over West India Dock Road. The two staircase buildings are clearly shown, with the up side being offset to clear the Custom House which was immediately to its south.

Above (right): The Second Edition 1:2500 map, as revised in 1893-4, with the station prior to its 1899 rebuilding. The platforms now extended over the bridge but had been shortened at their opposite end. The sidings on the north side of the line were used for goods traffic and were opened by the Midland Railway in 1882-3.

Right (centre): The station in its final form, as shown on the 1:2500 Ordnance Survey map of 1914. The signal box to the east of the up platform remained in use until 26th February 1928.

Right (bottom): The exterior of West India Docks station at an unknown date, with the rear of the down side building clearly visible to the right of centre and a large nameboard on the bridge above the road. The horse-drawn tram and other vehicles in the foreground provide a nice period touch, but unfortunately they obscure the entrance. The large building on the left was West India Dock Fire Station.

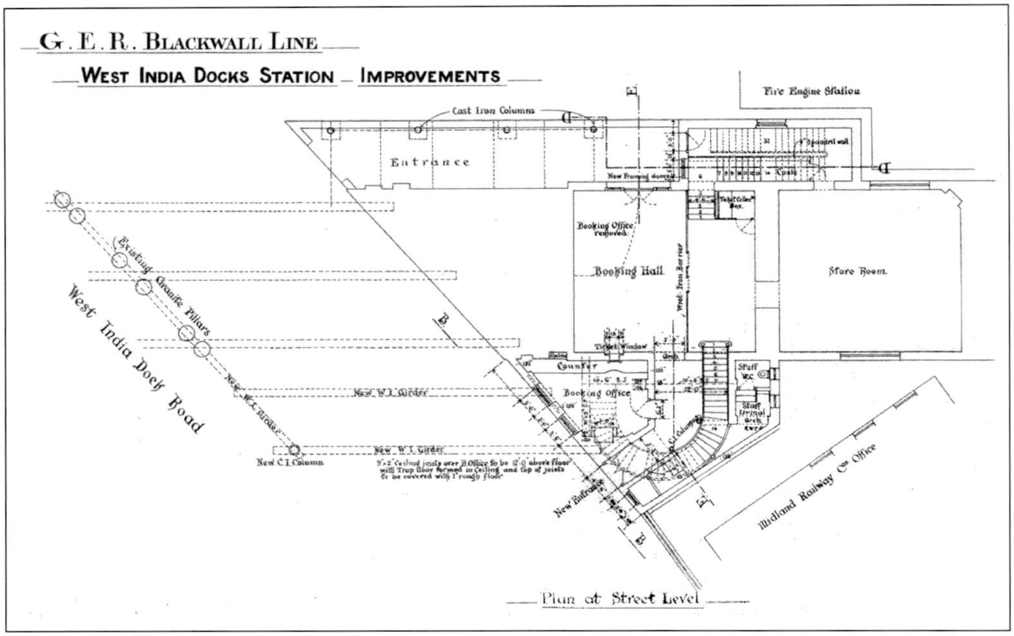

Plan prepared for the 1899 rebuilding, showing the street level accommodation with an additional entrance added on the up side. The original entrance was on the north side of the formation and was accessed from the east side of West India Dock Road by means of a footpath, which lay beneath the down platform building. This was constructed of wood and was supported by a row of four cast iron columns. The changes also saw the removal of the old ticket office and its replacement by a new office created within the building extension which contained the additional entrance.

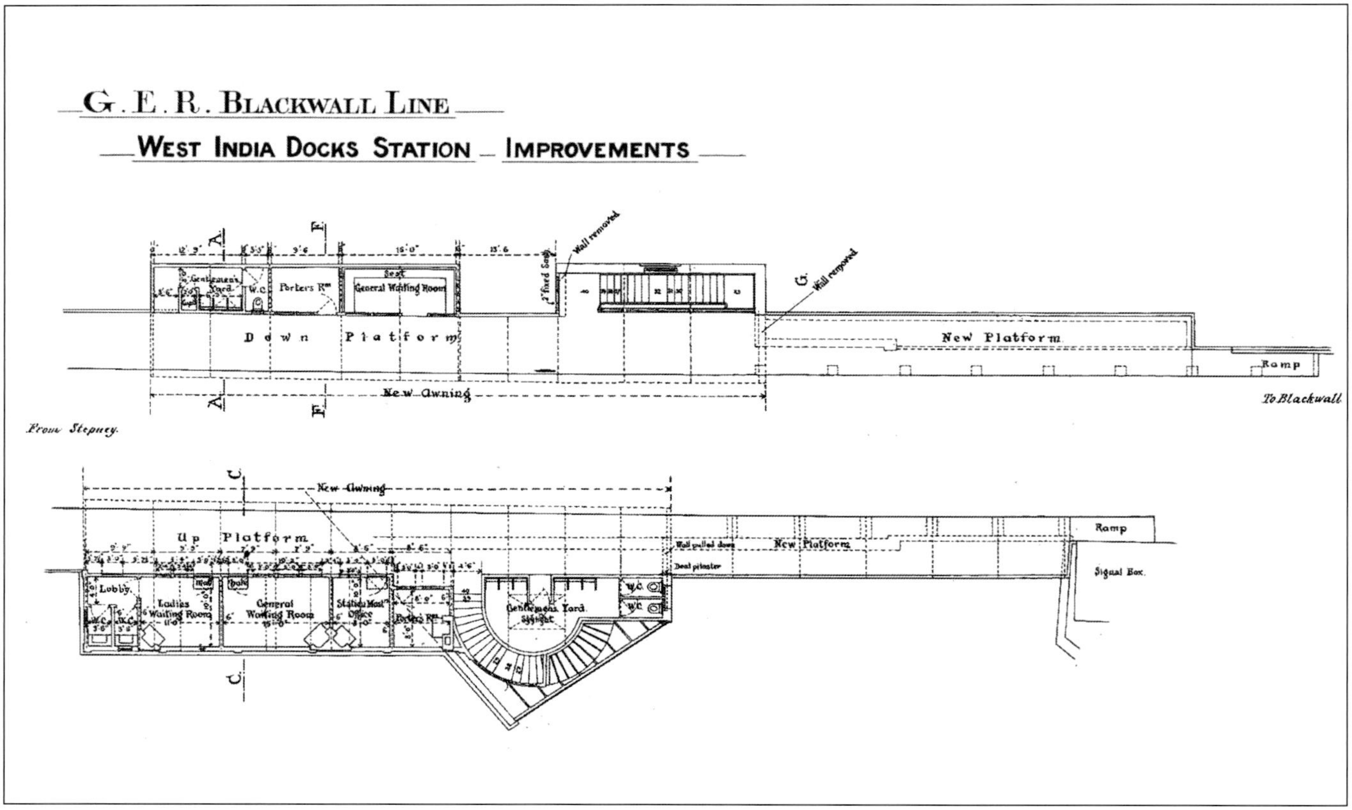

The new platform layout of the station, again as shown on a plan of 1899. The facilities at West India Dock had been in need of improvement for some time. When Major General Hutchinson from the Board of Trade was inspecting the adjoining Midland Railway sidings on 29th November 1882, he noted that *"At West India Dock station the platforms are objectionably narrow and the* (parapet) *walls of the viaduct close to the station are too low. This could lead to accidents in the case of trains stopping short of or overrunning the platform."*

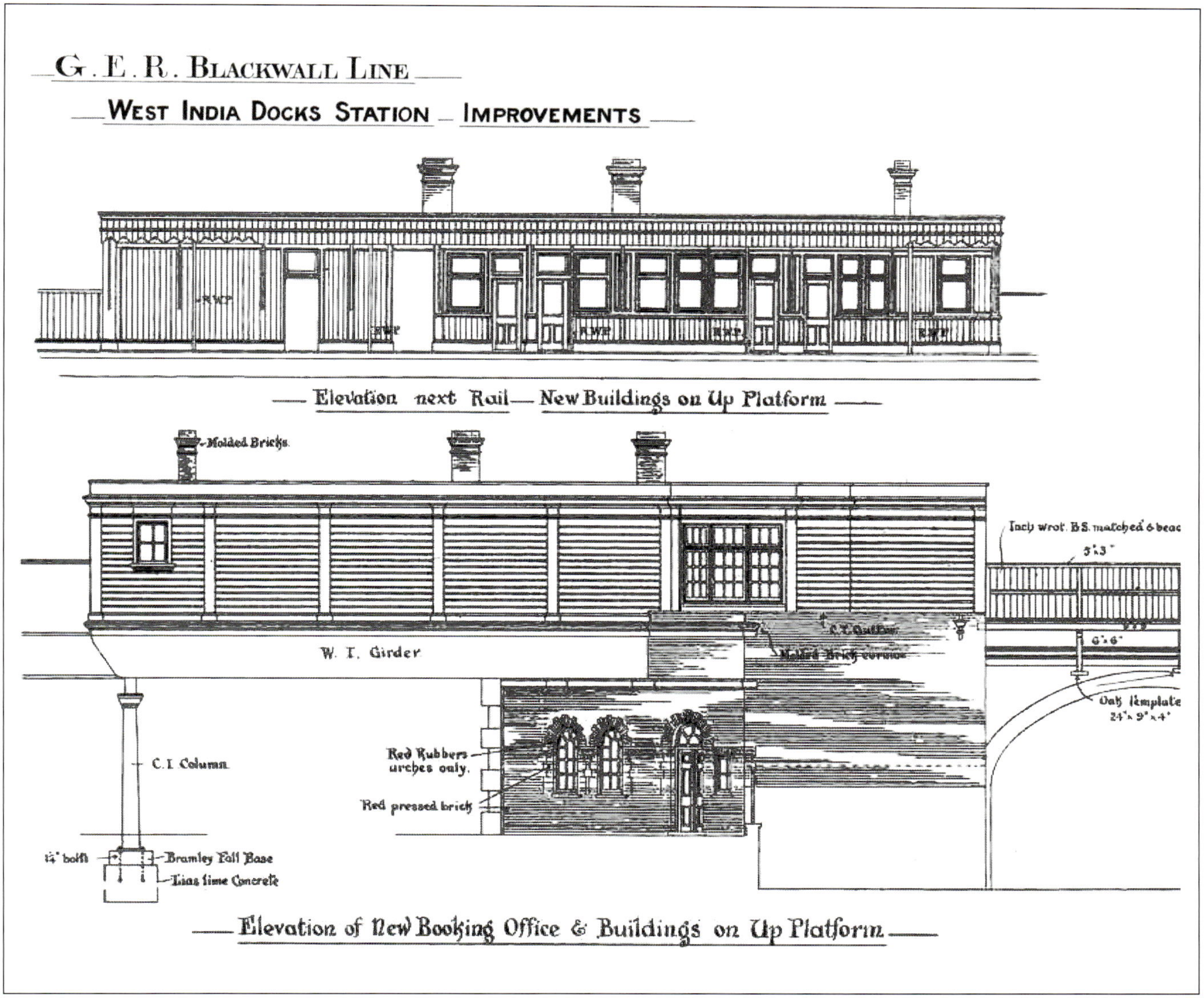

Front and rear elevations of the new buildings erected on the up side at West India Docks during the rebuilding of 1899. The section at street level, which included the new entrance and replacement ticket office, was constructed of brick, but everything above was largely of wood. The style of canopy valance was typical of that which was being used by the Great Eastern Railway at the time and seems to have been the same as that at Leman Street. The section of platform building supported by a girder, was above the road. Unfortunately, no photographs of these buildings are known to exist, so it cannot be said whether any detail differences were incorporated when they were erected.

A selection of tickets. *Left:* GER third class single to Fenchurch Street issued on 9th November 1912. *Centre:* GER second class single to Stepney issued on 28th February 1906. *Right:* Issued on 10th July, but year unclear.

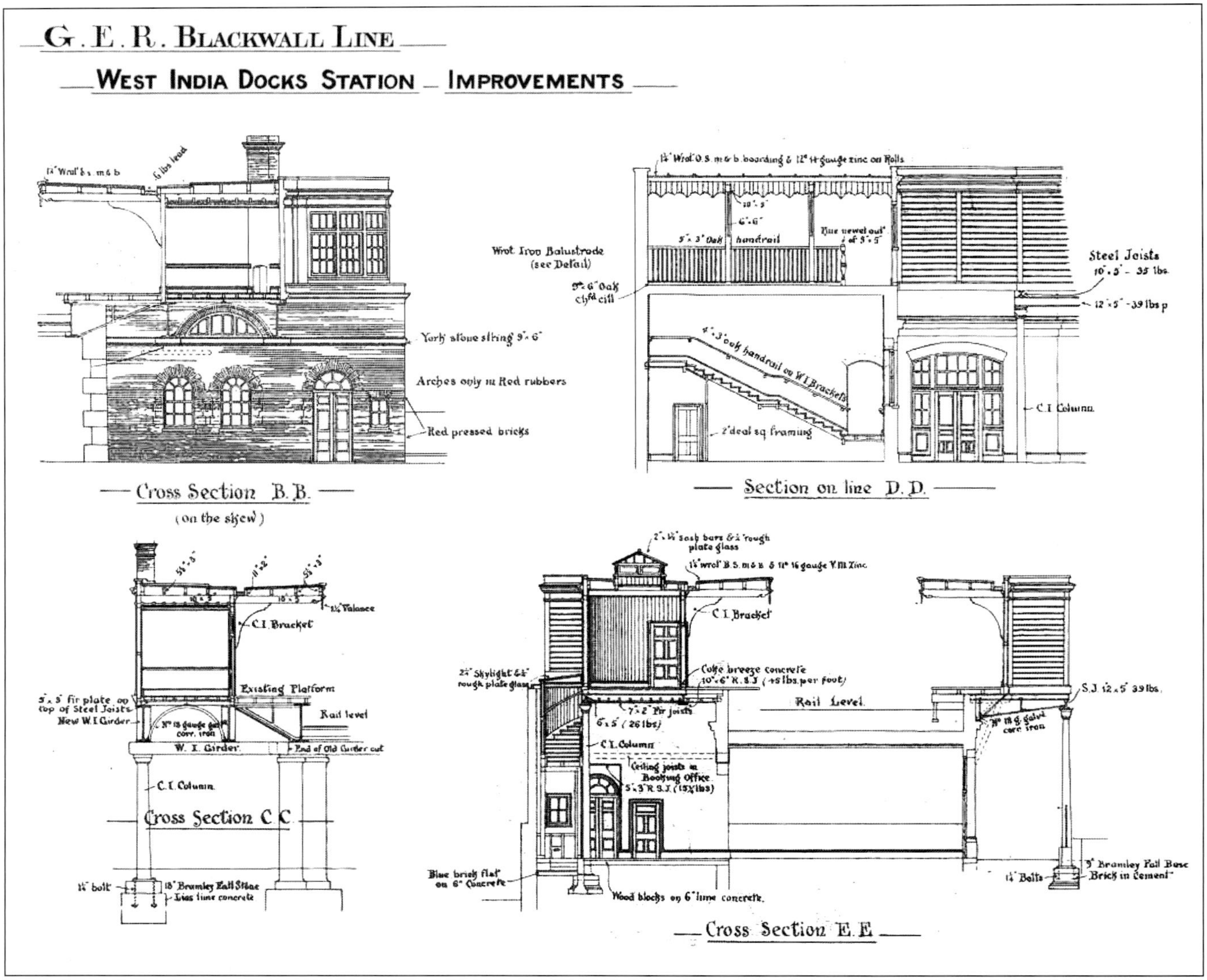

A selection of 1899 drawings, showing various sections and elevations for the new works.

Top left: The frontage of the new street level extension, with the entrance door to the right and two booking hall windows on the left.

Top right: The down side, with the original 1840 LBR entrance door on the right, together with one of the cast iron supporting columns and part of the wooden platform building above. To left of this is the protective screen at the top of the stairwell and a section of canopy supported on wooden posts.

Bottom left: A cross section of the up side building, with supporting columns below.

Bottom right: A cross section, showing the up side on the left, with part of the booking hall interior and curving stairway below the new wooden platform buildings.

Right: Looking east along the viaduct towards the site of the station in 1936. To the left is *'The Railway Tavern'* public house, better known locally as *'Charlie Brown's'*, whilst beyond this is the bridge over West India Dock Road, with railings marking where the west end of the platforms had once been. The low viaduct parapets in the foreground were seen as potentially dangerous by Major General Hutchinson of the Board of Trade, in the event of passengers alighting from a train that had pulled up short.

Looking west from the station site in 1967, with the bridge over West India Dock Road in the foreground and *'The Railway Tavern'* on the right, with the name *'Charlie Brown's'* just visible on the roof.

Millwall Junction

Opened (Great Eastern Railway): 18th December 1871.
Closed (London & North Eastern Railway): 4th May 1926.

Millwall Junction, disused but intact around 1936. The view, which looks east, shows the Blackwall line platforms on the left and the branch to North Greenwich on the right. Above the wagons standing on the left can be seen part of the footbridge which led from Harrow Lane, but the south end of this is completely hidden by the covered bridge linking the platforms.

Millwall Junction was opened on 18th December 1871 and was located between the earlier LBR stations at West India Docks and Poplar.

It was accessed from the south end of Harrow Lane, and comprised three platform faces, of which two served the Blackwall line and the other served the North Greenwich branch. This opened on the same day as the station, but initially only stretched as far as Millwall Docks and was not extended southwards until the following year.

From available information, it seems that the only station building was that on the island platform, which stood between the up Blackwall line and the branch. According to a signalling diagram of 1881, this was rectangular in plan and did not follow the line of the 'vee' shaped platform, but as the drawing was more concerned with trackwork, this may have been simplified.

Less than a year after the station opened, the GER Way & Works Committee discussed lengthening the platforms by 40 feet and requested that the Engineer should provide an estimate. After this, nothing seems to have happened until October 1873, when the same committee were advised that the outlay would be £320, but whether this work was carried out or not is unclear.

The subject of adding an inspectors and porters room at a cost of £90 was under discussion in May 1874, but this was deferred. It was subsequently agreed two months later and in August 1874, the Engineer was instructed to organise the necessary alterations.

During the 1870s, the North London Railway was in the process of constructing a large complex of sidings on the north side of the Blackwall line and as this affected the station approach, a new footbridge had to be constructed. This was agreed in July 1878 and the contract was awarded to the East Ferry Road Engineering Company. The bridge was to be of wrought iron on brick piers and the cost of £354 was shared with the NLR.

The subject of platform lengthening arose again in the autumn of 1885 and the company agreed to pay £275 for the work to take place. The extensions were added at the eastern end of the Blackwall side, but whether these were in addition, or instead of those first mooted in 1872 is not known.

A more significant alteration took place three years later, when the station building was replaced at a cost of £1,377. The contract for this was awarded to the firm of J.T. Chappell on 20th December 1887 and it was agreed that the work would be completed by 31st May 1888.

The new building was constructed of brick and had a rhomboidal floor plan to follow the shape of the island platform on which it stood. At its western end it had a double doorway which led into the booking hall and general waiting room. Two more doors on the side facing the up Blackwall line served the ladies' waiting room and station master's office, whilst tucked away at the building's eastern end were doorways which led into a goods office, a porters' room and a lamp room.

Opposite the porters' room was access to a gents toilet, which was a separate building containing five urinals and two cubicles.

Millwall Junction was served by two footbridges. The easternmost of these commenced at the south end of Harrow Lane and took passengers above both the NLR sidings and the station to a stairway which led down onto the south-eastern end of the branch platform. As this provided access to the booking hall it was probably used as an entrance, but no detailed plans have been located to confirm this. The other footbridge was covered and linked the two platforms. At the top of the down side stairway, there was a short section which connected it to the other bridge and this may have been intended as an exit, but again this cannot be confirmed.

The main building was protected on its northern southern and western sides by an awning, which was supported on iron columns and featured canopy valancing of the type then being introduced by the GER. The awning continued a short way east of the footbridge link with Harrow Lane, but did not cover the gents toilet, which had its own roof.

Millwall Junction closed when passenger services over the Blackwall and North Greenwich lines were withdrawn in 1926, but goods continued to be handled by the office in the station building until 14th November 1927. After that it fell into disuse, although everything remained intact and seemingly in good order well into the next decade.

The station itself does not seem to have received any serious damage during the Second World War, although the signal box, which was located to its west, was more or less destroyed on the night of 19th March 1941. It was subsequently rebuilt, but lost its glazing when a V1 flying bomb landed nearby on 18th August 1944 and was further damaged by a V2 rocket during the small hours of 24th March 1945.

For many years it remained possible to walk onto the bridge from Harrow Lane and look down on the old platforms below. By the postwar era its south end had been extended to provide access to the adjoining dock property. During the 1950s and into the 1960s, the occasional enthusiasts' special train would venture onto the Blackwall line and stop at Millwall Junction, where those on board could get out and briefly look around before continuing on their journey.

The station building remained standing for much of this period, partly boarded up, but largely intact until 1965, when it was reduced to a pile of broken bricks.

The platforms survived until the mid 1980s, but

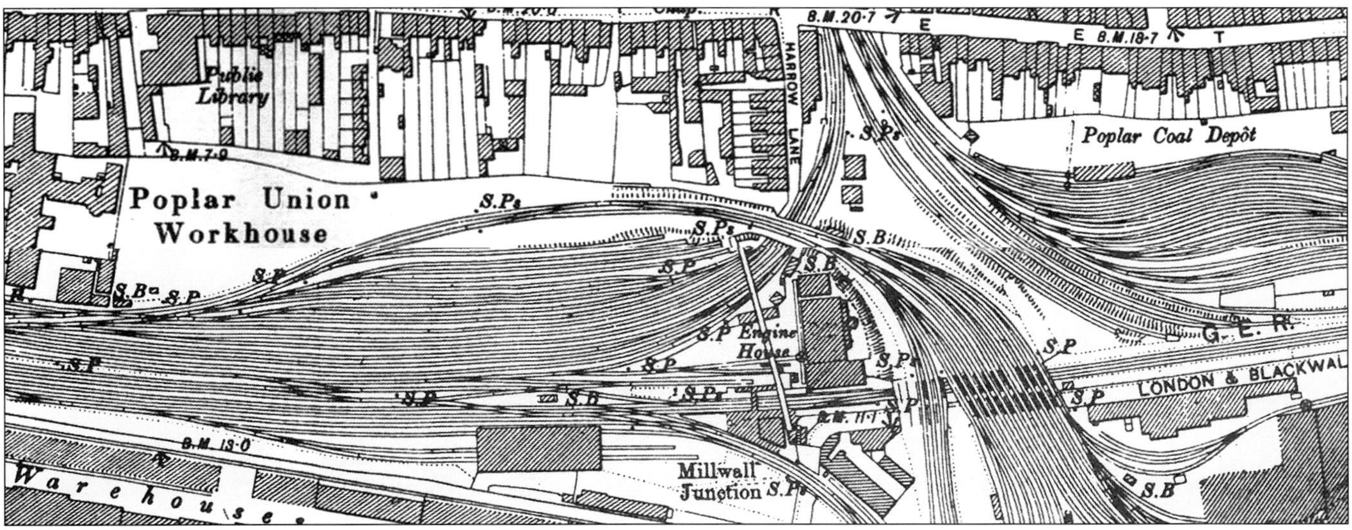

An extract from the 1894 1:2500 Ordnance Survey map, showing the station and its immediate surroundings, with their mass of railway lines, largely intended for goods traffic to and from the docks. Poplar High Street appears near the top, with Harrow Lane heading southwards to the right of centre. From the south end of this, the footbridge leads above the NLR sidings and in front of the associated hydraulic engine house before reaching the east end of the island platform. The rectangular building to the left of the station was the three-road Millwall Junction locoshed.

Above: Manning Wardle 2-4-0T No 6 awaits departure from Millwall Junction with the branch train to North Greenwich. Three of these diminutive locomotives were built at the Boyne Engine Works, Leeds, and supplied for working the line in 1880. Prior to this, the fear of lineside fire hazards resulted in services being worked by horses from Millwall Junction to the southern boundary of the Millwall Docks, where a locomotive was attached for the remaining stretch into North Greenwich. In this view, the locomotive is seen fitted with a spark arrester on top of her chimney. The gents' toilet is visible on the right, tucked between the station building and the pier of the easternmost footbridge.

disappeared when work was being done elsewhere on the former Blackwall line in connection with the Docklands Light Railway, which was then under construction. With later DLR expansion and complete redevelopment of the surrounding area, it is now very difficult to pinpoint exactly where the old station once stood.

Left: Manning Wardle No 6 again, but taken at a different date when she was not fitted with a spark arrester. The three locomotives, which were numbered 3, 4 and 6, were the smallest ever built to work a standard gauge passenger line in Britain and were originally only provided with hand brakes. Westinghouse equipment was fitted in 1891 and the brake pump can be seen on the left side of the smokebox in both views. At one time the engines were painted dark yellow and carried advertisements for Pear's Soap on their tank sides. This was later changed to brick red, lined out in black and a lighter colour, thought to be white. After working the branch for twenty five years, all three locos were in need of a thorough overhaul, so they were rebuilt locally at the East Ferry Road Engineering Co in 1905.

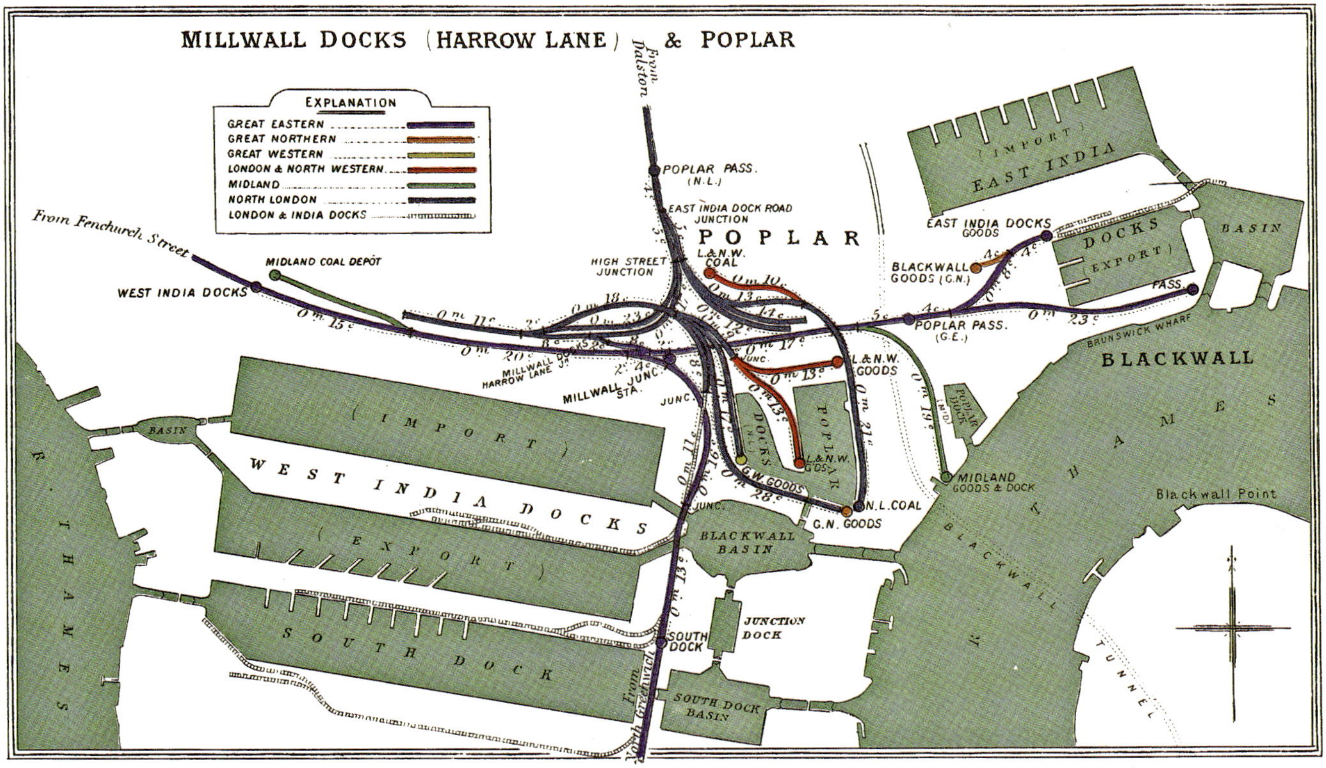

Above: The Railway Clearing House junction diagram of 1906, showing the complexity of lines in the area. The station was actually located in Poplar, but got its name as it was junction *for* Millwall.

Right: The island platform at Millwall Junction, as it appeared in 1936, with the up Blackwall line in the foreground and the North Greenwich branch curving off behind. For a station that had been closed for ten years when the photograph was taken, it was remarkably intact and in very good condition. It is not known when the awning, stairs and covered footbridge were removed, but from photographic evidence it is apparent that they had gone by 1946.

Above: A general view of the station, taken from the Stepney end in February 1950, after the awnings, stairs and covered footbridge had been removed. The bridge leading from Harrow Lane crosses the site behind the station building, in front of the former NLR hydraulic engine house which can be seen on the left. Near these, a cleaner section of brickwork marks where the connection between the two bridges had once been, whilst to the right an additional span has been added to serve the adjoining dock premises.

Left (upper): A closer view of the station building seen on the same day. The door in the end closest to the camera led into the booking hall and general waiting room, which was lit by the window to its right. The window on the left served the ladies room and this was entered by means of the door immediately around the corner, facing the up Blackwall line. The other door on that side led to the station master's office, whilst the windows looking out onto the North Greenwich platform belonged to the ticket office, porters lobby and lamp room.

Left (lower): Looking towards the station on 20th November 1954, with a group of extra-mural students from the University of London, led by the late Dr Edwin Course, standing on the island platform. The signal box in the foreground had been rebuilt following war damage in 1941 and was still standing in 1964.

Above: Looking along the up platform towards Blackwall on 22nd February 1964, with the 1888 station building in the right foreground and the surviving footbridge immediately behind. The bridges beyond carried ex-North London Railway goods lines over the LBR route linking depots at Poplar Dock with the yard at Harrow Lane, and fell into disuse during the 1960s.

Right: The station building viewed from the footbridge around the same time, with the door and window belonging to the station master's office on the left and the boarded-up ladies' waiting room window on the right. By 1964 the building was becoming increasingly derelict, as is apparent from the narrow window opening near the centre, which once lit the lobby serving the ladies' toilet, but by then was completely devoid of both glazing and frame.

Left: GER third class single ticket to Stepney issued on 12th April 1905.

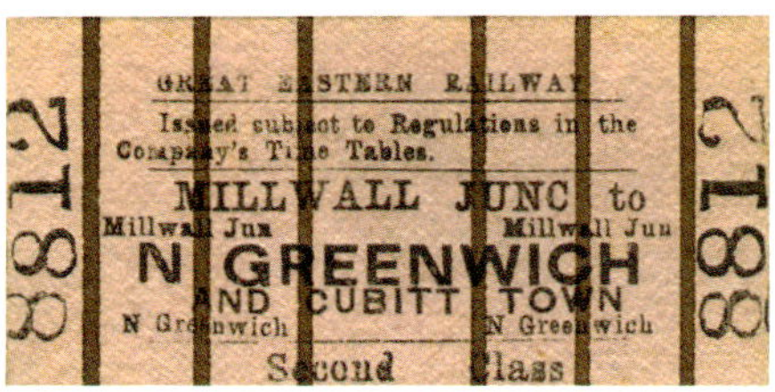

Left: GER Second class single ticket to North Greenwich & Cubitt Town issued on 19th April 1886.

Saturday 21st October 1967 brought the Railway Correspondence & Travel Society 'East London No 4' railtour, which was formed of three 2-car diesel multiple units and ran into Harrow Lane sidings. Whilst there, tour participants alighted and explored the surroundings, including the remains of Millwall Junction station, as seen in these two views. The upper photograph shows the former North Greenwich side, after the platform line had been lifted, but whilst the adjoining goods track was still in position. The grounded coach body on the right had become very derelict by this time, although its remains survived into the mid-1980s. The lower view looks along the Blackwall side, with the down platform on the left and stored wagons on the right. The bricked-up gap between the bridge girders is where the short section linking the two footbridges had once been.

Poplar

Opened (London & Blackwall Railway): c.July/August 1840.
Resited to east (London & Blackwall Railway): 1845.
Closed (London & North Eastern Railway): 4th May 1926.

The remains of the second London & Blackwall Railway station at Poplar, viewed from the east side of Blackwall Way (formerly Brunswick Street) in 1968. By this time all that remained of the track work was the former down line, which is seen on the left, curving off to serve a scrap yard. This yard was on the site of a former Great Northern goods depot, which went into decline during the postwar period and closed around 1961. The route to Blackwall continued ahead, but the stretch leading into the terminus disappeared in 1946 when the site was being prepared for the Brunswick power station.

THE FIRST STATION

Poplar was one of the original stations on the London & Blackwall Railway, and it had long been believed to have opened with the line on 6th July 1840. However, evidence exists that suggests this may not have been the case and that it was brought into use a little later. *The Times* of 6th July 1840 carried a report on the ceremonial opening of the route, which took place two days earlier, and stated that only three of the intermediate stations had opened on time. These were listed as Stepney, Limehouse and *'The Marsh'*, which is understood to have been West India Docks. *The Railway Times* of 18th July also said that only three stations were in use, but *"another would be open in a few weeks"*.

Unfortunately, from here the trail runs cold and an actual opening date for Poplar has not been traced.

The station comprised two platforms and was located between the future site of Millwall Junction and Prestons Road. The area was later covered by railway sidings, and the street which served as its approach completely disappeared.

It seems that having been open for four years, the LBR directors were unhappy about its siting as on 12th November 1844 they were *"Read a report from the Superintendent suggesting the erection of a temporary Station at Brunswick St Poplar with a view of giving greater facility to the inhabitants than by the present Poplar Station. The report also suggested that from its*

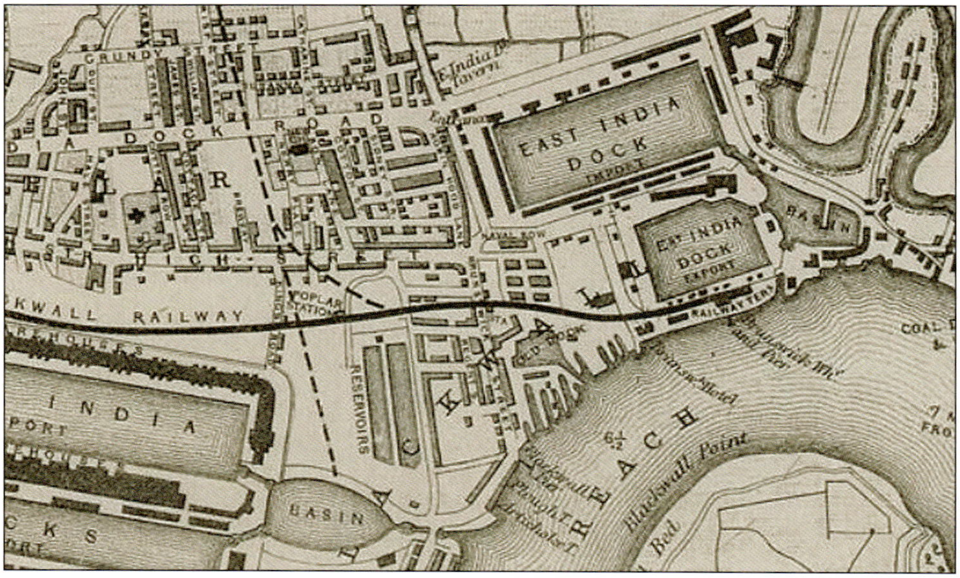

An extract from the Post Office Directory map of 1849 showing the east end of the London & Blackwall Railway. The original station of 1840 appears to left of centre and is labelled *"Poplar Station"*, whilst its 1845 replacement is shown simply as *"Sta"* on the east side of Brunswick Street. Beyond here, the line continues to the terminus at Blackwall, which can be seen immediately below the East India Export Dock.The railway shown as a broken line running from north west to south east and joining the LBR between the two Poplar stations, was the East & West India Docks & Birmingham Junction, which was then under construction. The section between Bow and Poplar opened for coal traffic in 1851 and two years later the E&WID&BJR was renamed the North London Railway.

central position the Station might take the place of the Terminus itself after 7 o'clock in the evening during the winter months and that a saving in gas (for lighting) *might thereby be effected with other advantages."*

A plan was submitted for consideration and it was stated that the cost of erection would not exceed £150. At the next meeting *"The Board determined that the Station at Brunswick Street, Poplar should be proceeded with at once according to the plans submitted... the work being done in the most convenient way consistent with completeness"*.

Details of opening do not seem to have been recorded, but the statement of half yearly accounts dated 8th August 1845 included *"Cost of Brunswick Street Station £351.1s"*, therefore indicating that the work had been completed. As the final bill was in excess of £200 over the original estimate it seems that the work was of a more substantial nature than envisaged and not *"temporary"* as originally stated. H.V. Borley in his *Chronology of London Railways* made no mention of a resiting as such, but recorded that the station's *"permanent buildings"* were opened c.1845. After closure, the original premises were demolished and no illustrations of them are known to exist.

Around the time that the second station opened, the company seemed to be considering building another close to the original site. A Board minute of 27th May 1845 suggested the *"making of a Passenger Station"* at Harrow Lane, but this came to nothing and the locality had to wait until 1871, when Millwall Junction was added.

THE SECOND STATION

The new Poplar station platforms were positioned in cutting and were accessed from the east side of Brunswick Street. The First Edition Ordnance Survey map of 1867 showed a street level building, with a covered stairway descending to the down platform, which was provided with an awning; but the up side, including its stairs, appears to have been open to the elements.

By this time, a new connection had been added at the east end of the down platform, where a line diverged northwards to serve a goods depot, leased to the Great Northern Railway.

The station seems to have had a poor reputation with some members of the travelling public and it was also prone to flooding. One such incident occurred on 26th July 1867, and this was due to problems with the local

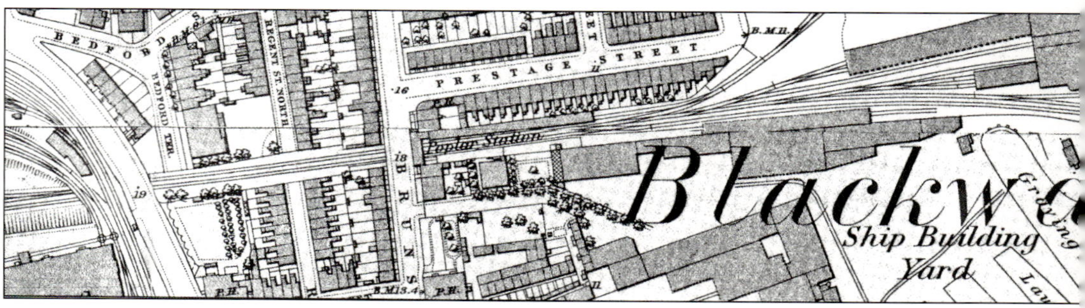

Extract from the First Edition 1:2500 Ordnance Survey map of 1867, showing the second Poplar station near the centre. The down platform appears to be roofed for its entire length, but there is no cover on the up side, apart from a small section on a toilet block near the eastern end. As can be seen, the platforms were slightly staggered and what appears to be a short narrow section on the up side continued west of the Brunswick Street bridge.

The 1:2500 Ordnance Survey map of 1894 shows the station after a canopy had been added to protect the up platform, and that on the down side had been shortened. The map also includes some of the railway goods facilities which served the area, with the Great Northern Railway depot north of the passenger line and the Midland Dock to the south. The line serving the GNR depot curved off a short distance east of the station at Brunswick Junction, whilst the Midland branch diverged at Poplar Junction to the west.

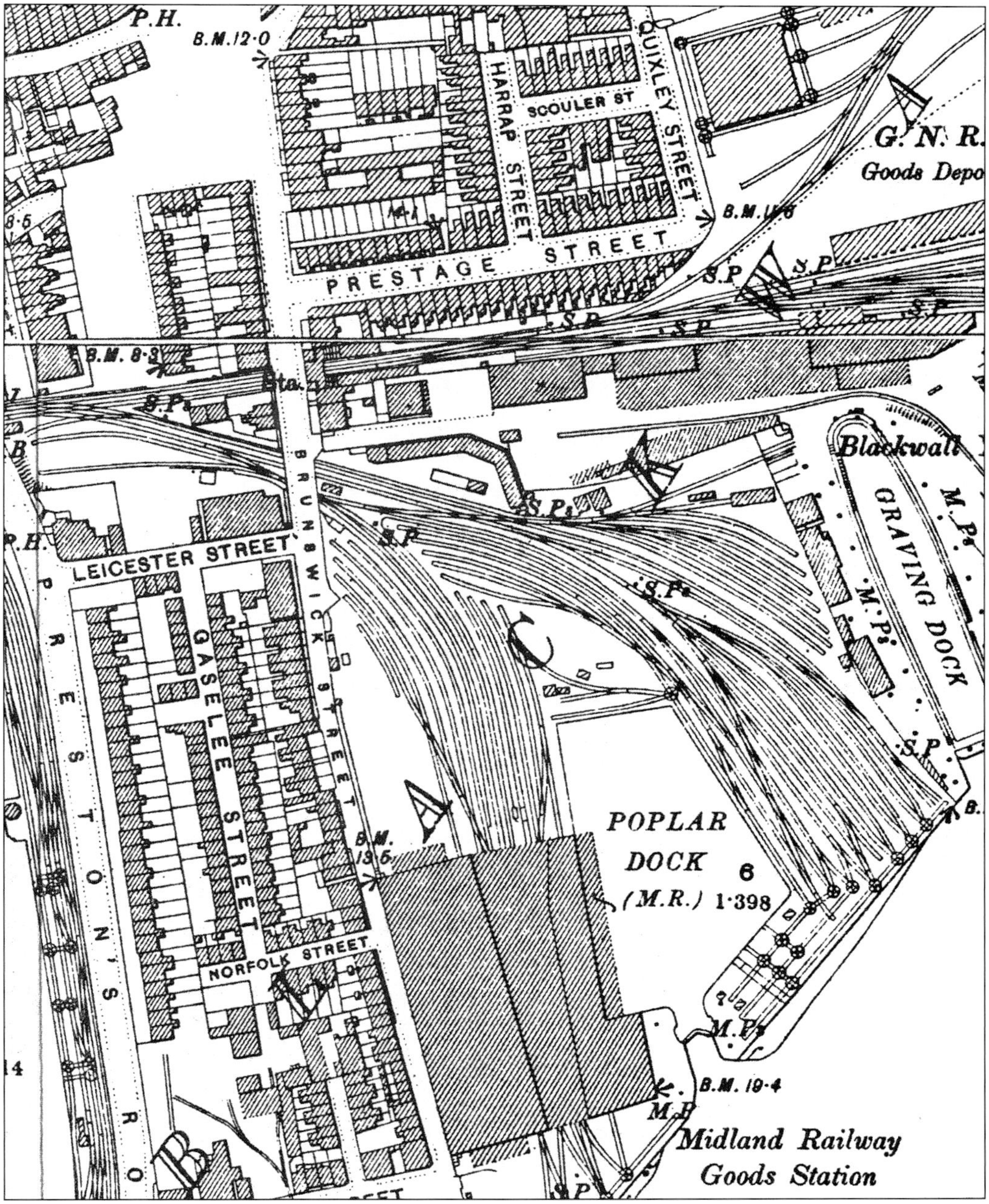

sewers. Eventually, an attempt was made to remedy the situation, as on 4th June 1870, *The Tower Hamlets Independent* reported that *"East Londoners accustomed to use the Poplar Station of the Blackwall Railway, have been agreeably surprised during the past few days by evidence that some attempt to improve the accommodation and get rid of some of the filth is being made; and the way is being brought up to a considerably lower level - an alteration rendered possible by a systematic attempt at drainage."*

The reason for this attention was probably because the North London Railway was about to extend services beyond its Poplar East India Road station to Blackwall. This arrangement came into being on 1st September 1870, but as *The Tower Hamlets Independent* recorded *"The trains do not stop at the Poplar station* (LBR), *which will act prejudicially to the success of the extension."*

Early in 1871 there was a plan to provide *"Additional accommodation at Poplar Station"* at an estimated cost of £250. Four companies were invited to tender and the resulting quotes ranged from £295 to £415. The matter was discussed by the Way & Works Committee on 27th April 1871 and the contract was awarded to

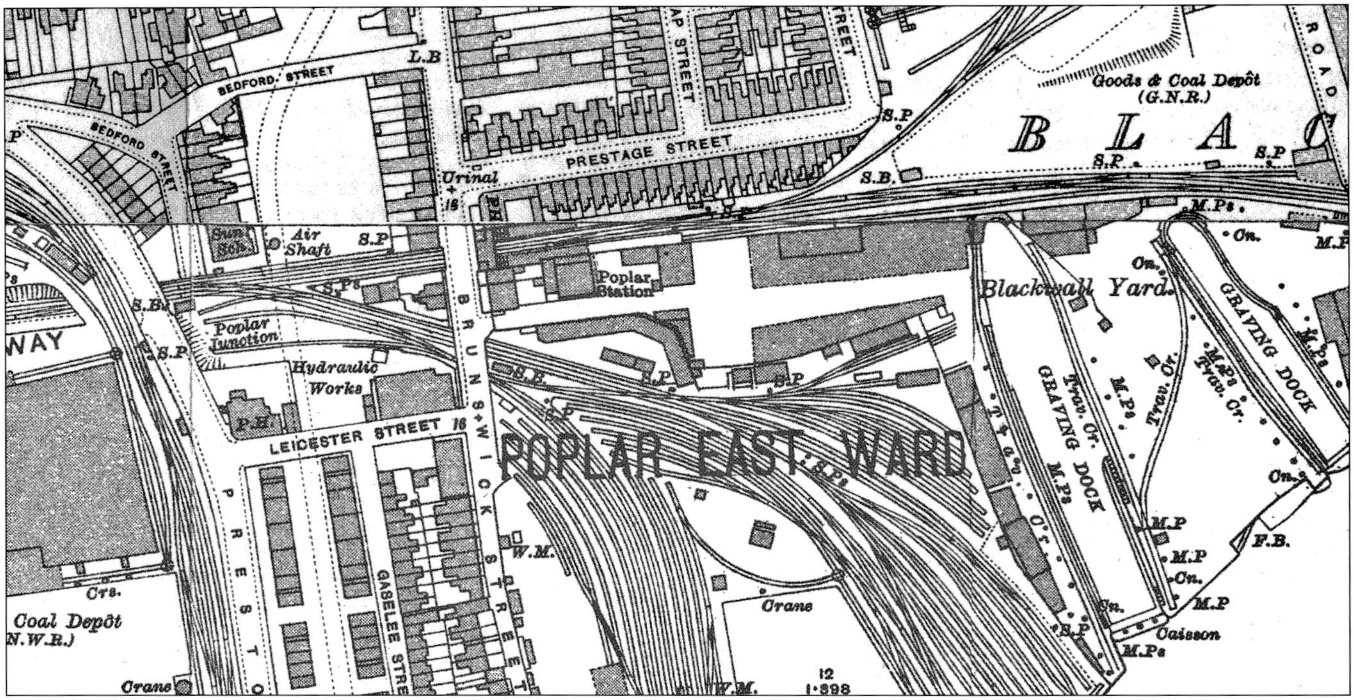

Extract from the 1914 1:2500 Ordnance Survey map, revealing that the down platform canopy had been lengthened and was now only a little short of its counterpart on the up side. Brunswick Junction signal box can be seen just beyond the divergence of the line serving the GNR goods depot, whilst the cabin controlling Poplar Junction appears on the left, immediately east of the bridge carrying Preston's Road.

Messrs Garland of Camberwell, who agreed to carry out the work for £295. Unfortunately the plans have since disappeared, so details of the alterations are not known.

In the autumn of 1873, it was decided to lengthen the platforms at various Blackwall line stations, but the work at Poplar must have been fairly minimal, as the estimated cost was just £25.

In June 1892, an expenditure of £145 was authorised to improve the booking office, with a further £477 in the following year for *"New covered ways and staircases"*, which were subsequently erected by the Ramsey firm of A.J. Bateman.

From the 1:2500 OS map surveyed in 1893-4 it appears that the floor plan of the street level building had changed since the survey of 1867. Both stairways were now covered and although the up platform had been fitted with an awning, that serving the down side had been shortened. As no photographic evidence is known to exist, we have to work out for ourselves what was done in 1871 and during the improvements of 1892-3.

Mr C. S. King, a signalman who worked on the Blackwall line in later years, produced some sketches of the station as it was around the time of closure and portrayed the up platform as having an awning of the ridge and furrow type, with sawtooth valancing. This style was used at a number of GER stations in the 1870s and into the 1880s, although by the middle of that decade the design had been largely superseded. It therefore seems likely that the up side awning dated from the early 1870s and was erected as part of the £295 Garland's contract. The illustration showed the down side awning more or less end-on, which made its design unclear, but as the 1893 alterations specifically included *"new covered ways"*, the contemporary term for platform awnings, it seems possible that the earlier down side canopy was replaced at that date, whilst the up side may have been left as it was.

The sketch also indicated a small building close to the east end of the down platform, which had once been the station master's office. Mr King also sketched the rear of the street level building and its two stairways. From the illustrations these appear to have been constructed of wood, but again with no known photographs, confirmation is not possible. There was a single doorway beneath the stairs on either side, with that on the up platform serving a coal store and that on the down leading into a lamp room. The rear of the street level building was shown as having four windows, with a bracketed signal between the pair on the left.

On 19th December 1893, the GER Way & Works Committee discussed the widening of both platform ends and approved an outlay of £370, but once again no further details have been located.

According to the minute books it seems that little happened to the station during the early twentieth century, other than it being repaired and repainted a couple of times.

After closure in 1926, Mr King said that *"A lot of movable stuff* (had been) *taken away by 1927. The hut on the down side was there then... There was no sign of a porters' room or 'gents' when I saw Poplar first in 1927."* Elsewhere in his reminiscences he stated that the up side platform awning had also been removed *"before 1927"*, but if this was indeed the case, how come he produced a sketch with it in, if he never saw the station until it had been removed? Was he slightly out with the date when the up side canopy was demolished? After all, the line had only closed to passengers the previous year, so although easily removed items may well have been taken away soon after, it seems a little early to undertake awning demolition, unless of course it was required for station renovations elsewhere, or it had to be taken down quickly for some other reason.

A further puzzling comment is that concerning the gents, as platform level toilets definitely existed and it seems unlikely that these were for the use of ladies, as a ladies' room was included within the street level building.

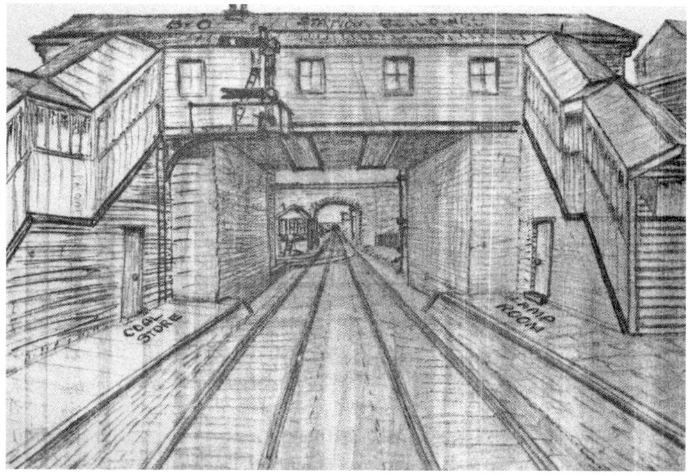

Above: Two of Mr C.S. King's sketches, drawn from memory in the 1970s. With the absence of any photographs it is impossible to confirm their accuracy, but, although simplified, they largely seem to comply with known facts. The 'Xs' on the lower drawing were added by Mr King to indicate items which were removed prior to 1927.

Below: The station layout, extracted from an undated plan produced by the London Midland & Scottish Railway in the 1920s in connection with their goods depot and Poplar Dock. The street level building of Poplar station is shown on the left, with the ticket office on one side and a ladies room on the other.

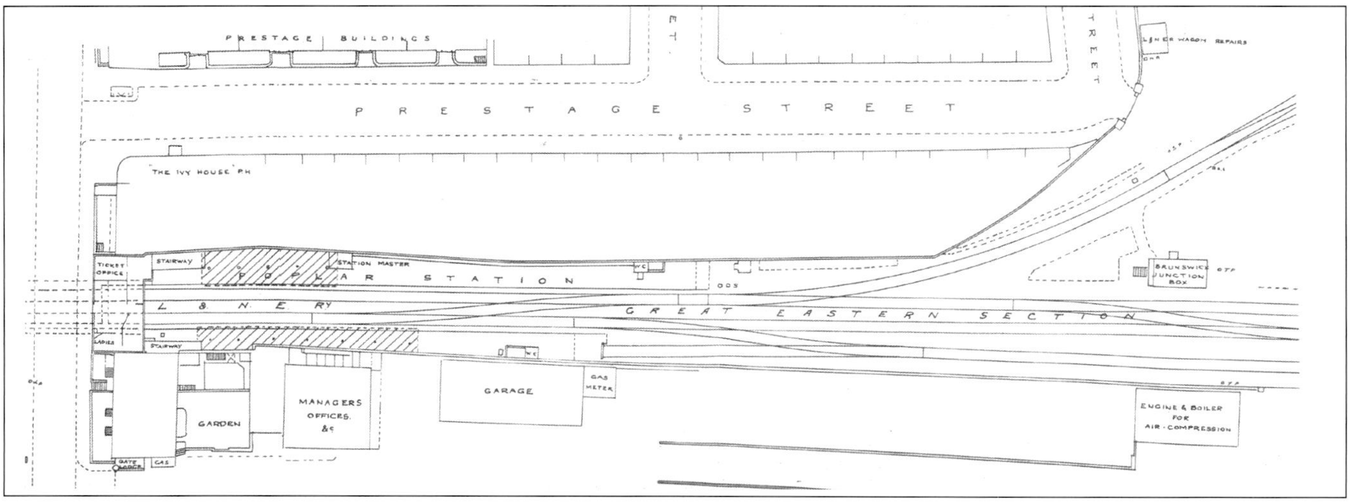

The July 1936 edition of the *Railway Magazine* included a photograph which was captioned *"Poplar Station, partly dismantled"* and this must have been taken during demolition, as there was rubble strewn along both platforms. Whether the street level building went at the same time cannot be confirmed, but it seems very likely that it did.

After this, the residue of the station's fabric remained unchanged for another three decades, but it looked very bare, with its two derelict platforms and little else. There were traces of buildings, but nothing of significance except a few surviving vestiges of the section which once supported the street level building on the down side. There were also the shells of the former toilets which continued to stand near the Blackwall end of both platforms, but comparison with a plan dating from the 1920s, shows that these appear to have been reduced in length.

Above: Poplar station looking towards Blackwall whilst partial demolition was under way in the 1930s. The 1907 Brunswick Junction signal box can be seen beyond the end of the down platform, with the track serving the ex-GNR goods depot curving left and the line to Blackwall continuing on the right.

Left: The station viewed from its opposite end in 1950, with a small toilet block on the left. Trackwork details appear very similar to those shown on Mr King's sketch, although the lamp room accommodation which had been beneath the down side stairs differs from that shown in his illustration.

Right: Poplar Junction, looking east on 5th April 1956, with the signal box on the right and the station in the distance to the left. Between the two we see the Midland Dock branch curving off and a brick building in the 'vee' of the junction, which according to an LMSR plan of the 1920s was the *"Hydraulic Department's Workshop Stores"*. This stands on a platform, which was once thought by many, including Mr C.S. King, to have belonged to the original 1840 passenger station, although this was actually sited some distance to the west. The box was brought into use in late 1882 and had an eighteen-lever Saxby & Farmer frame. It had fallen into disuse by the early 1960s and its derelict remains were subsequently demolished.

At the Stepney end of the up platform was an old signal, complete with two arms, which had presumably been resited from its earlier elevated position by the rear of the street level building.

As the years progressed, the track around the station began to disappear, until all that remained was the former down line. This was subsequently lifted and the site was buried under infill. However, until the 1980s, part of the up side stairway wall, complete with evidence of its handrail could still be seen from the east side of the erstwhile Brunswick Street, which had been renamed Blackwall Way in 1937.

A view of the station taken on the same day, with the old lamp room on the left. As can be seen, the platforms had survived their years of closure very well and, as the line was still open for goods traffic, the former station was still fully signalled. The demolition work carried out during the 1930s had resulted in the removal of all buildings, apart from the lamp room shown here and the toilet blocks at the opposite end of both platforms. The street level building presumably went at the same time and was replaced by a brick parapet on the east side of the bridge.

Left: The signal at the west end of the up platform, viewed on 5th April 1956. Behind it can be seen the wall which had once backed the up side stairway, complete with its painted plaster finish and brackets which had previously supported the banister.

Above: Looking towards the station from its eastern end around 1958, with Brunswick Junction signal box on the right.

Below: The Railway Correspondence & Travel Society *Northern Heights* railtour is seen visiting the station on 1st October 1960.

Above: The former Midland Railway Hydraulic Department's workshop stores in 1965, with the Blackwall line on the left and the Poplar Dock branch on the right. Seeing the 'platform' complete with its ramp, it is understandable that it had once been mistaken as being part of the original passenger station. The red brick accumulator tower just visible on the right continues to stand and is now used as commercial premises.

Right: The remains of Poplar station looking west in 1965, after the track had been singled. The parapet on the bridge carrying Blackwall Way over the formation is that which was erected when the street level building was demolished.

Above: Poplar station looking towards Stepney in 1965. The signal post in the foreground had been stripped of its arms, but those on the up side signal were still in position and can be seen close to the Blackwall Way bridge.

Below: The 1907 Brunswick Junction signal box around the same time, with Brunswick power station behind it. The box had been disused since the previous decade and its remains were finally demolished soon after the photograph was taken. Some withdrawn locomotives from Stratford ended their days in the scrap yard on the left, including the last surviving Class Y4 0-4-0T, which carried the Departmental number 33.

Blackwall

Opened (London & Blackwall Railway): 6th July 1840.
Closed (London & North Eastern Railway): 4th May 1926.

A hand-coloured postcard view of Brunswick Wharf and pier, as they appeared in the early twentieth century, with the frontage of Blackwall station on the left.

The terminus at Blackwall faced onto Brunswick Wharf and Pier and was located 3 miles and 43 chains from Fenchurch Street. It was initially brought into use for a ceremonial opening on Saturday 4th July 1840, but public services did not start until the following Monday.

The contract for building the eastern end of the route, was placed with the firm of Grissell & Peto in January 1839 and a further contract was awarded to the same company to construct Blackwall station. An article which subsequently appeared in *The Mirror* 2d magazine gave this description: *"Its general arrangement is pleasing and highly creditable to the taste of the designer, Mr Tite, architect of the New Royal Exchange, and of this Railway. The elevation consists of a rusticated basement, and an upper floor with five windows, which is crowned by a bold block cornice of Roman Doric character. The basement has square-headed compartments, which are virtually filled with windows resembling Venetian ones. The upper windows have triangular and segmental pediments alternately, and also rustic blocks on their jamb-mouldings. In addition to this principal centre structure (which measures 105 feet in length by 45 feet in height, and is chiefly executed in Portland Stone), there are wings on either side which considerably recede from it. Each of these wings consists of nine arches, making the entire frontage to the river about 400 feet. The centre building contains, on the ground floor, a spacious pay office, besides the convenient waiting rooms, and others for the police; while the whole of the upper floor, with the exception of two waiting rooms, is appropriated to a warehouse for the examination of steam-boat goods. The wings contain the arrival and departure sheds, comprising three lines of rails and covered by a light iron roof; the arches are filled with doors of imitative oak, with upper panels of plate glass, and they communicate with the adjoining wharf".*

The customs office on the upper floor was necessary, as Brunswick Wharf was used to embark and disembark passengers from ships. Back in 1837 William Cubitt had told the directors of the newly formed London & Blackwall Railway that the location was *"the chief landing and shipping place for the large steamers"* and it was *"well adapted for transport to and from town, of goods and passengers by steamers, to and from all parts of the coast and continent; likewise from its proximity to the East and West India Docks, for the conveyance of merchandise to and from these great depots of foreign produce."*

In his 1847 book *The Practical Railway Engineer*, George Drysdale Dempsey described the track layout at Blackwall: *"On entering the station, the left-hand or 'down' line diverges into two branches, the northern one of which is connected with the main line by a switch, and is intended for the reception of spare carriages. Two turn-plates are fixed on each branch of the down line, and are placed obliquely, there not being sufficient width to place them at right angles. By these turn-plates carriages may be transferred from the main down line to the siding, and vice versa... The southern or 'up' line runs uninterruptedly until stopped against the building."* Although referred to as such in the description, the tracks on the LBR were not designated as being up or down at the time. They were known simply as the North Line and the South Line, as the method of cable haulage meant that both could be used for carriages travelling in either direction. If a service left Minories on either the North or South Line, it remained on it all the way to Blackwall, then returned on the same track.

The winding engines and machinery at Blackwall were located west of the station and were described in the *Civil Engineer and Architect's Journal* of March 1848 as being similar to their counterparts at Minories, but smaller. The writer stated that *"The railway* (at Blackwall) *passes by the side of the engine-house on the ground, and therefore the ropes are gathered at the lowest part of the circumference of the drums, instead of at the highest point as at the Minories, where the railway passes over the engine-house."* To reduce the speed of incoming trains and to give impetus to those that were departing, the station was approached by a short incline of 1 in 150.

The ceremonial opening certainly seems to have been memorable, although not necessarily for the right reasons. Everything started off as planned, but, unfortunately, the event ended in chaos. The first train, conveying the Lord Mayor, the sheriffs and other civic dignitaries, set out from Minories at mid-day and arrived at Blackwall fifteen minutes later. Throughout the East End, the route was lined by dense crowds who cheered and applauded as the train went past. One eye-witness described how the inhabitants of two tenement houses, close to the line, removed some of the roofing tiles so they could poke their heads through the holes and get a better view of the proceedings. Further trains followed, but these took a little less time to reach their

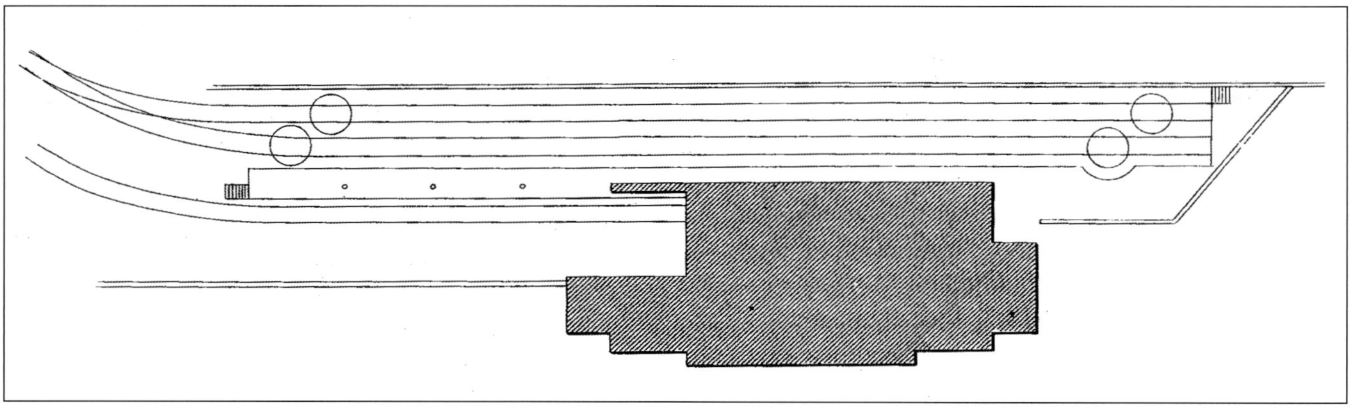

Above: Track plan of Blackwall station drawn c.1847, showing the carriage siding at top, followed by the North and South passenger lines either side of an island platform. As mentioned in the text, the North Line and its adjoining carriage siding were linked by turntables, with the eastern end of the platform cut away to accommodate one of them. The space between the South Line and the western wing wall is known to have accommodated a further platform by 1867, but it is not known when this was constructed.

Opposite: Drawing showing the building at Blackwall, as erected in 1840, with the front elevation at top, followed by the floor plan and two cross sections. On entering the station, passengers passed a police office on the right and the entrance to a stairway on the left. This was described at the time as being "spacious" and led to the upper floor. Beyond these was the booking hall, which had a length of 63ft 2ins and width of 30ft. To the left of this was the 19ft 7in x 17ft 9in gentlemen's waiting room, whilst to the right was similar accommodation for ladies, measuring 25ft 8ins x 17ft 8ins. Both of these included toilet facilities. The cross section at bottom left illustrates the eastern end of the building and includes a span of the overall roof. The other cross section shows part of the internal arrangement and the style of roof construction.

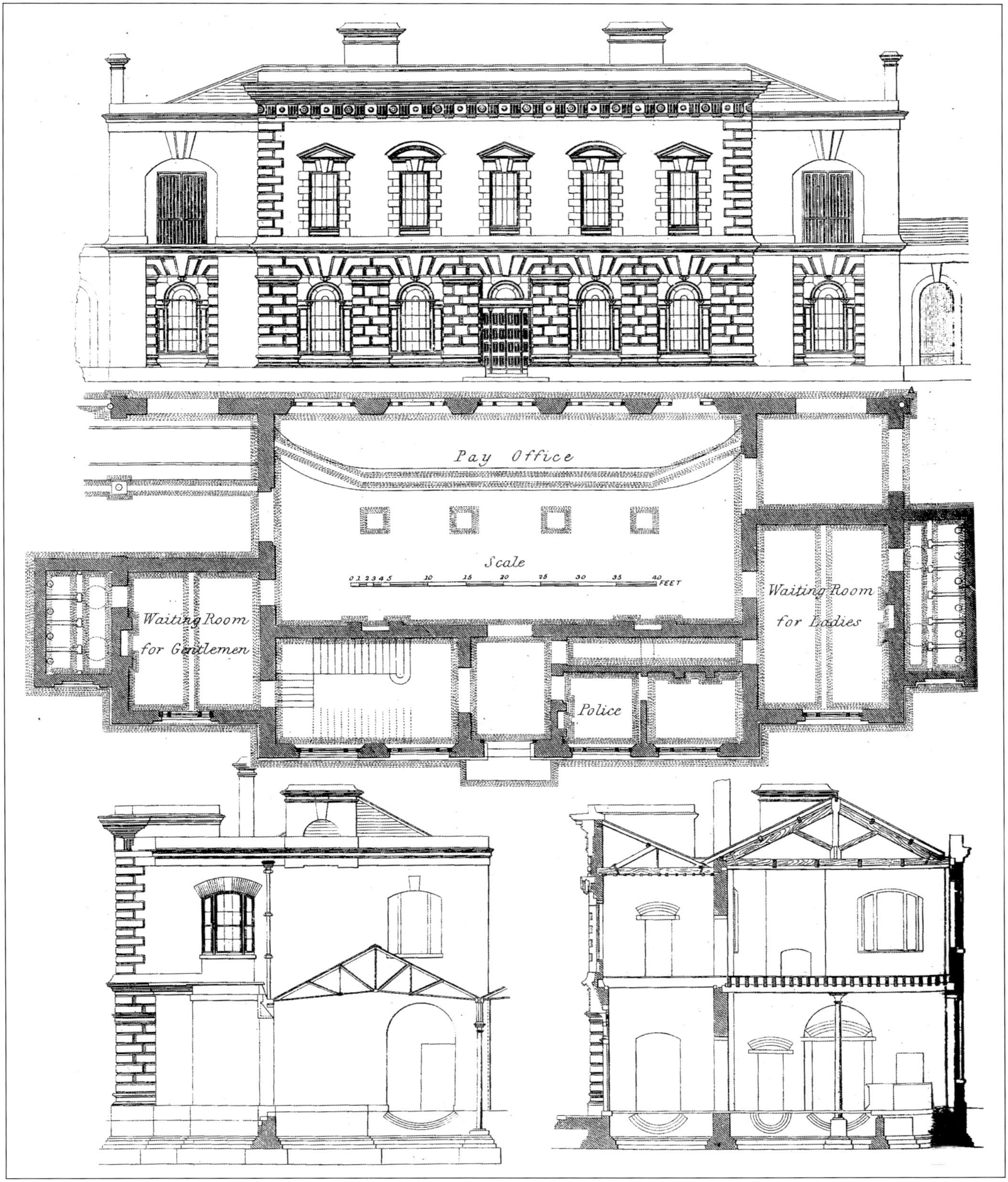
Pay Office
Scale
0 1 2 3 4 5 10 15 20 25 30 35 40 FEET
Waiting Room for Gentlemen
Waiting Room for Ladies
Police

Drawing showing the eastern wing of the station, viewed from the front.

destination, and arrived at Blackwall in just ten minutes.

On arrival, the guests assembled on Brunswick Wharf and were entertained by the Woolwich Marine Band. Then, at 3pm, the doors of the nearby East India Company's warehouse were opened and the banquet commenced. The building had been specially carpeted and flags were hung from the walls to add a touch of dignity. In a large room on the first floor, Mr Lovegrove, the owner of the adjoining Brunswick Tavern, provided the guests with a gourmet meal which included turtle with iced punch, whitebait with champagne, and grouse with claret. There were upwards of 1,500 guests, including *"elegantly dressed"* ladies and the majority were undoubtedly in a party mood. However, as the punch, champagne and claret began to take effect, an argument broke out, which brought the festivities to an abrupt end. *The Tablet* of 11th July 1840 reported: *"The affair, we regret to state, had a rather disagreeable termination, owing to the brutal conduct of Sir Peter Laurie and a certain company of tailors who were marshalled under his directions. The health of Mr O'Connell - who had been one of the most active promoters of the railway in the House of Commons - was proposed by the chairman. This announcement (Which we believe was made without any concert with Mr O'Connell) was no sooner made than there commenced the most extraordinary exhibition of yelling and hooting, howling and screaming, that was perhaps ever witnessed, except on the Conservative side of the House of Commons. The Tory gentlemen present were excessively disgusted. One of them, Mr Gordon, MP for Lymington, came over to Mr O'Connell, and declared that though he had never spoken to him before, he could not refrain from coming to shake him by the hand on this occasion, and expressing his disgust at the conduct of Sir Peter and the aforesaid Tory tailors. The harmony of the evening however, was now completely at an end. The entertainment was to have wound up with music and a dance. The company returned sulkily home, and the altercation, we believe, was not quite ended when they reached London."* Whether the *"altercation"* actually resulted in physical brawling does not seem to have been recorded, nor if it took place in more than one of the trains. Prior to the event, the LBR felt that some guests might prefer to take a more leisurely river trip back to the City so chartered the vessel, *Ariel*, from the Woolwich Steam Packet Company. There was no mention of this in *The Tablet* report, so presumably the passengers on board had a more peaceful and less fraught journey than those who went by rail.

The LBR were not authorised to operate their own shipping services, so a number of directors grouped together and financed the construction of three iron ships. These were named *Blackwall*, *Brunswick* and *Railway*, and they took between seventy minutes or an hour and three quarters to complete the journey between Blackwall and Gravesend, depending on the direction of the tide. The coloured lithograph shows the station as seen from the river in the 1840s, with the steamer *Brunswick* on the right.

Despite this initial hiccup, Blackwall soon established itself as a place to go for dining out, having travelled down from the City by train. *The Mirror* of 27th March 1841 stated that *"...such repute extends far west of Temple-Bar, and alike attracts to this neighbourhood the gourmand and the gourmet, to enjoy its peculiar delicacy of whitebait, with the luxurious accompaniment of cold punch. And thither, by aid of the Blackwall Railway, he may be wafted in less than 10 minutes! ... Having arrived at the wharf, or pier, nothing can be more invigorating, or repellent of dyspepsia, than the river breeze to be enjoyed in a few turns along the esplanade..."*

Much more importantly, the LBR eyed the river traffic as a source of revenue and they reached an agreement which allowed them to rent the pier at Brunswick Wharf from the East & West India Docks Company. The Railway's main aim was to obtain a share of the profits then being made by the steamers sailing to Gravesend and beyond.

Another source of income gained from collaboration with river operators was obtained by running trains which connected with short sailings between Blackwall and Woolwich. In fact, the relationship between the Railway and ferry owners became so good that by 1844, through tickets to Woolwich began to be issued from all the stations on the line. In January 1844, a correspondent wrote to Herapath's Journal and stated *"Your readers will be pleased to hear that arrangements have been concluded between the Directors of the* (LBR) *and the Directors of the Old Woolwich Steam Packet Company, and the Directors of the Waterman's Company, for despatching a boat from the Brunswick Wharf to Woolwich on the arrival of every railway train; besides which there are several of the boats running between London and Woolwich which call at the Brunswick Wharf, and land and embark passengers there, so that no hindrance or delay is experienced by passengers in the journey from London to Woolwich, which will in future occupy half an hour only."*

A hand-tinted print, showing the station frontage soon after opening.

In the following decade another company, the East & West India Docks & Birmingham Junction Railway, decided that they would like to share in the profits offered by river traffic, and sought permission to connect its line with the LBR at Poplar. It extended its

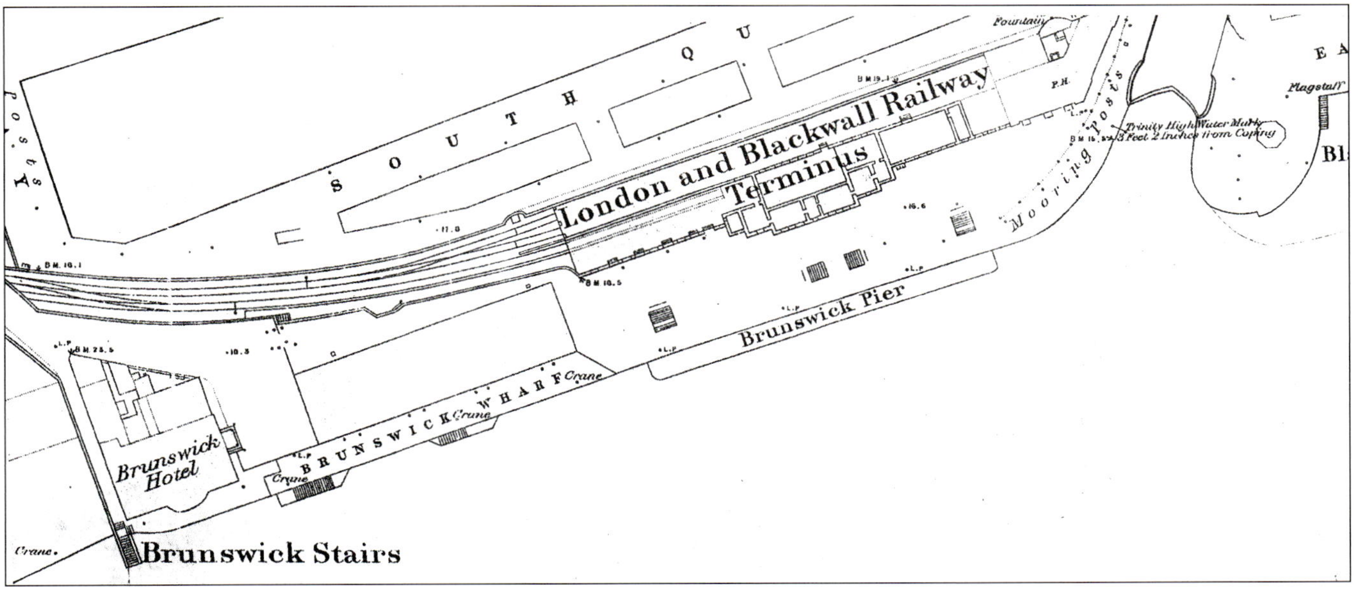

Extract of a map produced by the Midland Railway and based on the Ordnance Survey of 1867, showing the station around the time that the LBR was leased to the Great Eastern. The track layout appears very much as it did twenty years earlier, although changes were presumably made with the introduction of locomotive haulage in 1849. A platform is now shown on the south side, but nothing can be seen of the arrangement beneath the overall roof.

route south of Bow, but for various reasons the scheme didn't go to plan, and when it opened in October 1851, the extension was only used by freight traffic. An agreement between the two companies reached during the previous month mentioned that leaving the branch free of passenger traffic would *"give additional facilities for working the Goods and Coal trains"*.

The E&WID&BJR, which was renamed the North London Railway in 1853, never lost sight of its goal and a Parliamentary Act was eventually passed, which permitted NLR passenger trains to serve Blackwall. Before this could happen however, various alterations and improvements needed to be made to the terminus which, from 1st January 1866 would be leased to the Great Eastern Railway, along with the rest of the LBR system.

Although river traffic continued to attract patronage, it seems that the new lessees did little in the way of upkeep on their latest acquisition. In fact, conditions on the line were becoming a cause of public complaint as illustrated by a paragraph in the *Tower Hamlets Independent* of 3rd July 1869, which stated that the ex-LBR third class carriages were *"filthy, stifling and unsightly"*. He went on to suggest that those who wished to reach the Poplar area did so by North London services and *"that travellers should abstain from patronising the Blackwall line..."*

Eventually, it seems that the GER took heed of such comments as, on 13th October 1869, it was reported that there were problems with both the booking and toilet facilities at Blackwall, although the matter was left in abeyance until the other changes were under way.

On 24th November, the same Committee heard that the necessary NLR track alterations were due to start, then, the following month, the firm of Garland & Co were awarded the contract for modifications at Blackwall station, which they agreed to undertake at a cost of £3,320. This must have seemed a reasonable price, as ten months earlier, the GER Board of Directors agreed an outlay of £7,000 in connection with extending North London services, although it is not known whether this figure included work other than at Blackwall station itself.

The NLR services were extended from Poplar to Blackwall on 1st September 1870 and the new link was greeted enthusiastically by the *Tower Hamlets Independent* nine days later: *"The North London Railway extension to Brunswick-pier, Blackwall, brings the whole North of London in direct communication with the docks and the steamboat traffic of the river Thames, and will be an especial boon to the Gravesend, Ramsgate and Margate traffic. The Blackwall station, which hitherto formed no exception to the other dirty and disgraceful stations on the Blackwall Railway, has been entirely renovated, and on the day of opening presented quite a gay and animated appearance. The interior and exterior of the station was profusely decorated with bunting, as well as the engines of the North London Railway."* Although the paragraph referred to the *"especial boon"* to river services, the Gravesend steamers were already in decline by the time that NLR trains reached Blackwall.

Ex-Great Eastern Railway J65 0-6-0T No 158 leaving Blackwall on 25th July 1925 with the 1.35 train to Fenchurch Street. In common with some of her classmates, the front section of her coupling rods had been removed, so she was running as a 2-4-0T.

In the October of 1870, the GER agreed to provide two extra lamps at the station for the North London, with a NLR coaling stage and water column following two months later.

Part of a waiting room at Blackwall was let to the General Post Office in March 1871, to be used for telegraphic purposes, but apart from that, no more significant changes took place at the station itself for the remainder of the nineteenth century.

A subsequent amendment in the agreement between the Great Eastern and North London Railway resulted in the withdrawal of passenger services between Poplar (NLR) and Blackwall. At the North London Board meeting held at Euston on 19th June 1890, it was stated that *"The General Manager reported that it has been arranged with the Great Eastern Company that the respective running powers referred to in clauses 5 & 6 shall be suspended for a period of 30 years... The payment by the North London Company in respect of Blackwall to cease on the 30th instant, when the train service will be discontinued between Bow and Blackwall"*. The short spur linking the two lines officially closed from 1st July 1890 and the points at the eastern end were removed the following month. On 26th June 1891, a General Notice was issued stating that *"The disused curve to the Blackwall line has been converted into Carriage Sidings for trains of the Poplar service, and the present sidings will in future be used as standing roads for coal."*

As the century drew to a close it seems that patronage of the Blackwall branch began to decline and on the 5th March 1902, the GER Board of Directors decided to reduce the service from four trains an hour to three. To justify this it was stated that the traffic was *"not expanding"* and had shown a slight decrease since 1896.

The passage of time had also been unkind to the old trainshed roof, so it was decided to replace this with standard GER awnings above the concourse and island platform. At a meeting of the Way & Works Committee on 18th December 1906, a contract was let to the firm of Kirk, Randall to erect new roof steelwork at a cost of £544, then, five months later, the same company were asked to add cladding for a further £515.

By now, the decline in patronage was beginning to accelerate, but despite competition from LCC trams, it was still making a small profit in 1908. At a meeting on 31st July that year however, the Directors considered closing the line on Sundays and reducing the service on Saturday evenings to cut down on operating costs.

Three months later it was announced that Sunday trains would cease from 4th October 1908.

Unfortunately the decline continued and it seems that the service was now very poorly patronised. In his book *First and Last Loves*, John (later Sir John) Betjeman recalled *"Those frequent and quite empty trains of the Blackwall Railway"* which stopped *"at black and empty stations, till they came to a final halt at Blackwall"*. On alighting *"there was nothing to see but a cobbled quay and a vast stretch of windswept water."*

Despite the lack of public enthusiasm, the branch soldiered on throughout the First World War and all of its stations remained open at the time of the grouping in 1923, even though passenger numbers continued to fall. On a one day count, the number of those using the route fell from 8,153 in October 1912 to just 4,331 in October 1925 and it was estimated that the branch was losing £4,000 per annum. Closure of the route was therefore considered, but before any notices could be posted, fate stepped in and brought passenger services to a hasty end.

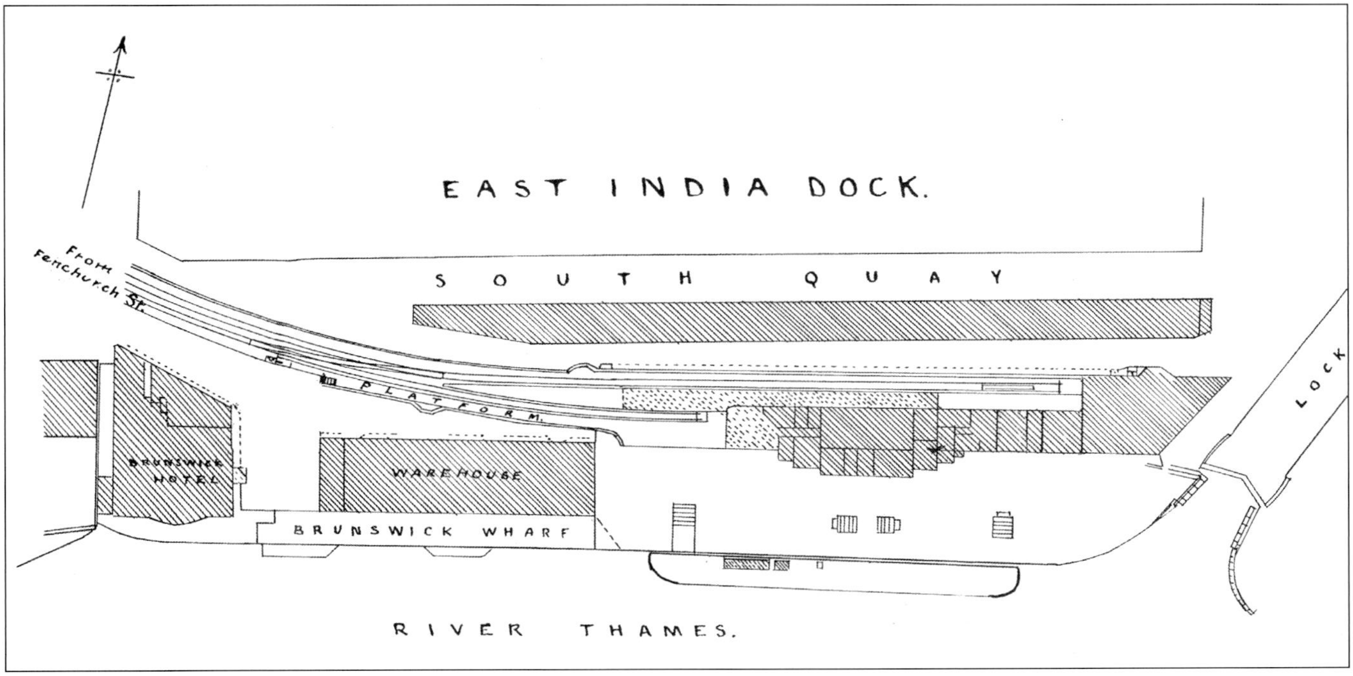

A plan of the station drawn by the LNER in 1927, showing the track layout soon after closure to passengers. The south side platform, shown on the 1867 map is still there, but one of the tracks had been removed to allow for a widened island. It is not certain when these changes took place, but they were probably done in connection with the introduction of NLR services in 1870. The overall roof, which was taken down in 1907, has been replaced by a conventional awning and an engine pit is evident near the buffer stops on the down side. At one time it seems that a locomotive would be employed on station pilot duties. However, this practice appears to have ceased in 1895, as the minutes of a GER Way & Works Committee meeting held on 19th February that year recorded that the Blackwall *"waiting engine"* was no longer required.

1926 was the year of the General Strike and railway services throughout the country were drastically affected. The last passenger trains into Blackwall ran on 3rd May, and when the strike ended the service was not resumed. At a meeting held on 29th July 1926 at Marylebone station, the London & North Eastern Railway Traffic Committee was presented with a memorandum written by the Chief General Manager the previous day, recommending that the stations along the line should close permanently. It stated that the Chief Legal Adviser was of the opinion that it was not necessary to give any public notice under Statute or otherwise, although normally such advice would have been desirable. The memorandum continued: *"Inasmuch as the service has been discontinued since the beginning of the Strike it does not seem advisable to give a public notice... but it is recommended that any parties complaining of the discontinuance of the service should be informed that we have found it unremunerative and do not propose to re-instate it... The district is well and cheaply served by tram and 'bus, and it is not thought that any objections will have serious weight, or can be effective in*

Two views of William Tite's fine building at Blackwall, taken whilst the station was still in passenger use. The photograph above dates from 1925 and includes a refreshment stall on the left, seemingly tended by two young girls, although trade appears to have been very slack at the time. The GER Way & Works Committee minutes of July 1870 recorded that Blackwall was to be provided with a refreshment room *"subject to cost"*. This was to be leased by the well-known catering firm of Spiers & Pond, but no further details are known. The view to the left was taken at an unknown date and shows the opposite end of the building, together with the wings on either side of it.

compelling the Company to continue incurring a heavy annual loss on the services... It should be understood that the existing goods services over the Blackwall branch will be maintained, but it is proposed to terminate the passenger service altogether."

With that statement, the Blackwall branch was consigned to the history books.

The main building had some of its windows boarded up, although it still appeared to be in good condition when photographed for a *Railway Magazine* article in 1936. It continued to stand throughout the Second World War, and does not seem to have been significantly damaged, although it is thought to have been struck by an incendiary bomb during the dreadful overnight air raid of 10th and 11th May 1941.

After the war, the site of the old terminus was required for a new power station, so the buildings and platforms were razed to the ground in 1946. Brunswick Power Station, as it was known, lasted into the late twentieth century, but it was subsequently demolished and the site has again been redeveloped.

Above: The platforms at Blackwall, seen in 1925, with the 1907 awning prominent on the left. The NLR trains seem to have used the track on the right, as H.L. Hopwood wrote in *The Railway Magazine* of February 1919: *"There is one long platform with a short bay line; the latter is now disused, but formerly accommodated trains of the North London Railway..."* He also noted that *"very few passengers are seen at the station, which consequently has a deserted appearance and an air of departed glory."*

Right: Blackwall station, looking east in 1936, ten years after closure.

Above: A photograph taken from the north side of the island, looking towards Poplar in 1936. Blackwall station was still largely intact at the time, although the platform lamps had been removed from their posts. In October 1870 it was noted that two extra lamps were to be fitted at a cost of £10 in connection with the extension of North London services.

Left: The view from the side platform, looking west in 1936. The 1840 winding engines were beyond the bridge, as was a later shed, which was erected to house locomotives after cable haulage ceased in 1849.

Blackwall in the early stages of demolition during 1946, when the site was being cleared to accommodate the Brunswick power station.

South Dock

Opened (Millwall Extension Railway): 18th December 1871.
Closed (Port of London Authority): 4th May 1926.

Millwall Dock Company 2-4-0T No 3, built by Manning Wardle & Co in 1880, stands at South Dock station around 1905 with a train from North Greenwich. The passing loop was located on the opposite side of the island platform, behind the station building and is not visible in this photograph, whilst the track in the foreground was used for goods traffic.

South Dock was located on the East & West India Dock Company owned section of the North Greenwich branch, 33 chains from Millwall Junction, and comprised a single island platform. It had the only passing loop on the line and housed the head office of the MER Managing Committee. The building was largely wooden, with a slate roof and valanced awning. It stood within the dock estate, with timber yards on either side and was not directly served by a public road. Not surprisingly, it was used mainly by the local dockers and had no service after 6.30pm on weekdays, or on Sundays.

The line between Millwall Junction and *"Millwall Docks"* was inspected on behalf of the Board of Trade by Captain Tyler on 29th November 1870, but he refused to sanction it being brought into use on safety grounds. He made further visits on 7th January and 1st February 1871, but still felt it was unfit for passenger traffic, so its opening was further delayed.

The Managing Committee arranged for various alterations to be made and, on 13th December 1871, informed the Board of Trade that the work had been completed. One of the main problems had been the existence of three swing bridges, which were thought to be too weak to take locomotives, so this time the company stated that they would use horses instead and these would each haul a single carriage or tramcar.

A further inspection was hastily arranged and Colonel Yolland visited the line three days later. Although very little in the way of improvements seem to have been done, he was content that the line was safe enough for horse traction and therefore sanctioned its opening.

In his report, he said that the steps at the ends of the platform at *"West India Dock"* should be replaced by ramps, but there was no mention of a passing loop, so this may have been a later addition. South Dock was close to the West India Export Dock, so must have been

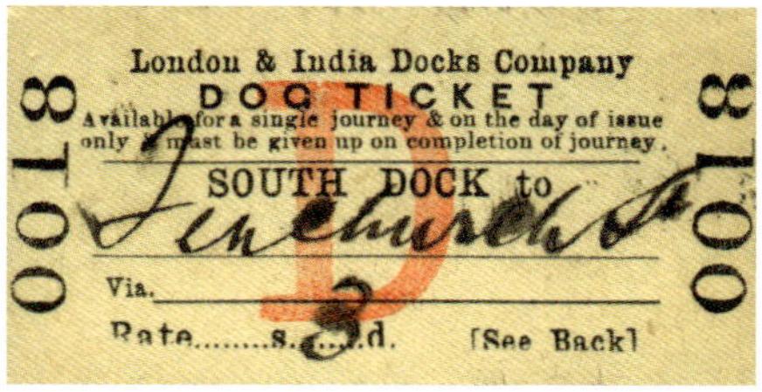

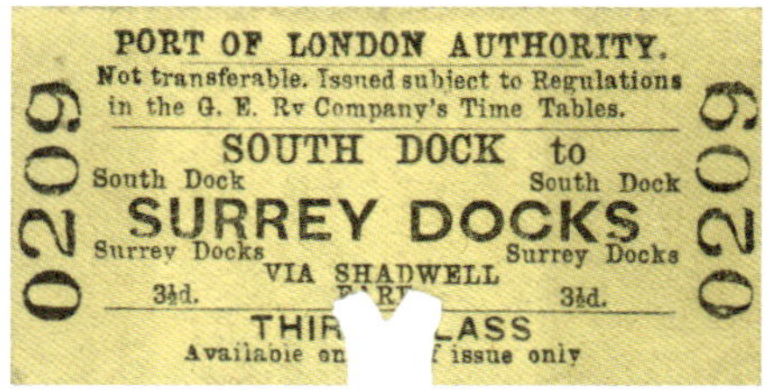

A Selection of Tickets. *(Left):* East & West India Dock Company Second class single to Millwall Junction issued on 27th May 1899. *(Centre):* London & India Docks Company dog ticket issued to Fenchurch Street on 21st May 1901. The East & West India Dock Co and the London & St Katharine Dock Co amalgamated in 1888 as the London & India Docks Joint Committee. *Right:* Port of London Authority third class single to Surrey Docks, issued on 23rd May 1915. The PLA was formed under the Port of London Act of 1908, and became operative the following year.

the station he was referring to.

Eight years later, after it was agreed to use locomotives instead of horses, Colonel Yolland returned and made a further inspection. For the first time there was mention of the *"Loop line at back of South Dock Station for crossing two trains"*, so it is assumed that this was when the facility was added. He also required the *"lengthening of station platform to the required length, together with a complete system of fencing and gates to be carried out."*

When inspected by Colonel Yolland, the station signal box at South Dock was recorded as having nineteen levers, of which one was spare.

There can be little doubt that the line was successful in its early days, as traffic returns for the first five weeks since the introduction of loco-haulage throughout recorded that 11,163 return tickets were issued to South Dock, along with 7,416 singles.

On 25th February 1917 at around 11pm, a fire broke out at the station, badly damaging the building and signal box. Despite being tackled by the London County Council Fire Brigade and the Port of London tug *Lea*, the blaze continued for around two hours, resulting in the destruction of the ticket office, waiting room and Inspector's office.

A year earlier, it was suggested that the northern section of the branch could be diverted in connection with a proposed dock improvement and because of this, the repairs following the fire were only intended as temporary.

Like the Blackwall line, the North Greenwich branch went into decline during the first two decades of the twentieth century and closure notices were put up towards the end of March 1926. These stated that passenger trains would cease from 1st July, but, as with Blackwall, the service was suspended after 3rd May due to the onset of the General Strike and was never restored.

Subsequent dock enlargements necessitated various changes, and to make way for these, the disused South Dock station, along with part of the formation which served it, was demolished in 1929.

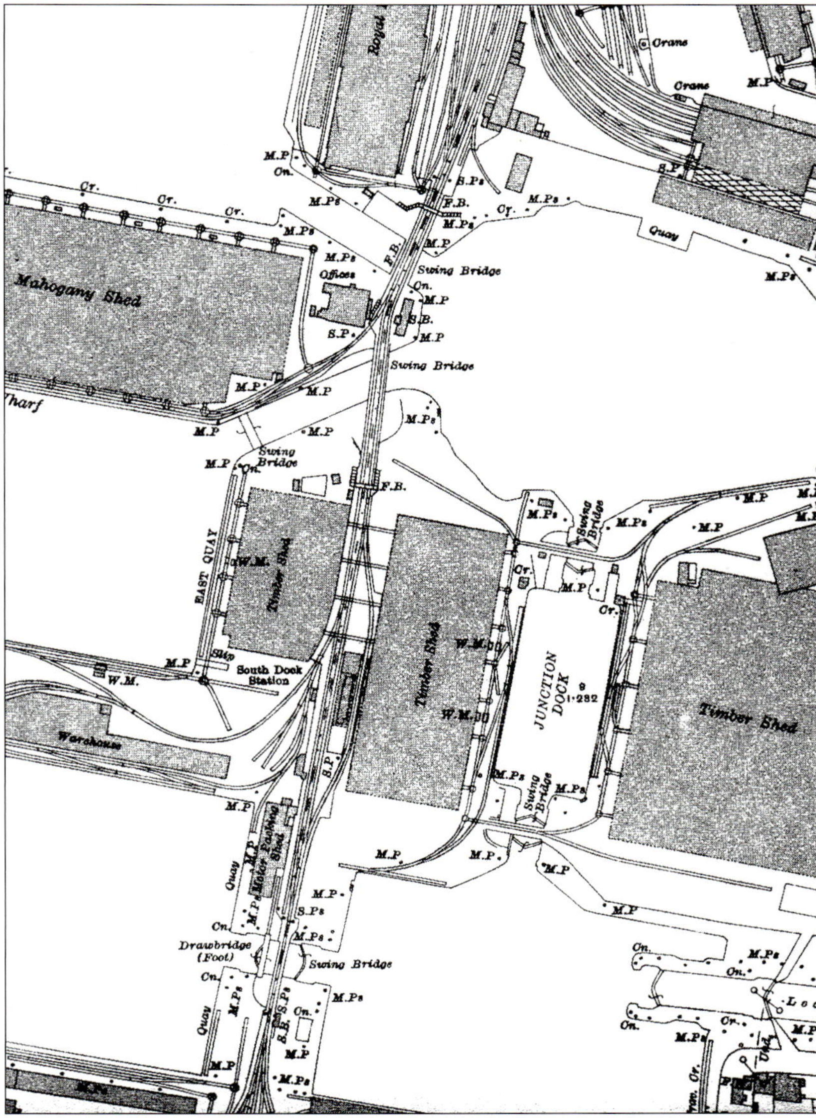

Extract of the 1:2500 Ordnance Survey map revised in 1914, showing South Dock station between the timber sheds near the centre, along with the three swing bridges, which restricted the weight of locomotives and stock employed on the route. Apart from the passing loop at South Dock, the North Greenwich branch was single and the other lines shown on this map were part of the internal dock network.

Millwall Docks

Opened (Millwall Extension Railway): 18th December 1871.
Resited to south (Millwall Extension Railway): 29th July 1872.
Closed (Port of London Authority): 4th May 1926.
Sometimes referred to as 'Glengall Road' or 'Millwall Docks (Glengall Road)', but neither of these were official names.

A Millwall Junction to North Greenwich service is seen at Millwall Docks station, around the early years of the twentieth century. Interestingly, the nameboard reads "Millwall Dock", whereas it was shown on tickets as Millwall Docks. The station was on the section of the MER owned by the Millwall Docks Company, which subsequently became part of the Port of London Authority.

For a little over seven months, Millwall Docks served as the southern terminus of the MER and originally stood to the north of Glengall Road.

When Colonel Yolland made his Board of Trade inspection on 16th December 1871, he stated that alterations were required to the stairs leading up from street level and that a fence was needed near the platform end. Apart from these minor snippets however, nothing seems to have been recorded about the temporary station, other than it was located six furlongs and five chains from Millwall Junction.

Just four days after opening, the Railway again contacted the Board of Trade and told them that the extension would be ready for inspection in a month. Their letter made reference to the permanent facilities at Millwall Docks and stated that the works included a passenger station *"in connection with the portion of the railway situated on the eastern side near the point where the railway crosses the Glengall Road"*. Unfortunately construction was far from complete, as when Colonel Yolland returned on 4th May 1872 he discovered that *"At Glengall Road, a crossover road* (was still) *to be taken out and the platform* (was) *only 18-20 yards long."* A further visit on 4th June found that progress had been made on the platform and that its lengthening was nearly finished. Some fencing had also been erected on the abutment of the adjoining bridge over Glengall Road, but as other tasks still needed to be carried out, the line did not open until the latter part of the following month.

The permanent station was located about 88 yards south of its predecessor and was approached by means of an uncovered stairway which led up from the south side of Glengall Road. At the top of this stood the wooden buildings, but with the absence of plans, full details of these are not known. Down below, adjoining the bridge, was a doorway, which presumably led into the booking hall, but again this cannot be confirmed. The station was staffed by the GER, but tickets issued there were headed *"Millwall Docks Company"* until the Port of London Authority was formed in 1909 and the title was changed accordingly.

It is understood the Millwall Docks was the only station on the North Greenwich branch to issue platform tickets, although why this should have been is uncertain. One explanation, provided by an elderly resident many years ago, was that there was a refreshment room at platform level, which was popular with dock workers, and they thought it was a penny well spent to partake of the tea, which was served in large, generous mugs. On the face of it, a small station such as Millwall Docks appears to have been unlikely to have a refreshment room, but from photographic evidence it seems possible.

The wooden platform was built on top of the embankment and stretched southwards, alongside East Ferry Road. Beyond this stood the signal box, but details of this have not been located.

Like South Dock, the station was well used in its early days with 12,978 single tickets being issued to there during five consecutive weeks in 1880, along with 6,931 returns.

Such success was not destined to last however and four years after taking over, the PLA began to seek economies. Sunday services were withdrawn from 28th December 1913 and around the same time, Millwall Docks ceased to have its own station master. More cuts came from April 1917, when weekday trains ceased to run after 8.30pm, but still the branch continued to lose money. During the period 1920/1 the revenue received from the North Greenwich line came to £2,222, but in 1921/2 it only reached £1,245.

Millwall Docks closed with the line in 1926 and although it remained standing for a while afterwards, it was subsequently demolished and being built of wood, disappeared completely.

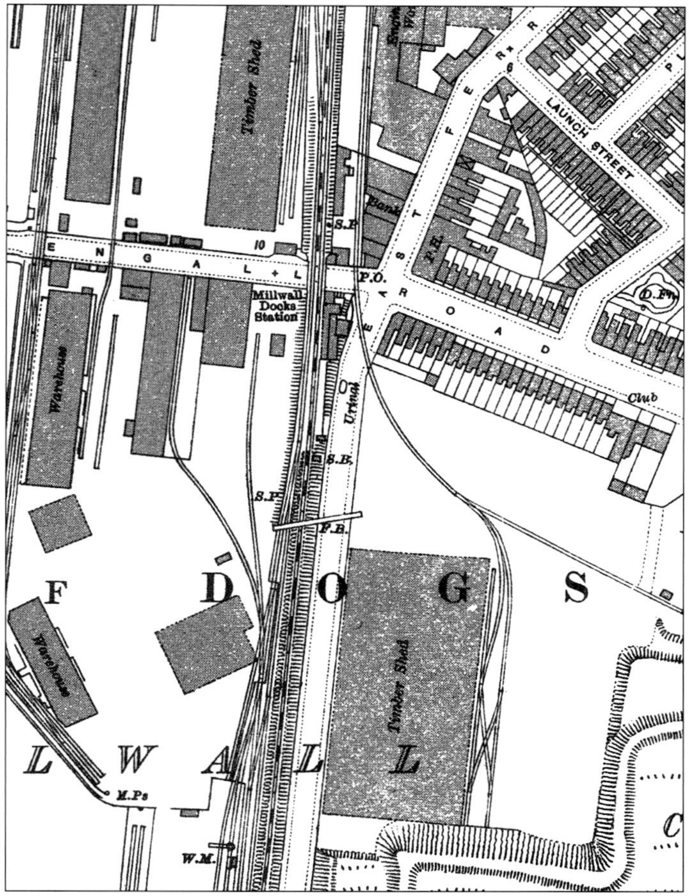

Right: An extract from the 1914 1:2500 Ordnance Survey map showing the station at centre, with Glengall Road to its north and East Ferry Road to its east. Millwall Docks signal box is seen a little to the south of the platform. At an unknown date, this replaced an earlier cabin known as Glengall Road which, when inspected by the BoT in 1879, had six working levers and four spare, within a Saxby & Farmer frame.

Looking east along Glengall Road at an unknown date, with the station on the right. Just beyond the bridge can be seen a window and door, which presumably formed the entrance.

The station exterior seen from the corner of Glengall Road and East Ferry Road. A sign at the top of the stairway promoting Cadbury's cocoa and chocolate, hints that the eastward extension of the building may have housed a refreshment room, as it does not appear to be a standard vitreous enamel advertisement of the time. If the doorway shown on the previous page was indeed the station entrance, then the roof just visible above the fence on the right, presumably sheltered the booking hall.

Looking north along East Ferry Road, with the station on the left. The windows of the eastward extension of the building have curtains, which again hints that it may have accommodated a buffet. It appears as if this was a later addition, but again, as no detailed plans have been located, this cannot be confirmed. Cast iron gents' urinals, such as that seen below the station buildings, were once a familiar sight around the docks.

Railway staff pose for the camera beside PLA 2-4-0T No 29, as she pauses at the station with a three-coach train to North Greenwich. The locomotive was built by Manning Wardle & Company in 1880 and was originally numbered 4. She was one of three engines which worked the line until November 1922, when they were all withdrawn and replaced by steam railmotors, which were acquired secondhand. The track in the foreground was part of the dock network and was not used by passenger trains.

North Greenwich & Cubitt Town

Opened (Millwall Extension Railway): 29th July 1872.
Closed (London & North Eastern Railway): 4th May 1926.

Postcard produced by the Cynicus Publishing Company in the first decade of the twentieth century, poking fun at the service between Millwall Junction and North Greenwich.

North Greenwich & Cubitt Town was located south of Manchester Road, on the east side of Johnson Street, or Ferry Street as it later became and was the only station on the MER owned by the Great Eastern.

When opened in 1872, horses continued to operate the service between Millwall Junction and the southern boundary of the Millwall Docks, where a locomotive would back on for the remaining part of the journey. The loco would therefore work in complete isolation and when it was sent away for mechanical attention, it had to be towed through the dock estates by horses.

The station building at North Greenwich had a brick frontage and a slate roof, but was otherwise constructed of wood, as was the single platform. North of this was the signal box, which was also wooden. It had a Saxby & Farmer frame, which comprised seventeen levers, although not all of these were used.

The front of the station was very plain and had a doorway at either end with a row of four windows above. Between the tops of the doors and the window ledges was a stone course, which displayed the legend *"GER North Greenwich Station Frequent Trains GER"* in incised lettering.

The line ended at a set of buffer stops, with a bell alongside, although the exact purpose of this is uncertain. Beyond the stops were a wooden fence and the Thames.

On the east side of the line was a single-road engine shed which dated from opening and accommodated the branch locomotives. Facilities at the depot included an engine pit and a coaling stage with water tank above.

The booking office received new barriers and a lamp room was added in September 1882, but no other changes seem to have been recorded over the years that followed, other than the addition of a carriage siding in 1885.

GER 2-4-0T No 17A stands at North Greenwich with one of the original carriages used on the line. This locomotive operated branch services from opening until 1875, and although restricted to the section south of the Millwall Dock boundary, was fitted with a chimney spark arrester to reduce the likelihood of lineside fires. No 17A seems to have endeared herself to the locals and was nicknamed the *"I Can Do It"*.

Just short of the station was a 490 yard brick viaduct, which was the most noteworthy engineering feature on the branch. It accommodated a single track and stretched northward from the bridge over Manchester Road.

"North Greenwich" was very much a misnomer, as the station was located at the southern end of Millwall and not in Greenwich at all. There was a connection however, as since the 17th century, the two places had been linked by a service provided by the Potter's Ferry Society. With the coming of the new line, the London & Blackwall Railway directors realised it would be advantageous to take this over and operate it themselves so, by an Act of 1873, they acquired the rights at a cost of £8,000. By this time of course, the LBR was being worked by the Great Eastern, so it fell to them to make the necessary arrangements. To better integrate services, a new pier was constructed beside North Greenwich station in 1877 and through bookings onto the ferry were introduced from stations along the route three years later. The landing stage on the opposite side of the river was referred to as "South Greenwich". This was provided with a booking office, which issued GER tickets for journeys to North Greenwich and beyond.

In 1880 the Company announced in the press that: *"This line is now worked by Engine Power throughout and that a new and greatly improved Service of early and late trains is in operation, affording direct communication with Greenwich, Blackheath and the South side of the Thames. Greenwich passengers cross the Thames by a large and commodious Steam Ferry, and step from the train to the steamer and vice versa, at the new Railway Pier at North Greenwich Station".*

The ferry service was well used, but often proved unreliable in bad weather. Added to this, it seems that the access at North Greenwich was less than satisfactory and complaints were frequently made about the poorly lit stairs.

All this would soon pass into history however, as an Act of 1897 authorised the London County Council to construct a pedestrian subway under the river to link Millwall with Greenwich. The Great Eastern objected to this proposal, but the scheme went ahead and the subway opened on 4th August 1902. The ferries continued as normal until the end of the month, when operations were drastically reduced, although final closure did not come until 31st October. On 19th May 1903, the GER

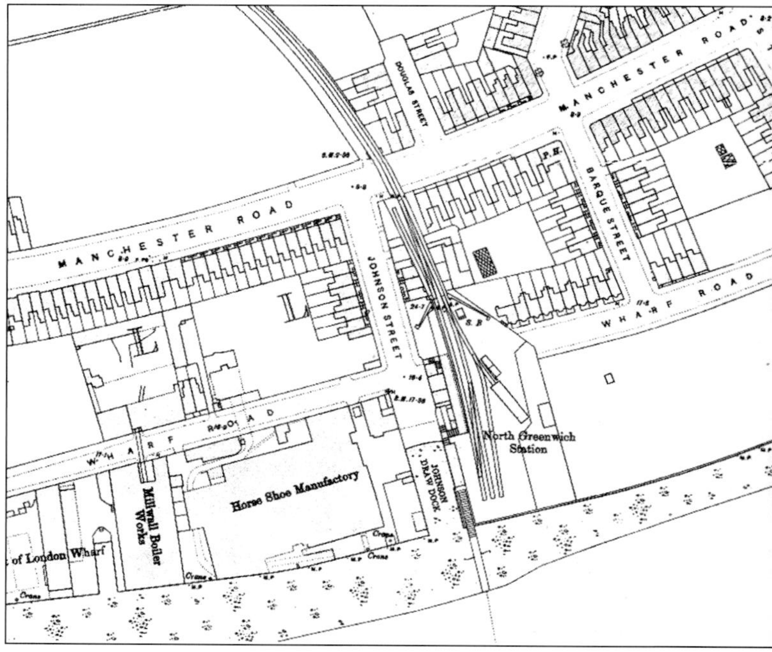

Reduced extract of the 5ft to 1 mile Ordnance Survey map of 1893-5, showing North Greenwich station, with the bridge over Manchester Road at the top and the river at the bottom. The doorway at the north end of the building led to a stairway which provided access to the platform, whilst that to the south served the stairs used to reach the ferry. With no detailed plans of the interior known to exist, it seems likely that the ticket office was at the northern end, but whether this was just inside the door at street level, or on the platform, is not known. There was a short section of viaduct on the south side of Manchester Road, but the station itself was built on embankment. The signal box is shown at the north end of the site, with the line serving the coaling stage and engine shed branching to the right below it. The arrangement leading to the ferry is near the bottom of the map, adjoining the Johnson Draw Dock. In 1902, a subway was provided beneath the station in connection with the new foot tunnel, with the cost of £1,075 being shared equally by the GER, the LCC and the Poplar Borough Council.

Way & Works Committee recorded that the pontoons and gangway at North Greenwich were sold to Moss Isaacs for £65 and the ferry service was never restored.

Despite this setback, North Greenwich station could still be busy, particularly on Saturday afternoons, when Millwall Football Club were playing at home. On these occasions, the trains were strengthened by an additional two coaches, thereby increasing the load to five crowded vehicles. This must have been the upper limit that the tiny locomotives could manage and it's perhaps understandable that all three had to be rebuilt by the East Ferry Road Engineering Company in 1905. The extra revenue earned on match days came to an end in 1910 however, when Millwall FC relocated to New Cross, so their followers no longer needed the branch when travelling to games.

The trains continued to ply back and forth between Millwall Junction and North Greenwich, but as the twentieth century progressed there was less and less demand.

After closure in 1926, the track serving the station was lifted and the bridge over Manchester Road was removed. The brick viaduct remained untouched for a while, but 160 yards at its northern end were demolished

Above: The bridge over Manchester Road, looking east in April 1922. The station was at the far end of Johnson Street, which is seen branching off, immediately in front of the viaduct on the right. The structure in the middle of the road is a cast-iron gents urinal.

Right: One of the Manning Wardle 2-4-0Ts awaits departure from North Greenwich, with the combined coaling and watering facilities to the left. The engine shed was immediately beyond these, but was painted out by the photographer, presumably to give a clearer background to the loco.

in 1937. The station itself was subsequently used for storage and remained substantially intact into the 1950s, albeit with its canopy valance rationalised. The building later provided accommodation for a local rowing club and as such lasted into 1969. After demolition, its site was redeveloped to provide new facilities for the club and all trace of the old station disappeared.

The bridge abutments on the south side of Manchester Road survived however, as did the viaduct, but otherwise there was little to be seen of any significance. By a strange twist of fate, the old viaduct was renovated and brought back into use, when the first section of the Docklands Light Railway was opened in 1987. A new bridge was erected above Manchester Road and a terminal station provided at Island Gardens. This was located to the north of the old North Greenwich site and consisted of two platforms, which were laid out in a "vee", either side of a glazed stair and lift tower with a domed roof. The DLR was built as double track, but widening the old viaduct would have proved expensive, so the two lines were merged into one near its northern end. The points leading to the station were located on the new bridge, which splayed out to carry the lines towards their respective platforms.

This arrangement did not last very long however, as plans to extend the DLR to Lewisham resulted in the south end of the earlier route being diverted into a new tunnel beneath the river and replacement stations being built at Mudchute and Island Gardens. The last train departed from the 1987 terminus at around 1.09am on a very wet Saturday 9th January 1999 and the viaduct fell into disuse for the second time in its existence.

After closure, the original Island Gardens station was demolished, along with the DLR bridge over Manchester Road and a brief chapter in east London's long railway history drew to a close.

A Manning Wardle 2-4-0T has been uncoupled from her train after arrival at North Greenwich and is seen running round in readiness for the return run to Millwall Junction. To the right of the locomotive is the bell referred to in the text, whilst to the left, on the opposite side of the river, are the towers of Greenwich Hospital. The three locomotives of this type were owned by the Millwall Dock Company and were numbered 3,4 and 6. They were taken over by the Port of London Authority in 1909 and became Nos 28, 29 and 31 respectively.

2-4-0T No 4 stands at North Greenwich having just arrived from Millwall Junction. To the left can be seen the top of the stairway which served the ferry, by way of the southernmost door in the station frontage.

A train is seen prior to departure from North Greenwich at an unknown date, headed by a Manning Wardle 2-4-0T. To the right can be seen part of the running-in board, which was presumably of vitreous enamel within a wooden frame. Interestingly, this had a lower section from which the sign had been removed. No other photographs showing the nameboards are known, but it seems likely that this section had advised passengers to alight for the ferry, but was removed after the service was withdrawn in 1902. The station was invariably shown on tickets as 'North Greenwich & Cubitt Town', but the suffix was probably omitted from the nameboards.

The station frontage in Johnson Street, probably taken in the 1930s, showing the incised lettering above the doorways which is mentioned in the text. Although the ferry pontoons and gangway were recorded as being sold in 1903, the entrance which led to them remained standing and can be seen to the extreme right, seemingly still sporting a nameboard.

After closure the track was lifted and North Greenwich was used for storage. This view is undated and shows that although the station was still largely intact, the stairs which once led to the ferry had been removed. By 1952, most of the canopy valancing had been taken down, with the awning itself disappearing in the years that followed.

Above: Looking towards the station from the short section of viaduct to the south of Manchester Road, again at an unknown date. Just to right of centre, a row of iron railings have been installed beyond the brick parapet to allow more light to filter into the upper floor windows of the adjoining houses.

Below: A photograph taken in the opposite direction showing the main section of viaduct north of Manchester Road. The old car adds to the air of dereliction.

By 1964, when this photograph was taken, the building had lost its three chimney stacks, but otherwise appeared to be fairly intact, even though becoming progressively derelict. The view was taken from near the site of the ferry entrance and looks north to Johnson Street, or Ferry Street as it had been renamed, and shows the south end of the station with the former stairway access boarded-up on the right.

The exterior of the station, viewed from its northern end in 1968. The incised lettering in the stone course above the door seems to have been filled with cement, as none of it remained discernible.

Two photographs showing North Greenwich station as it appeared in 1967. The view above was taken from the southern end and shows how much the building had deteriorated during its years of closure. For some time it had been occupied by a rowing club and a roof had been erected over part of the platform, to protect the premises below from inclement weather. The view on the right looks south and includes the twisted and warped remains of the platform. Demolition followed a couple of years later and the building disappeared completely.

Above: Manchester Road, viewed from Ferry Street in 1968, showing where the bridge had been removed. The site of the short section of viaduct, partly seen on the right, was subsequently redeveloped in connection with the DLR.

Below: The main section of viaduct on the approach to North Greenwich station, seen from Millwall Park in 1968.

Above (left): A Docklands Light Railway vehicle is seen crossing the old single line MER viaduct on 31st August 1987, which was the first day of public service. The DLR also revived a section of the old route beside East Ferry Road, but this was formed of embankment and not viaduct.

Above (right): The new section of formation, built to support the original Island Gardens station, faced in brick to match the original viaduct. The replacement bridge over Manchester Road is partly visible on the extreme left.

Right (centre): Looking towards Island Gardens from a DLR vehicle in 1987, showing part of the original 1870s viaduct in the foreground and the new formation beyond, including the bridge over Manchester Road.

Right (bottom): The first Island Gardens station, showing its rather unusual layout with platforms either side of the domed structure which provided both lift and stair access.

Burdett Road

Opened (Great Eastern Railway): 11th September 1871.
Closed (London & North Eastern Railway): c.21st April 1941.

Looking north along Burdett Road in the early twentieth century, with the station on the bridge in the middle distance. The entrance was on the east side and the booking hall was located within an arch, although this is hidden in the photograph by an open top 'bus. The rear of the up side platform buildings can be seen spanning above the road and includes two large signs of similar size. That above the centre arch was the station nameboard, whilst that to the right promoted the removals firm of A. H. Barker.

For those unfamiliar with the East End, Burdett Road is a wide thoroughfare linking Limehouse with Mile End. It was completed in 1862 and took its name from the banking heiress, Angela Georgina Burdett-Coutts, who paid for its construction.

The road passed beneath the London & Blackwall Extension Railway, but initially there were no thoughts of erecting a station there. However, it was subsequently decided that one would benefit the area and construction commenced around the beginning of June 1871.

The station was located 26 chains north-east of Stepney and comprised two platforms. The site of these had previously been occupied by a pair of tracks, which flanked the running lines and dated from 1854. These were known as the 'Bow Sidings' and were originally used for marshalling wagons. One of these sidings had subsequently been adapted to provide an additional up line from Gas Factory Junction to St Pauls Road, and this was cut back to end at the north end of the station. The down siding was lifted completely.

As the formation had already been widened to accommodate the sidings, there was no need to create further space and the contractors lost no time in proceeding with the work. Within a couple of months, the station was reported as nearing completion and it opened for traffic on 11th September 1871.

The entrance was on the north-eastern side of Burdett Road and took the form of doorways beneath the arch. These led into a booking hall, which had been built within an existing viaduct arch and, from here, stairs led up to the two platforms. At first these seem to have been very basic and lacking in facilities, but the situation was remedied in 1872 when accommodation for staff was provided.

During 1875-6 it proved necessary to renew the bridge over Commercial Road and trains which normally stopped at Stepney called at Burdett Road instead. Unfortunately the existing platforms proved to be too short for some of these, so both sides were provided with temporary wooden extensions. These were presumably removed when they were no longer required and the platforms were returned to their earlier length.

As traffic grew, the waiting rooms were added in 1880 at a cost of £300.

Initially only Great Eastern trains called, but from 1st November 1891, the station was also served by the London Tilbury & Southend Railway.

The booking office was enlarged towards the end of 1893 and the height of the platforms was raised five years later, but very little else in the way of alterations appears to have been recorded in the company minute books.

Burdett Road signal box, which stood at the north-east end of the up platform, was abolished from Sunday 3rd March 1935 in connection with the introduction of electric signalling between Fenchurch Street and Bow Junction. It was replaced by a two-lever ground frame which was necessary to work the station crossover and from photographic evidence it is known that the former cabin disappeared completely within seven months

By this time a fair amount of traffic had been lost, as a result of competition from other forms of transport. The opening of the Whitechapel & Bow Railway station at Mile End in 1902 had provided an alternative rail link between the area and central London. When this line was electrified three years later, many of the passengers that had previously used Burdett Road turned to Mile End instead. This, together with tramway and bus improvements, brought about a decline in the station's fortunes. An enthusiast recalled visiting there in the late 1930s and said that *"there seemed to be very few passengers."* Nevertheless the station was still fairly busy during the peaks but by then, fate was to ensure that its days were numbered.

During the Second World War, the line serving Fenchurch Street was subjected to bombing on numerous occasions, with the earliest incidents being recorded around the onset of the Blitz. The first of these to affect Burdett Road took place on the night of 7th/8th September 1940 but, although the line itself was damaged, the station was stated to be "safe". In the small hours of 9th September a bomb caused two nearby arches to collapse and Fenchurch Street services were temporarily suspended, but again the station seemed to have escaped any serious damage. Early in the morning of 10th September a bomb landed on the track, but it fortunately failed to explode. A disposal team was quickly on the scene, but services were again suspended whilst the bomb was dealt with. The station was not so lucky on 19th September however, because at around 10pm, a high explosive bomb penetrated the booking hall ceiling, damaging the arcade and passimeter ticket office. Both tracks were blocked, but against all odds, the down line was clear by 1pm the following day and normal working was resumed on 23rd September. The station seemingly reopened, but the death blow came on 10th April 1941, when it was badly damaged for the second time. The East End of London suffered

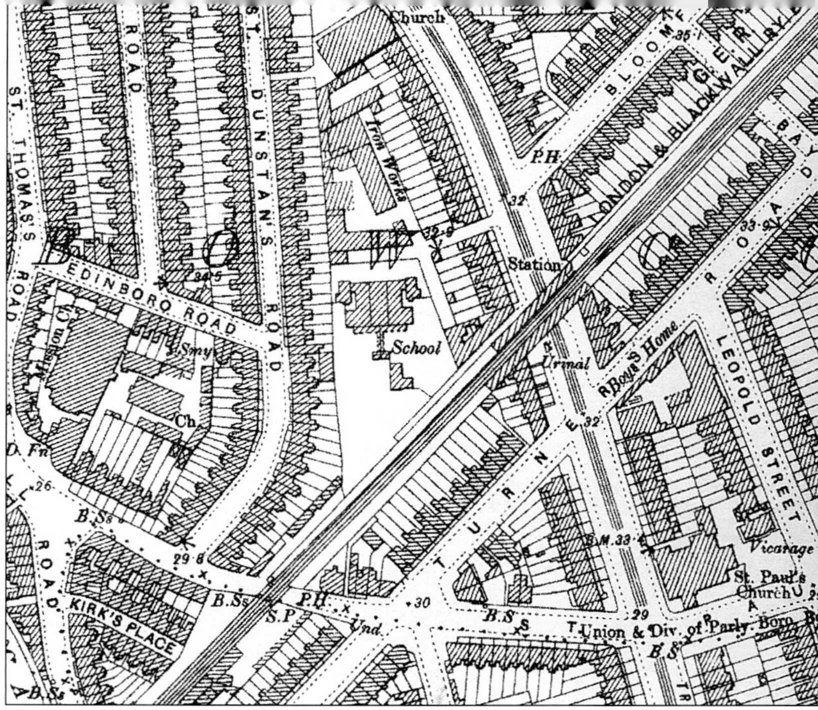

Extract from the 1: 2500 Ordnance Survey map of 1894, showing Burdett Road station at centre.

dreadfully during the Blitz, so it is difficult to say with any certainty exactly what happened at Burdett Road in this raid. However, an undated photograph exists which, although taken from street level, clearly shows that the wooden buildings on the up side had been more or less destroyed. This may have been taken after the incident of 19th September 1940, but is perhaps more likely to date from April 1941. Either way, the station was very badly damaged and was officially closed soon after.

At a meeting of the LNER Traffic Committee on 24th October 1946 it was decided that Burdett Road would remain permanently closed and demolition was approved on 5th October 1950, although from photographic evidence it is known that the wooden platform buildings had gone by 1946. However, the sections which contained the gents' urinals were constructed of brick and these, together with the platforms themselves, survived the initial demolition. The gents continued to stand until the mid-1950s, but the platforms remained a little longer.

Down below, the former street level accommodation remained disused and empty and was shown in Kelly's Directory simply as "Burdett Road Railway Station (Closed)" for many years. It seems to have been used by a sack merchant for a short time around 1957, but then seems to have reverted to being unoccupied. A firm of shop fitters eventually moved in during the early 1960s and were replaced by a furniture manufacturer about 1964. After this, the old booking hall continued to be used for wood working purposes for a number of years, but by the early 1980s was again disused. It remained

easily identifiable throughout its period of closure, being located within a pedestrian arch and therefore set back from Burdett Road itself. The 'station arch' and that on the opposite side of the road, were decorated with stucco rustication, although some of this disintegrated with the passing of time.

At track level, the platforms had certainly gone by 1964, leaving just the stairwell openings, with a few crumbling stairs at the top. The Burdett Road bridge was renewed in 1984 and the surviving station relics were swept away. The widening of the viaduct where the 'Bow Sidings' and later platforms once were is still evident, but other than this, Burdett Road station has gone without trace.

Above: LMSR 4-4-2T No 2113 arrives at Burdett Road with a Fenchurch Street - Southend via Tilbury train on 20th October 1935.

Left: Ex-LTSR 0-6-2T No 2225 approaches Burdett Road on the same day, with a goods train for Commercial Road. The colour light signalling had recently been installed at the time and the former signal box had already been demolished. To the right can be seen part of Bow Common gas works.

Above: Looking north along Burdett Road in 1941, with the badly damaged station up above. As can be seen, the wooden buildings on the up side had all but disappeared, leaving just the brick-built gents standing on the left. Those serving the down platform appear to have fared better, although the north-eastern end of the awning had lost its valancing.

Below: A southward view, dating from 1952, which shows the station after all the platform buildings had been demolished, leaving just the gents toilets on both sides. The entrance to the booking hall was within the pedestrian arch on the left.

The remains of Burdett Road station, viewed from the Stepney end in 1956, by which time only the platforms survived. Note the reverse curvature of the lines, due to the viaduct widening in 1854 being done 15ft on the up side but only 5ft on the down side.

A Selection of Tickets. *Top left:* GER third class single to Shadwell & St George's East issued on 1st October 1902. *Top centre:* GER third class single to Bow Road issued on 12th February 1901. *Top right:* GER third class single to Stratford issued on 7th October 1903. *Bottom left:* LTSR third class single to Bromley issued on 31st January 1904. Although operated by the GER, Burdett Road was also served by London, Tilbury & Southend Railway trains. *Bottom centre:* Midland Railway (LTSR Section) third class single to Plaistow issued on 5th April, but year unclear. The LTSR was taken over by the Midland Railway in 1912. *Bottom right:* LNER third class single to Fenchurch Street issued on 8th May 1930.

Two views of the former booking hall arch, as it appeared in 1967. The photograph above was taken from the north side, whilst that below is seen from the south. The rusticated stucco surrounding the arch was in a pretty poor state and had partially dropped off, presumably as a result of air raid damage. The north end of the pedestrian arch had been repaired using a concrete lintel, but the former station entrance which it served had changed little since closure.

Above (left): The former station entrance on the east side of the pedestrian arch, seen in 1967.

Above right: The remains of the down side stairway photographed in 1984, shortly before final demolition.

Left: The station site in 1984, with the two former stairwells behind broken brick walls in the foreground.

Bow Road

First station opened as Bow & Bromley (London & Blackwall Railway): 2nd April 1849.
Closed (London & Blackwall Railway): 26th September 1850.
New station, Bow Road, opened on same site (Great Eastern Railway): 1st October 1876.
Resited to north (Great Eastern Railway): 4th April 1892.
Temporarily closed (London & North Eastern Railway): c.21st April 1941 - 9th December 1946.
Temporarily closed again (London & North Eastern Railway): 6th January 1947 - 6th October 1947.
Permanently closed (British Railways Eastern Region): 7th November 1949.

A commercial postcard showing Bow Road prior to 1907. The street level building of the 1892 station is seen on the right, whilst part of its 1876 predecessor is just visible to the left. The wooden structure showing the station's name is projecting forward from the bridge side and is supported by a fairly substantial post seen to the right of the passing bus. This seems likely to be the rear of the up side 1879 platform extension, but as no track level photographs of Bow Road from this period have been located, this cannot be confirmed.

BOW & BROMLEY STATION (1849-1850)

Bow & Bromley stood on the south side of Bow Road and was opened with the London & Blackwall Extension line from Stepney in 1849. It was built on viaduct and comprised two platforms. It seems to have been little patronised and closed in September 1850, when the East & West India Docks & Birmingham Junction Railway introduced a service linking Fenchurch Street with Islington by way of its own station at Bow.

The E&WID&BJR was renamed the North London Railway in 1853 and the London & Blackwall was leased to the Great Eastern Railway in 1866.

Bow & Bromley remained standing for at least twenty years after closure and appears on the 1870 edition of the 1:2500 Ordnance Survey map.

THE FIRST BOW ROAD STATION (1876-1892)

By the 1870s suburban traffic on the GER was increasing substantially and thoughts turned to bringing the old Bow & Bromley back into use. At a Board meeting on 24th March 1875, it was decided to build a new station on the site, at an estimated cost of £2,500, and the project was subsequently passed to the Way and Works Committee. Five companies were invited to tender, although in seven months, the engineer's estimate had increased by £1,000. On Wednesday 6th October 1875, it was agreed that the contract would be awarded to the local firm of Messrs Wicks, Bangs & Co, who stated it could be done for £3,640 and completed within eighteen weeks.

Whether work started immediately is not known, but in the following spring, it was clearly under way.

On 3rd April 1876, a Mr Edwin Phillips of *The Railway Service Gazette* wrote to Captain Tyler of the Board of Trade expressing his fears that the station's location was potentially hazardous. In his letter he said *"There is a station being constructed adjoining the Great Eastern Company's bridge over the Bow Road on the line to Fenchurch St. There is a very sharp curve at this point, and the position of the station is in my opinion extremely dangerous. At the place where the station is being constructed, there has for many years been a dilapidated unused station (showing that at some past time passengers were taken up and set down at this place, but for some cause the arrangement has been discontinued.)"* It is not certain whether Captain Tyler replied but four days later, Mr Phillips again wrote to the Board of Trade, and this time addressed his letter to Sir Charles Adderley. The wording was basically the same, but he expanded on his theory regarding potential danger, by saying that because of the sharp curve, the station *"cannot be seen by Drivers approaching from Stratford until they are very close to it."* He apparently had little knowledge of events twenty-six years earlier, as he thought the presence of the derelict Bow & Bromley seemed *"to shew that the Company had discontinued to deal with public business at this place in consequence of the dangerous situation of the station."*

At the time, the Board of Trade had not been officially informed that the work was in progress, but five months later, on 25th September, the GER Secretary wrote stating that the station was complete and ready for inspection.

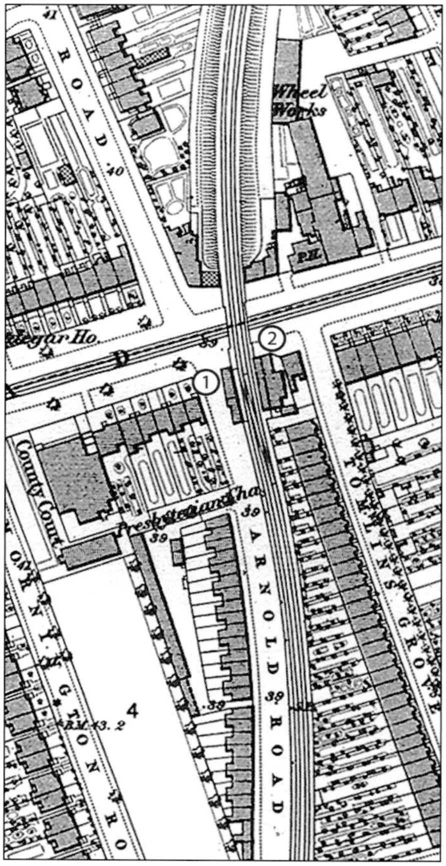

Extract from the 1st Edition 1:2500 Ordnance Survey map of 1870, showing the disused London & Blackwall Railway station at Bow & Bromley, on the south side of Bow Road. A similar plan to other LBR stations was used, with 'staircase buildings' adjoining the viaduct. 'No 1' indicates that on the down side, whilst 'No. 2' refers to the up. The 1892 station was later built on the stretch of embankment to the north of the main road.

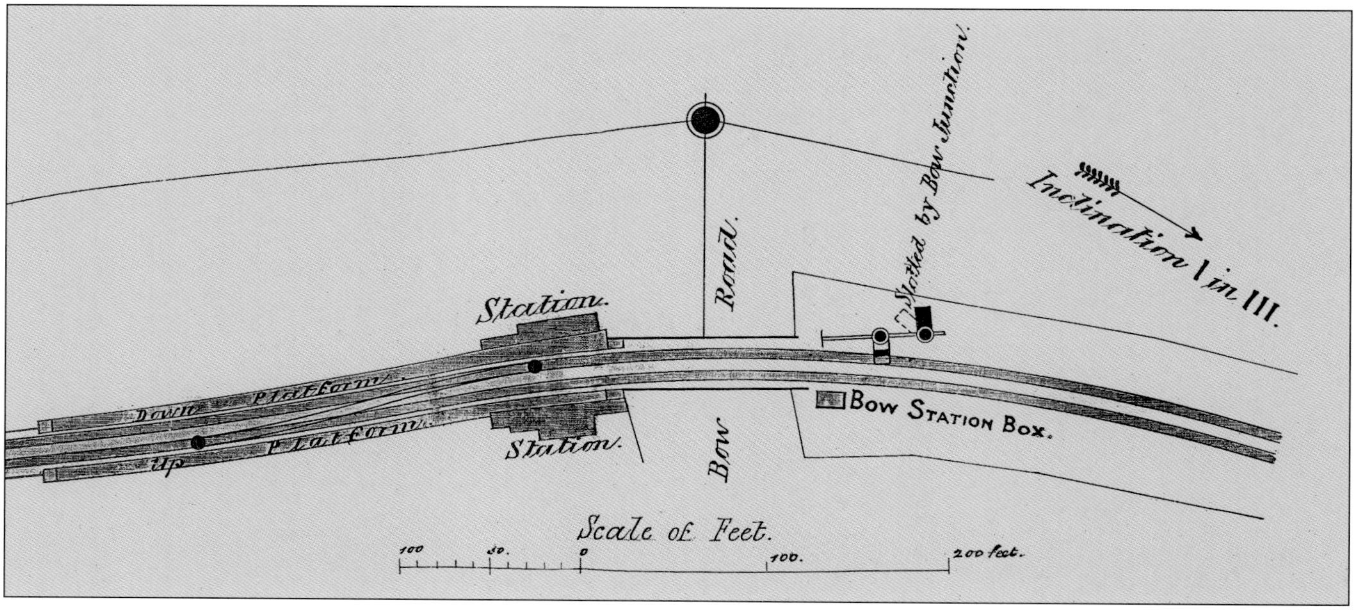

A signalling diagram produced in connection with the opening of the first 'Bow Road' station in 1876. Comparison of the main buildings with those on the 1870 Ordnance Survey indicates that the originals of 1849 were possibly brought back into use or their replacements were built to the same plan. The signal box shown here opened with the station in 1876 and closed with it in 1892.

Left: An enlargement taken from the postcard reproduced on page 137, showing, at left, a fragment of the up side 'building' of the 1876 station, whilst being leased to an auctioneer named John Bussey, who subsequently had it converted into a cinema. The single-storey angled section was a coal office, then occupied by Charles Abbott, but this was not part of the station itself.

Above: A view from 1979 showing the former coal office, with part of the 1876 street level building to its right. Very little of the original had survived however and the frontage seen here had been substantially rebuilt. Up above, the parapet shows signs of earlier demolition, but a date when this took place has not been located.

Colonel Yolland was appointed as Inspecting Officer and he duly visited the new station on 29th September. Apart from the necessity to remove some old fencing, which may have been vestiges of the original Bow & Bromley, he was satisfied that all was well and his report ended *"The new station is a great improvement on the old one and I recommend that the sanction of the Board of Trade may be given for it being opened for traffic."* The GER were subsequently informed of this and trains began to call on 1st October 1876.

From opening it was known as Bow Road, although prior to this it was recorded in minute books as just plain "Bow" and was even shown as such in the Traffic Committee entry for 3rd October.

As there appears to be a total lack of photographic evidence of both the 1849 station and its 1876 successor, it is difficult to assess what Colonel Yolland meant by "a great improvement", but it seems that both buildings shared similar floor plans.

Unfortunately no plans of the station at street level have been traced by the author, but the building was located on either side of the viaduct and no doubt used an existing arch as its booking hall. From contemporary editions of *Kelly's Directory*, it is apparent that the entrance was located on the west side of the formation, whilst the section of building on the opposite side of the line adjoined a small coal office. Up above, both platforms were a little over 300ft in length and stretched back towards Stepney on a falling grade of 1 in 339.

The signal box was located north of the station and adjoined the up line, just beyond the bridge over Bow Road. When inspected by the Board of Trade in 1876, it was equipped with seven levers and twelve years later was recorded as also having *"two block instruments and a speaking instrument"*.

The active life of the station proved to be comparatively short, but during its sixteen years a number of alterations took place. Of these the most significant occurred in the spring of 1879, when both platforms were extended northwards over the Bow Road bridge. The work was carried out under contract by M. Patrick & Sons and cost £644. Later in the same year, the Poplar Borough Council erected a urinal in nearby Arnold Road, whilst in May 1887, the GER Way & Works Committee agreed to spend £65 on improving the toilets on the station itself.

Since 1869, the Great Eastern had operated a shuttle service between Fenchurch Street and Bow on the North London Railway, but as time progressed this began to lose money.

Since the opening of the new GER Bow Road station in 1876 there was certainly no need to retain the shuttle for local purposes, but the connection with the NLR proved useful for interchange traffic. In a report dated 16th June 1890, the GER General Manager, William Birt, stated that the half-hourly service no longer paid and that each train only conveyed an average number of twenty-eight passengers. Their operation also restricted the number of additional trains which the Great Eastern could run between Fenchurch Street and Forest Gate or Romford and, as this was a more profitable route, it deserved a more intensive service.

The decision was therefore taken to withdraw the shuttles and replace them by providing a better interchange between the two companies at Bow. To achieve this, Bow Road station would be resited north of its existing location and be furnished with a covered walkway which led directly onto the North London station in the cutting below.

There then followed months of discussions between William Birt and his opposite number on the NLR, George Bolland Newton, before a proposal was put to the Board whereby *"The Great Eastern is to erect a new station at Bow Road, which shall afford a means of interchange for passengers with the Bow station (North London)...*

The expense of that part of the new station which shall be upon Great Eastern property to be borne by the Great Eastern, about £12,790.

The expense of that part which will be on North London property to be borne by that Company, about £1,650.

The Great Eastern to bear the expense of the staff at the new station employed exclusively for the Great Eastern Office."

The proposal was duly approved and the London & Blackwall, which although leased to the GER was still nominally independent, was informed of the forthcoming changes.

The site largely consisted of embankment and, as the new station was intended to be substantial, the platforms and associated buildings had to be constructed on brick arches. Ten building firms were invited to tender and on 20th January 1891, the contract was awarded to Kirk, Knight & Co who provided an estimate of £9,276.

Six months later the plan was submitted for Board of Trade approval and by 19th January the following year, work was sufficiently advanced to arrange for the subway floors to be surfaced in *"best rock asphalt"* by the firm of W. Griffiths.

By early spring, everything had been completed and on 16th March, the Great Eastern Railway informed the Board of Trade that the new premises were ready for inspection. Major General C.J. Hutchinson was duly appointed to carry this out and his report, written on 19th March 1892 stated *"The new station has been constructed close to and on the Stratford side of the existing Bow Road station which is to be closed. It is to serve as an exchange station with the North London Company's Bow Station (which is almost directly underneath it)."* Subject to the completion of signalling alterations and the addition of a handrail on the Stratford-end bridge parapet, the Inspecting Officer was satisfied with the standard of workmanship and recommended that the new premises be brought into use.

Services began to call on 4th April 1892 and the following day, William Birt reported *"that this station was opened yesterday the 4th instant. Commencing on that day the trains which hitherto have run to the North London station at Bow, began running through the new Bow Road station, and finished their journeys at Stratford or Forest Gate."*

It is not known how long the platforms of the old station survived after closure, but vestiges of the 1879 extensions may have still been standing until 1907 when the bridge was renewed. Down below, the street level premises were used by a coal merchant and a firm of auctioneers, before being converted into a cinema known as the 'Bromley Picture Theatre' during 1912. In his book *London's Lost Railways*, Charles Klapper recalled that the former station entrance was *"a typical road-level booking hall under viaduct platforms"* and *"... for a time it was in use as a 'fleapit' cheap 'electric theatre' showing low-quality films"*.

The cinema was originally provided with 428 seats, but the number was subsequently reduced to 374. It was used for storage during the latter part of the First World War, but briefly reopened in 1920, before being permanently closed three years later. The two arches which accommodated it were adapted for other uses, but all traces of the former station entrance have long-since disappeared.

THE SECOND BOW ROAD STATION (1892-1949)

The new station was considerably larger than its predecessor and was entered by way of a red brick building on the north side of Bow Road. Access to the trains was afforded by two stairways, which were covered in light iron and glass roofing, and led to the London end of both platforms. These stretched over 500ft towards Stratford and were covered from end to end by substantial awnings. Wood-fronted buildings were provided about half way along their length and immediately north-east of these, on the down side, a new signal box was constructed. When inspected by Major General Hutchinson, this was reported as having fifteen working levers and five spare. Apart from this, little is known of the cabin, other than it was built of wood and fitted with a McKenzie & Holland frame.

The replacement box was necessary because the original fell foul of the resiting plans and had to be demolished. There was a crossover at the southern end and another towards Stratford, although the latter was beyond the end of the platforms.

The station was situated on a sharp curve and at its north-eastern extremity could be found the interchange stairs leading to the North London Line. These were constructed in a similar manner to those already described and had white glazed brick at the bottom, where they led into a subway. At the far end of this was an inconspicuous little red brick booking office which kept stocks of both GER and NLR tickets, and was used by passengers who needed to re-book before continuing their journeys. Great Eastern tickets from here showed the point of origin as 'Bow Road (EO)', with the initials denoting 'Exchange Office', whilst North London issues displayed 'Bow No 2'.

Beyond this office, interchange passengers continued into a covered footway which brought them directly onto the Broad Street-bound side of Bow station, or else to a footbridge which provided access to the other platforms. There was a doorway leading into the footway from what is now Kitcat Terrace, but this is thought to have been for staff use only.

The station remained little altered throughout much of its existence, although a few minor changes took place in its early years. Initially it seems that there was an insufficient number of platform seats, as on 17th March 1896, the company agreed to provide *"improved seating accommodation"* at a cost of £35. Three years later, on 19th September 1899, the same committee approved the outlay of £107 to add a room for porters and transhipped parcels, although the location of this is not indicated within the relevant minutes.

As with many inner suburban stations, Bow Road's fortunes declined as a result of tramway and Underground competition. As patronage fell, the number of people using the interchange facility between Bow Road and Bow stations also dropped, so this was closed as a wartime economy measure at the beginning of 1917 and never reopened.

The decline continued in the years that followed, but a brighter future seemed to beckon when a modernisation scheme was announced for the line into Fenchurch Street. As part of this, new electric signalling would be introduced from the City terminus to both Bow Junction and Campbell Road Junction. The new arrangements were brought into use on Sunday 3rd March 1935 and resulted in the abolition of nine boxes, including that at Bow Road. A notice issued a few weeks earlier on 11th February by Mr H.H. Mauldin, Superintendent, Eastern Section, LNER said of Bow Road: *"The existing Down Starting Signal will be worked from Bow Junction LNE, as Down Outer Home (No.2), the Bow Junction Down Distant arm on the same post being dispensed with, and Gas Factory Junction Down Starting Signal (No GF35) will also act as Bow Junction Down Distant Signal.*

The crossover road will be locked with Hodgsons Locks, the keys of which will be kept in a cupboard on the wall of the Up side of line at Stepney end of Bow Road station. The key of this cupboard will be kept in Gas Factory Junction Box..."

With this in operation, Bow Road box became redundant and was subsequently removed, although the date of its demolition has not been traced.

Bow Road station lost its Sunday services from 5th May 1935, but late in the following year, the LNER announced that the Fenchurch Street - Bow Junction line would be included in the Shenfield electrification scheme. As part of this, two bay platforms were to be constructed at Stratford and a shuttle service of electrics

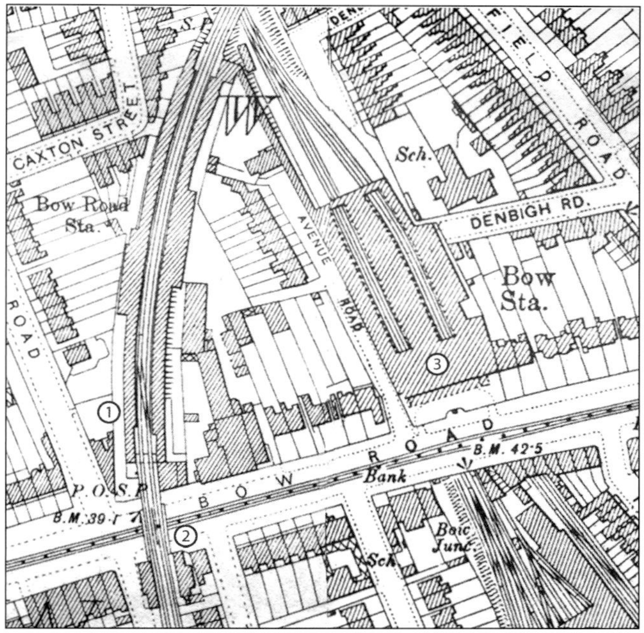

Extract from the 2nd Edition 1:2500 Ordnance Survey map of 1894, showing the new station as 'No.1' and its predecessor as 'No.2'. At the north end of the new platforms can be seen the stairs which descended into a subway beneath the tracks and led to the *'Exchange Booking Office'* on the east side of the line. From here, the interchange passageway follows the west side of the North London Railway formation and ends at a footbridge which provided access to the four platform faces at Bow NLR. This station is indicated by 'No. 3' and, as can be seen, it was much larger than its Great Eastern counterpart. The old 'staircase buildings' of 1849/76 are still in evidence at the pre-1892 station and it appears that the redundant platform extensions remained on the bridge over the main road.

introduced between there and Fenchurch Street. Work subsequently started on the project, but the Second World War intervened and progress ground to a halt.

Stairway glazing at Bow Road along with the roof of the street level building was damaged in an air raid on the night of 7th/8th September 1940, but otherwise the station fared reasonably well during the Blitz. Some nearby arches were hit on 19th/20th April 1941 however and LNER Fenchurch Street services had to be suspended. From 21st April, Bow Road station was closed and remained so until hostilities had ended.

The LNER Fenchurch Street service deteriorated seriously during the war and an interim report on the electrification scheme dated June 1944 stated that *"Seven trains are now run daily in each direction, five in the morning, and two in the evening peak hours, as compared with the normal service before the war of more than seventy trains per day in each direction."*

Nevertheless, the company intended to carry on with the work when peace returned largely because *"If this line were electrified, Fenchurch Street station would serve as an alternative terminal to Liverpool Street in the event of a mishap curtailing the electric line facilities between Bow Junction and Liverpool Street."*

For all this, a count of passengers using LNER services at Fenchurch Street and Stepney East on a weekday during October 1945, proved that the trains were under-used, so perhaps planners were beginning to have their doubts about electrifying the route.

At the time of this survey, Stepney East was the only intermediate station in use between Fenchurch Street and Stratford, but Bow Road was reopened on 9th December 1946, although possibly through lack of publicity there was clearly no demand. Ticket No 0000 for a third class journey to either Fenchurch Street or Stratford Market was sold to an enthusiast on the first day, but No 0001 remained in the rack for two more days before somebody bought it. The fact that the station closed again from 6th January 1947 probably came as no surprise, although plans were under way for its renovation and 'permanent' reopening.

An engineers drawing dated 28th March 1947 showed that repairs to the street level building roof were necessary and the passimeter ticket office needed *"refixing"*. The booking hall required a new coat of paint and the stairways leading up to the platforms had to be *"renewed"*. Up above, the waiting rooms and toilet facilities were shown as being in need of redecoration and repair. Surprisingly, it seems that the disused interchange stairs remained technically accessible until then, as the drawing stated that they were to be *"sealed off"*. Another point of interest is that the awnings were indicated in a rationalised, shortened form, although whether this was a job which needed doing, or one recently completed does not seem to have been recorded.

Bow Road made its reappearance in the public timetable which commenced on 16th June 1947, although its services were shown as being suspended. It reopened on 6th October 1947 however, but the service was far from good. On Mondays-Fridays, up trains left Bow Road at 7.17am, 7.40am and 8.44am, and there was an enormous seven and a half hour gap until the next departure at 4.14pm. Things were no better in the opposite direction with the 7.46am, service followed by the 8.15am and the 9.35am. After this there was a total lull until the evening, when down trains called at 4.51pm, 5.34pm and 6.09pm. On Saturdays, the situation was similar, although everything ceased around lunchtime. The early morning service remained the same, but additional up workings called at 11.14am and 12.29pm with trains in the opposite direction at 12.40pm and 1.02pm. With such a poor frequency, it was no wonder that potential passengers preferred to travel by trolleybus or else use Bow Road Underground station, which was just a few minutes walk away.

For all that, preparations continued on the electrification project and Bow Road LNER was equipped with smart new concrete lampposts, which although undeniably modern, displayed an affinity with the styles of the 1930s. Awnings were now restricted to short sections abovce the two London-end stairways and in front of the platform buildings. Elsewhere they had been removed and parts of the rear walls which once helped to support them were reduced in height accordingly.

The service improved slightly, but it was still extremely poor and scarcely attractive to would-be passengers. The evidence provided by surviving tickets shows that very few people were now using the station, with only ninety-four third class singles to Fenchurch Street being issued up to 7th August 1949.

By this time it had been announced that the proposed electric shuttle service between Stratford and Fenchurch Street would not now materialise and the route through Bow Road would close to passengers instead. It last appeared in the public timetable commencing 26th September 1949, but although this showed the relevant train times, Bow Road had already been deleted from the system map included at the back of the booklet.

Official closure came from Monday 7th November 1949, but as there were no Sunday trains, the end came on Saturday 5th November, when Thompson L1 2-6-4T No 67726 departed with the final 12.53pm ex Fenchurch Street. A little earlier, the last up train, the 12.12pm ex-Ilford had left behind L1 No 67727 and, according to the December 1949 edition of *Railway Observer*, it carried *"such items of the station's chattels as a chair and an immense kettle"*. The destination of the chair is not known, but the *"immense"* kettle was bound for the ticket office at Stepney East.

Electric services between Liverpool Street and Shenfield started working on a limited basis from 26th September 1949, and were fully operative from 7th November. Although it was not now to accommodate regular passenger workings, the section through Bow Road into Fenchurch Street was eventually equipped with overhead wiring and designated for use in emergencies. Electrification work on the route was completed a little over a year after the Liverpool Street - Shenfield line and was inspected by Brigadier C.A. Langley of the Ministry of Transport on 13th December 1950.

Bow Road station had lost most of its canopy roofing and valancing by 1951, although it retained short sections over both London-end stairways. The buildings continued to stand, although the up side gents was demolished around 1961 when its site was required for a 'telephone repeater station'. From photographic evidence it is known that a nearby platform nameboard was still in position in 1956 and this may have survived until the gents was removed. The next change came in 1962, when approval was received for the removal of the redundant station crossover, and this is thought to have been carried out during the following year.

Down below, the street level building remained empty for a while after closure and retained its nameboard

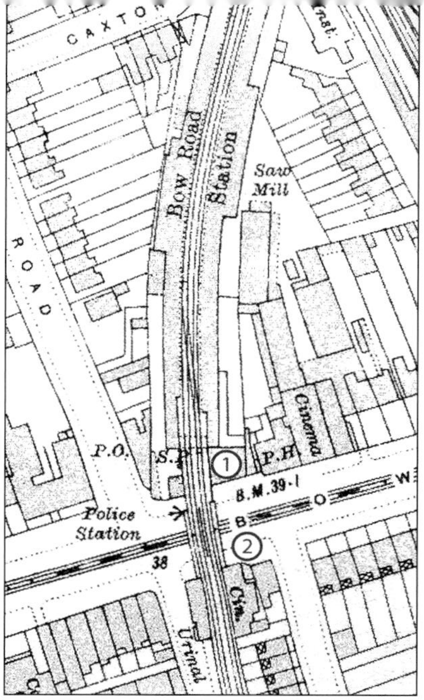

Left: Extract from the 1:2500 Ordnance Survey map of 1914, showing the 1892 station as 'No 1', and its predecessor as 'No.2'. The old buildings remain as before, although that on the up side displays the legend 'Cin.', as an abbreviation for cinema.

Above: The bridge over Bow Road seen in 1915, when about eight years old. Replacement of the earlier bridge was agreed by the GER Way & Works Committee on 16th July 1907 and the contract was let to Eastwood Swingler & Co Ltd at a cost of £989.16s.3d..

Below: Bow Road viewed from the Fenchurch Street end on 20th August 1942, during its first period of temporary closure, with its stairway glazing removed due to air raid damage. The station crossover is in the foreground.

until at least 1950. This had gone by 1952 however, although the iron bracket from which it had previously been suspended remained in position for a little longer. In 1954 it was leased to a firm of electrical engineers and remained under the same management until it was converted for use as a betting shop around 1980.

An enthusiast exploring the remains of the former North London Bow station in January 1965, discovered an LNER semi-circular enamelled lamp tablet from Bow Road lying in the undergrowth near the old interchange footway. This had presumably been removed when new lighting was being installed after the Second World War

Bow Road looking towards Fenchurch Street on 20th August 1942, showing the stairways which provided the interchange facility with Bow station, abandoned in 1917. The signal box was beneath the awning on the right but no photographs of it are known to exist.

The 1892 station, also seen in 1942, with doors and windows boarded up and the London end stairways minus their glazing. The view is taken from the site of the 1876 up side building, and includes part of what is thought to be the old street level accommodation in the foreground and the coal office roof on the right.

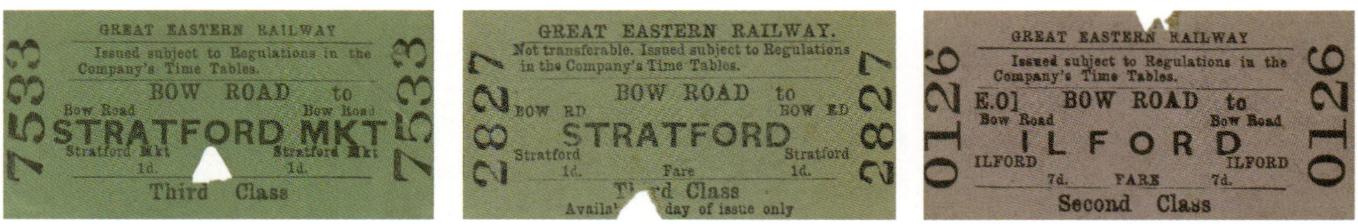

A selection of tickets. *Left:* Third class single issued from the 1876 station on 6th December 1890. *Centre:* Third class single issued at the final station on 8th April 1911. *Right:* Second class single issued from the GER/NLR Exchange Office on 15th October 1898.

and, having been discarded, ended up in the cutting below. Sadly this fascinating relic was not photographed at the time and it is not known whether it ever found its way into a collection.

Apart from the up side gents, the platform buildings remained derelict but largely intact until demolition took place during October 1967. Both of the London end stairways survived however, but the upper sections of the stairs which led to the interchange footway were demolished, as was the adjoining 'Exchange Office'. By the early 1980s, the up side stairway glazing was in a poor condition, so it was replaced by a plain flat roof. A few other changes have since taken place, but, at the time of writing, there are still some substantial remains.

Most notable of these is the former street level building, which although altered and provided with a rendered frontage, maintains some of its original features. A 'Bow Heritage Trail' plaque was fixed by

These views, taken on 10th July 1948, show the station after the awnings were rationalised and new concrete lamp standards erected in readiness for the anticipated electrification of passenger services. As mentioned in the text, the work also included lowering parts of the rear walls on both platforms and was presumably carried out during one of its periods of temporary closure. The top photograph looks north, whilst that below looks south.

Left: Class N7/2 0-6-2T No 9674 departs from Bow Road on 10th July 1948 with the 12.28pm Saturdays only train from Fenchurch Street to Ilford.

Below: Electrification work progressed during 1949, but public services were never introduced and the line linking Gas Factory Junction with Bow Junction closed to passengers instead. This view was taken a week before closure and looks towards Stratford. Although sections of awning were retained around the tops of the south end stairways, the same provision was not made with their north end counterparts as they had been out of use since 1917.

the entrance in 1990, but although it shows the correct station name it states that it dates from 1869. Both stairways are visible from Bow Road itself and a further view of these can be obtained from Addington Road, which follows the west side of the formation. From here it is also possible to see the arches, which were constructed in engineers' brick to support the platforms, but the red-brick rear walls have largely been reduced in height and topped with barbed wire to deter trespassing. The lower section of the down side interchange stairway also survives and can be seen from the open area at the north end of Addington Road. The track up above has long been singled, but both platforms remain standing. Being elevated, neither of these can be seen from street level, although the briefest of glimpses may be had from passing trains on the Liverpool Street line, just to the west of Bow Junction.

Above: N7/3 0-6-2T No 69733 pulls into Bow Road with an Ilford - Fenchurch Street train in August 1949.

Right: Having taken the train coming in, the photographer then recorded it departing, with the locomotive passing the up side stairway.

Below: A selection of LNER tickets. *Left:* Platform ticket issued on 12th March 1932. *Centre:* First ticket to Lea Bridge issued on reopening day, 9th December 1946. *Right:* Third class return issued on 5th November 1949, the last day open. It is endorsed on the rear in pencil *"Last issue. Stn closed"*.

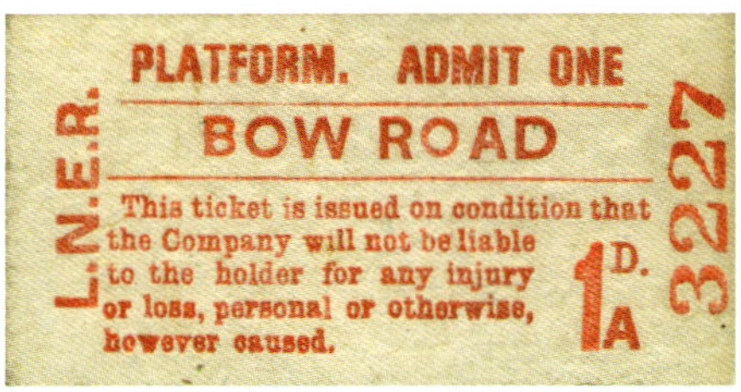

A view taken from the Railway Correspondence & Travel Society East London No.1 Railtour on 14th April 1951, as it headed back towards Stepney East from North Woolwich. By this time the awnings had already been removed, along with the platform coping, but the up side building was still intact and showed no sign of vandalism.

A photograph, thought to have been taken in the later 1950s, looking towards Fenchurch Street and showing the up side gents on the left, which was demolished around 1961 to provide a site for the 'telephone repeater station'. The stairs leading to the former booking hall were still accessible at the time and a nameboard still clung to the wall beside the toilet.

A general view of the station taken in the autumn of 1965, looking towards Stratford. The overhead wires were energised after closure and empty electric trains, nicknamed 'Sweepers', ran to and from Fenchurch Street to keep them clean.

The London end stairways were the last parts of the station to retain any canopy valancing, as the rest had been removed prior to April 1951. They also sported 'Way Out' signs and large boards advising passengers that they were not allowed to cross the line. Access to the stairs themselves had been sealed by breeze block walls by 1965, although staff could still reach the up side stairs by a doorway which was otherwise kept locked.

Above: The down side building, looking very much the worse for its years of disuse, is lit by the autumn sunshine in 1965.

Left: The same building seen from its north end in 1966.

Right: A view towards Stratford, showing the cast iron columns which once supported the awnings. The 'telephone repeater station' which replaced the up side gents around 1961 can be seen immediately beyond the wooden fronted building which is just on the right.

Below: The up side building viewed from its Stratford end in 1966, with a new section of wall on the left, erected in connection with the 'telephone repeater station'.

Above: The north end of the station seen in 1966, with the long-closed interchange stairways prominent in the foreground.

Left: The base of the interchange stairs in 1964, with the 'Exchange' ticket office right of centre. The commencement of the narrow covered footway link with Bow NLR can be seen on the left.

Right: The former station at Bow Road on 27th October 1967, with demolition well under way. When the work was completed. all that remained at track level were the platforms and London-end stairways.

Below: The 1892 street level building was leased to an electrical firm, before being converted into a betting shop in 1980. This view was taken on a day when the line between Gas Factory Junction and Bow Junction was being used as a diversionary route due to engineering works.

Victoria Park & Bow

Opened (London & Blackwall and Eastern Counties Railways): 2nd April 1849.
Closed (London & Blackwall Railway platforms): 26th September 1850.
Closed (Eastern Counties Railway platforms): 6th January 1851.

This station was located at Bow Junction and had platforms on both the London & Blackwall and Eastern Counties lines.

Details of it are very scant, but it is thought to have been accessed by means of a pathway on the east side of Fairfield Road, which led up to a building, stretching between the two formations and serving both sets of platforms.

It was intended as an interchange station between the two companies and opened with the London & Blackwall Extension Railway on 2nd April 1849. However, the relationship between the LBR and ECR was far from cordial at the time and the scheme seemed doomed to failure.

When opened, it was served by frequent trains to and from Fenchurch Street, but because the ECR workings often passed through without stopping, passengers found the interchange arrangements completely unsatisfactory.

In August 1849, just four months after opening, the LBR service was reduced to a shuttle between Stepney and Victoria Park & Bow, but this proved only temporary and through trains were reintroduced on 9th November 1849. The situation must have improved as the service was increased to run every fifteen minutes from 18th March 1850, but the ECR still failed to co-operate. The intended junction had still not been laid, and the Eastern Counties refused to issue through tickets, so the station's interchange potential remained very shaky.

The ECR eventually increased the number of its trains calling at the station, but the lack of through bookings remained a deterrent to many and during a survey in April 1850, the average daily number of passengers changing at Victoria Park & Bow was just eleven.

Back in 1846, a new line was promoted to link the docks around Blackwall with the London & North Western Railway at Camden. It was known as the East and West India Docks and Birmingham Junction Railway and was intended chiefly for goods traffic, but after construction commenced it was decided to introduce a passenger service as well. This would doubtlessly be of greater value if the trains could operate into a London terminus, but such a luxury was not included in the company's Act. Therefore, negotiations with the LBR were entered into and a junction was subsequently laid between the two lines south of Bow & Bromley station.

The EWIDBJR, which three years later was renamed the North London Railway, opened on 25th September 1850, and the LBR withdrew its service between Stepney and Bow from the same date.

The LBR platforms at Victoria Park & Bow fell into disuse and were subsequently removed, but ECR trains continued to call until January 1851.

The relations between the London & Blackwall and Eastern Counties Railways eventually improved and the planned junction finally became a reality in January 1854.

Victoria Park & Bow remained disused, but it seems that its station building and ECR platforms continued standing into the following decade. It was finally demolished however and all traces of it disappeared.

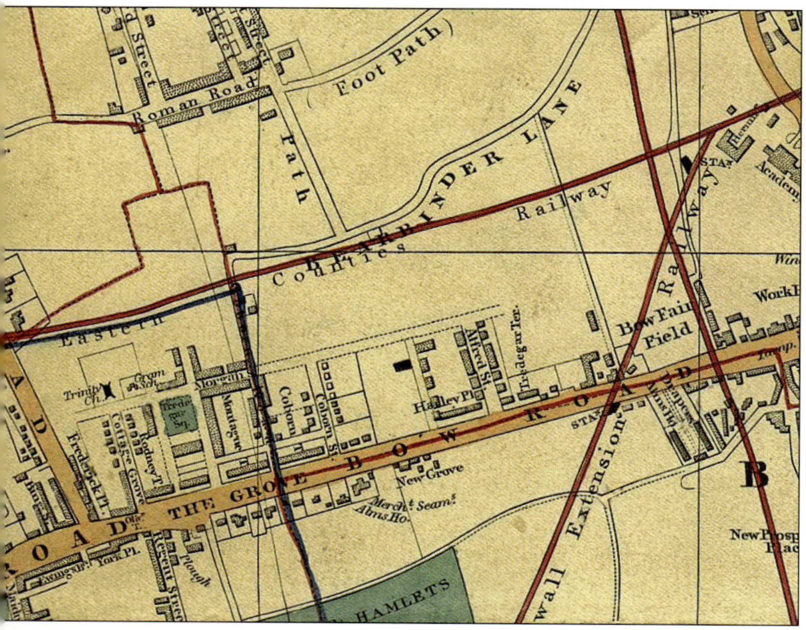

A section of Cross's map from 1850, showing the railways around Bow as maroon lines. Running from east to west is the Eastern Counties Railway, whilst coming up from the south west is the London & Blackwall Extension. Victoria Park & Bow is shown simply as "Sta" adjoining the junction between the two lines, whilst Bow & Bromley appears on the south side of Bow Road. The line running north to south is the East & West India Docks & Birmingham Junction Railway, but as no connection with the LBR is shown, the map was presumably drawn before the work had been completed.

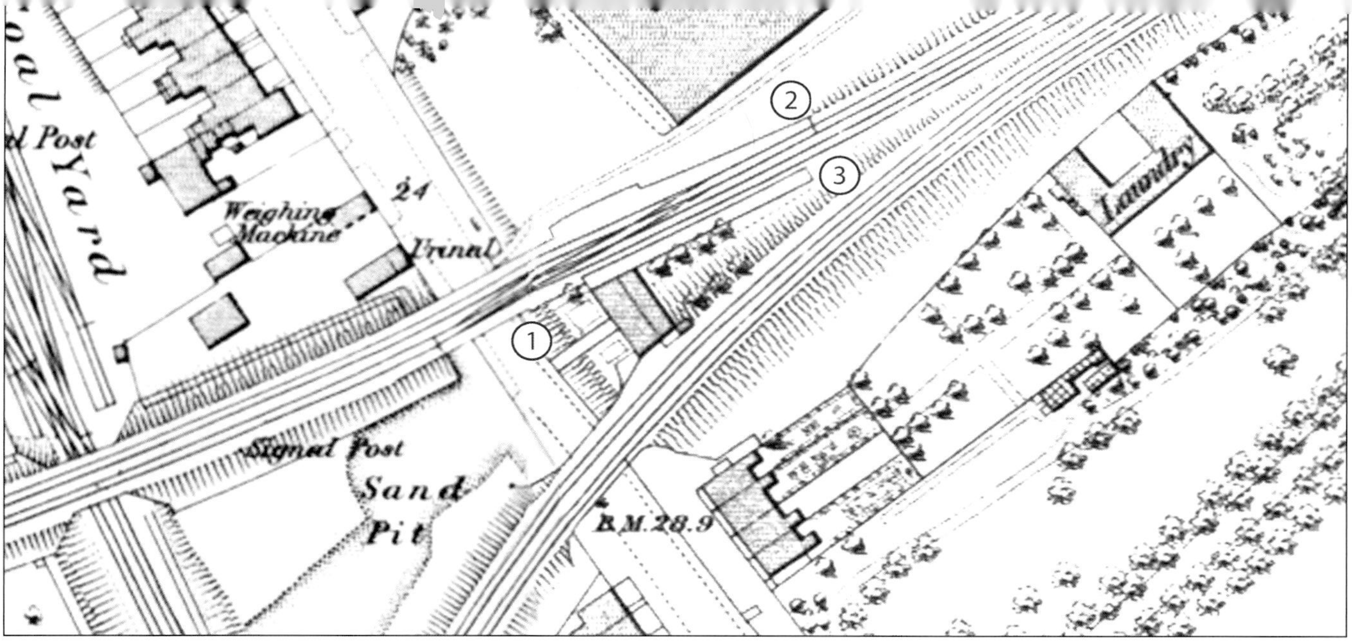

Extract from the First Edition 1:2500 Ordnance Survey map of 1867, enlarged to show details of the disused station at Victoria Park & Bow. Features of note are (1): The entrance on the east side of Fairfield Road, which led up to a building, presumably housing the booking office. (2): The ECR down platform, which had a wider section at its western end, possibly to accommodate a waiting shelter. (3): The ECR up platform which was slightly shorter. Both LBR platforms had been demolished by this time, although the site of that on the down side was still apparent, along with what appears to be a small structure.

Bow Junction looking west in GER days, showing the London & Blackwall route to Fenchurch Street diverging on the left beyond the signal box and the former Eastern Counties line towards Bishopsgate and Liverpool Street veering to the right. Victoria Park & Bow station had adjoined the junction, but had long-gone by the time this photograph was taken in 1911. The large building on the right is the match factory of Messrs Bryant & May.

Shoreditch

Opened (North London Railway): 1st November 1865.
Services suspended (London Midland & Scottish Railway): 4th October 1940.
Officially closed (London Midland & Scottish Railway): 17th November 1941.

Shoreditch was located on the NLR City Extension and opened with the line in November 1865. As built, the route comprised three running lines, with two for up trains and one for down. Shoreditch served all of these by means of a side platform and an island which were largely built on viaduct, but also stretched across above Old Street on a bridge.

The main building stood at the corner of Old Street and Kingsland Road and was one of the earliest to be constructed in the architectural style which became synonymous with the North London Railway. It featured round-arched windows and doorways and rose to a height of two storeys. The booking hall was at street level and from here stairs ascended to the platforms.

At track level, the main building accommodated a waiting room, ladies room and a station inspector's office. These were protected by a substantial awning and faced onto the easternmost up platform. Opposite this was the island, which served the down line on its east side and the other up line on its west. The island was provided with an awning of similar length to that on the other platform and had a signal box at its northern end.

Traffic on the NLR City Extension grew rapidly and it soon became apparent that an extra down line would be required. The widening took place on the western side of the formation and ultimately stretched all the way from Broad Street to Dalston Junction. The work was carried out in sections, starting from the northern end in 1872

The North London Railway station building at Shoreditch was located at the corner of Old Street and Kingsland Road and is seen here in the early twentieth century. The City Extension stations of 1865 established the architectural style which would be used by the Company into the 1880s, although detailing differed as the years progressed.

The up No 1 Lines platform at Shoreditch, looking towards Broad Street in 1966.

and was completed through Shoreditch in July 1874. The two tracks on the east side were referred to as 'The No 1 Lines', whilst those on the west became 'The No 2 Lines'. It was intended that trains using the new down track would not call at Shoreditch, so an additional platform was not deemed necessary. Both the existing platforms were subsequently lengthened however and the island was also widened by around 6ft.

The station alterations were carried out under the direction of the company engineer, Thomas Matthews and included three new wooden buildings on the island. That at the south end included ladies and first class waiting rooms, whilst that at the north housed a general waiting room. The central building accommodated a porters room and also the stairway providing access to and from street level. In addition to these there was a gents toilet beyond the southern limits of the canopy and a brick building at the opposite end. The full purpose of this is uncertain, although it contained urinals, so part of it at least must have been another gents lavatory.

The rebuilding of the island resulted in the signal box being moved about 40ft to the north, with the changeover taking place on 5th December 1875.

A further signal box was added in April 1893. This was located towards the north end of the station and adjoined the west side of the down 'No 2 Line'. The new cabin became known as 'Shoreditch No 2', whilst that built in 1875 became 'Shoreditch No 1'.

Tramway competition in the early twentieth century resulted in a decline of passenger receipts, but no significant service changes took place until 5th May 1918, when Sunday trains were withdrawn. Nine years earlier, in May 1909, the 'No 1' signal box was abolished and the other cabin became plain 'Shoreditch'.

The 'No 2 Lines' had been served by LNWR electric units since 1st October 1916 and although a few of these called in the up direction, there was no platform on the other track so down workings passed through without stopping.

A road improvement scheme undertaken by the London County Council in 1925, saw the widening of both Old Street and Kingsland Road, and because of this, the main building had to be reconstructed. Most of the original was demolished and replaced by a new three-storey structure of modern design, built largely of pale red bricks. Stonework was also employed on the frontage and the upper stone section was topped by a winged wheel emblem, then being used by the London Midland & Scottish Railway. Above this, the completion date was shown in three separate carved brick panels, which read "19 LMS 28".

Down below, passengers accessed the station by means of an entrance in the angled section at the junction of Old Street and Kingsland Road. This was protected by folding metal gates and led into the booking hall. The interior was clad in ceramic tiling, which was largely a medium buff in colour, but brown, burnt orange and black were used in detailing. Beyond the ticket office, a stairway ascended directly to the up 'No 1 Lines' platform whilst a subway branched off and led to the stairs which served the island. The original up 'No 1 Lines' stairway was retained, but its alignment had to be modified to fit in with the new layout. The subway leading to the island was lined in white glazed brick and also served an exit beneath the bridge on the north side of Old Street.

The new main building also included a parcels office and provided accommodation for two shops at street level, whilst up above, parts of the upper storeys were leased out for commercial purposes.

According to the contract for rebuilding the bridge over Old Street, it proved necessary for parts of the island platform buildings to be removed and subsequently re-erected like-for-like after the work had been completed. Presumably, this was duly carried out, although from photographs taken of the station in the 1930s, the buildings appear to have been covered in a uniform patina of grime and show no sign of having been disturbed a few years earlier. The canopy on the up 'No 1 Lines' platform was backed by a wooden screen on the bridge section and as this seems to have been altered, it is likely to have been completely renewed.

The following decade brought no further alterations of note, but the onset of war in 1939 resulted in the station's demise.

Enemy action at the beginning of the Blitz resulted in steam hauled services between Broad Street and Dalston Junction being temporarily suspended in September 1940. Trains officially ceased calling at Shoreditch from 4th October, although by that time it seems that nothing had stopped there for the best part of a month.

Despite the lack of services however, Shoreditch station remained technically open, but was officially closed from 17th November 1941.

Although the North London Line suffered badly from air raids during the Second World War, it seems that Shoreditch station received very little in the way of damage. The only incident affecting the buildings took place on 22nd August 1944, when a flying bomb landed nearby. The skylight above the up 'No 1 Line' platform stairway was damaged, along with a hoarding on the same side and the signal box glazing, but the results were not serious and there were no casualties.

Towards the end of hostilities, the decision was made to permanently withdraw passenger services over the Poplar line and although steam trains between Broad Street and destinations on the former Great Northern Railway were reintroduced in 1945, Shoreditch remained closed. There does not seem to have been any local pressure for it to be reopened, so it became permanently disused, with its folding gates at street level firmly locked.

In time, much of the building was taken over by a firm of dressmakers, but elsewhere little was changed.

The platform level structures remained intact, but some time between 1953 and 1956, the awning and rear wooden screen were removed from the up 'No 1 Lines' side.

The buildings on the island survived however, and although dirty and with a few broken windows, they appeared to be in a fairly good condition.

In April 1956, an enthusiast, who also happened to be a member of railway staff, walked the track from Broad Street in order to take photographs of features along the route. Having recorded Shoreditch, he headed for the island platform stairway to see if it was still possible to access the old entrance. He descended the dark and dusty stairs and walked through the subway into the booking hall. The gates were of course locked, but hearing sounds from behind a wall, he opened the former ticket office staff door and was amazed to find a number of ladies hard at work on their sewing machines making dresses!

A group of railway enthusiasts from a south London club made an organised visit to the station in December 1958 and again found the island platform buildings intact. Not only were they still standing, but one or more of the windows retained enamelled blue-on-white nameboards. At least two other similar signs were found, but these were smaller and may have been lamp tablets.

Apart from the loss of the up 'No 1 Lines' platform awning, the premises remained remarkably intact well into the next decade and weathered their years of closure very well.

The island platform buildings were still standing at the beginning of July 1965, but by January 1966 only that accommodating the stairway remained. The stairs themselves still led down, but were blocked off from

Above: The exterior of the main building at Shoreditch, after being reconstructed by the LMSR in the second half of the 1920s. The photograph was taken in 1968.

Above right: The interior of the old booking hall, again viewed in 1968, with the former ticket window to the right and the stairway leading to the up No 1 Lines platform on the left. Just visible near the base of the stairs is a red-on-white enamel sign advising passengers that the platform was for *"Broad Street Only"*.

the subway by what appeared to be a recently erected wall. The awning had been removed and a start had been made on demolishing the brick building at the north end, but for some reason, progress on this was halted. An actual date when the work was carried out has not been traced, although October 1965 has been suggested.

The derelict structures clung on into the early 1970s, although by this time the 'No 1 Lines' through the station had been lifted. The old buildings were now existing on borrowed time however and were removed in the second half of 1971.

Despite the demolition, both platforms continued to stand, along with the main building and the remains of a rusty lamp-post or two.

It is understood that the platform demolition was eventually carried out in January 2003, in connection with the East London Line Extension. This was opened on Tuesday 27th April 2010, when the Transport for London Overground service commenced operating to and from the rebuilt station at Dalston Junction.

The 1920s main building at Shoreditch survives and now accommodates a bar. The upper section, which once faced onto the up 'No 1 Lines' platform retains some original features and may be easily glimpsed from a passing train.

Below: There were once three wooden buildings on the island platform at Shoreditch, but these were reduced to just one in 1965. The surviving structure accommodated the stairs leading up from the passenger subway and had a porter's room at its northern end. The brick building on the right contained a gents' toilet.

Haggerston

Opened (North London Railway): 2nd September 1867.
Closed (London Midland & Scottish Railway): 6th May 1940.

Haggerston station was added to the City Extension in 1867. It was located between Shoreditch and Dalston Junction and, like Shoreditch, it comprised one side platform and an island.

Its main building stood at the corner of Lee Street and Queen Street (now Stean Street) and was designed by Thomas Matthews. It was constructed of stock brick, but also featured detailing in Portland stone. From the outside it appeared to be double storey, but the booking hall is thought to have been open from ground to ceiling. The parapet surrounding the roof included cement friezes on at least three of its four sides. That facing the platform stepped higher than the others and displayed what was presumably the company name, and *"Haggerston Station"* in two separate panels. Those on the northern and eastern elevations simply showed *"North London Railway"*, but no photographs of the southern end have been located, so it is not known if this featured a panel and, if so, what it displayed. At an unknown date, the elevation facing the platforms had the upper section of its pediment removed, thereby losing it *"North London Railway"* panel and leaving just that which showed the station's name. The lower section of the building facing onto Lee Street, projected forward and was covered by a lead or zinc covered roof.

The platforms stretched from Dunston Street in the south to Lee Street in the north. That serving the up No 1 'Line' was built on separate arches, but abutted the existing viaduct. The upper section of the main building faced onto its northern end, adjoining the stairwell which led to and from the booking hall. The island was slightly longer than the side platform, and extended northwards onto the bridge.

Both platforms were protected by equal length canopies, which stretched from Dunston Street to Lee Street. The bridge section of the island was beyond the north end of these however and therefore was not covered.

The widening of the City Extension took place later in the 1870s, although the work did not seem to result in any major changes to the platforms or buildings.

The southern ends of both station canopies were subsequently shortened and although an exact date for this has not been located, it seems to have been done after 1913.

As with Shoreditch, passenger numbers began to drop following the introduction of electric trams, but the decline was more drastic. Thomas Matthews' fine building deteriorated as the years progressed and by the 1930s, the booking clerk would place a bucket on

The remains of Haggerston station, looking towards Dalston Junction in 1969.

the floor of his office to catch raindrops which came in through a hole in the roof. With little demand for the station, Haggerston was closed as an economy measure after the onset of the Second World War and trains ceased to call from 6th May 1940.

The main building received bomb damage a few months later on 25th October, and a further raid on 17th April 1941 blasted the signal box.

From the available photographic evidence, it does not seem that the main building had been severely damaged, but this may be deceptive, as it is thought to have gone by December 1946. It seems likely that demolition at track level took place around the same time, as the 1:2500 Ordnance Survey map of 1952 shows the island platform with its eastern face partially cut back and both sides devoid of buildings.

The station remained in this condition for many years and was clearly visible from passing trains. Well into the 1960s, it was still possible to recognise the island platform stairwell, although this had been surrounded by a low brick wall and covered over for protection. Because of this it was not possible to see whether the stairs remained in position, although it seems likely that at least some of them survived at the time. Part of a large gents' toilet on the up 'No 1 Line' platform remained standing, but by 1968 the only other building to be seen was a more recent lineside hut which had been erected after the station had been largely demolished. A little to the north of this was a telephone for staff use, topped by a board which displayed the former station's name in metal lettering.

In the years that followed, the remains of the island platform were demolished, but traces of the up 'No 1 Lines' platform survived into the twenty-first century.

When the route was rehabilitated as part of the London Overground system, the broken platform surface was replaced by a waterproof covering to protect the arches underneath, which were used as business premises.

Whilst the line was in the process of being rebuilt, the engineers uncovered the island stairwell. By this time the stairs themselves had definitely gone, but apparently there was still some indication of painted plaster on the walls.

The entrance to the present booking hall is on the opposite side of Lee Street to its predecessor but the site of the old up 'No 1 Lines' platform can still be seen from the south end of the current station, opened in 2010.

Extract from the 1913 1:2500 Ordnance Survey map, showing Haggerston station at centre. North at right.

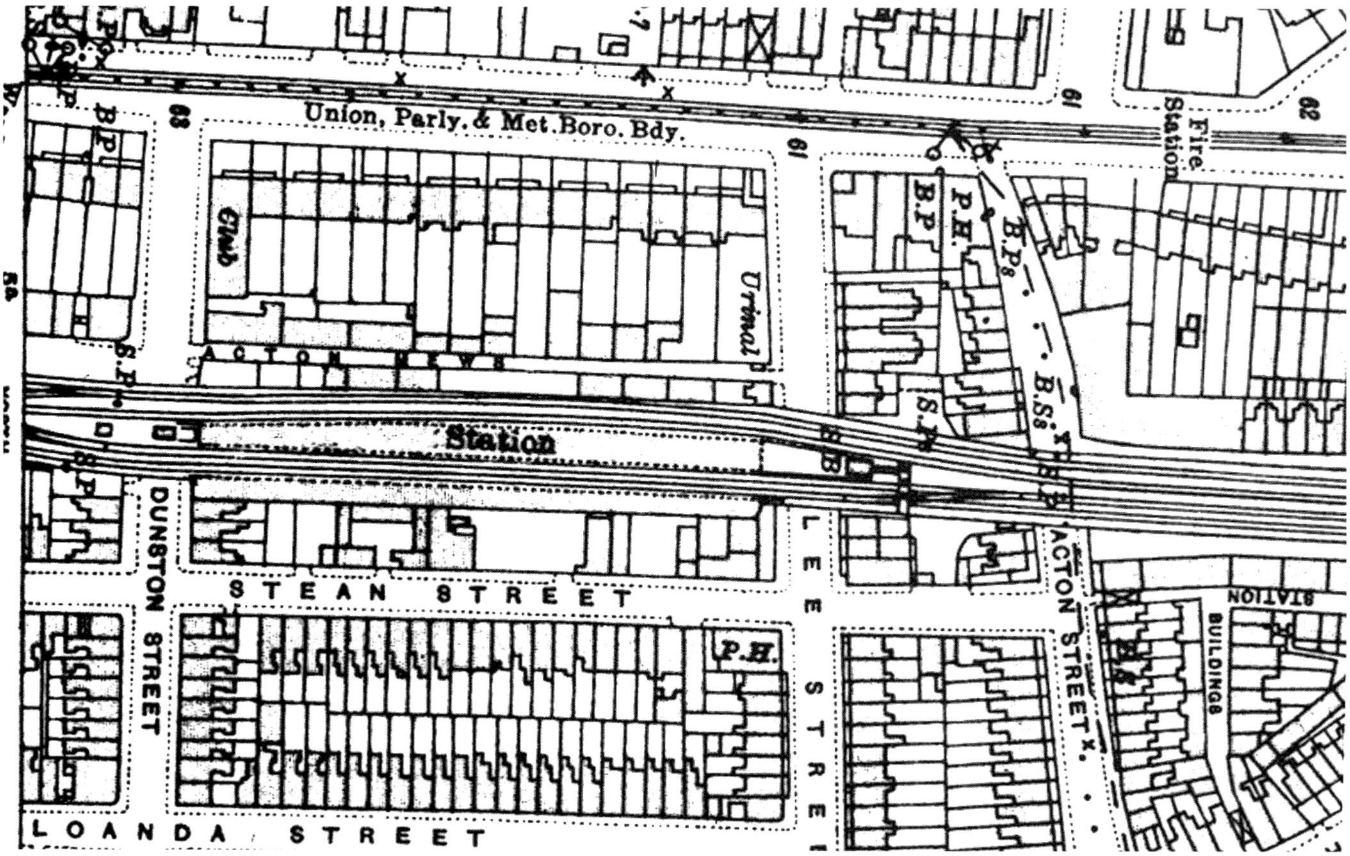

Hackney

Opened (East & West India Docks & Birmingham Junction Railway): 26th September 1850.
Resited to west (North London Railway): 1.12.1870.

A view of Mare Street taken in 1868, with part of Henry Martin's Hackney station building at centre, immediately left of the bridge. The station was resited to the opposite side of the road two years later.

Hackney was one of the original stations on the East & West India Docks & Birmingham Junction Railway and opened with the initial section of line on 26th September 1850.

The station boasted substantial buildings, designed by the engineer Henry Martin, and stood on viaduct to the east of Mare Street. It comprised two platforms, which were staggered and covered by awnings for part of their length. The booking arrangements are not known, but it is likely that the ticket hall was at street level and was connected to the west end of the platforms above by wide stairways.

The station signal box was located on the down side, close to the Mare Street bridge. Immediately beyond the opposite end of the station lay a coal yard, which opened later, on 20th October 1851.

During 1868 the NLR decided to transfer some of its coal depots to the London & North Western Railway and these included the facilities at Hackney.

The changes required moving the depot from the south to the north side of the line, but to do so it would be necessary to resite the passenger station. Other stations were being rebuilt or resited at the time, largely because of a widening scheme between Dalston and Camden Town, so Hackney was added to the list of those to be dealt with.

The replacement station was to be constructed west of the original and have its entrance on the opposite side of Mare Street. On 1st September 1869, the Permanent Way & Estates Committee agreed that the platforms should be constructed using spoil excavated as part of the Camden Town widening works.

Work on the new passenger station was carried out simultaneously with the other rebuildings and was nearing completion towards the end of 1870. Whereas earlier NLR stations were largely designed by engineers, the company decided to employ the services of architect Edwin Henry Horne for the new main buildings.

The North London Railway doubtlessly realised the value of what would now be referred to as a corporate image for its station architecture, and erected a number of distinctive buildings in an instantly recognisable style from the 1860s onwards. The engineer responsible for most of these was Thomas Matthews, who seemingly did so without the assistance of an architect. Horne's buildings were in the same basic style to those designed by Matthews, but their detailing was more ornate.

The new station opened on 1st December 1870, when its predecessor closed and was subsequently demolished.

Passenger services over the Dalston Junction - Poplar line were suspended in 1944 and Hackney, along with the other stations on the line, fell into disuse. It was later revived however, when new platforms on part of the old site were constructed and opened as Hackney Central on 12th May 1980.

The current booking office adjoins the eastbound platform, but Edwin Horne's fine 1870 building survives as a restaurant and bar.

The main building at the second Hackney station in 1967. It has since undergone various changes, but it remains as a good example of Edwin Horne's work.

Victoria Park

Opened to regular traffic (North London Railway): 14th June 1856.
Resited to east (North London Railway): 1st March 1866.
Closed (LNER platform): 1st November 1942.
Closed completely (London Midland & Scottish Railway): 8th November 1943.

On 15th August 1854, the Eastern Counties Railway opened a branch to link Stratford with the North London at a point known as Hackney Wick or Victoria Park Junction. A passenger service of NLR trains began using this two months later on 16th October and regular goods traffic commenced on 1st January 1855.

To serve the new line, certain North London Hampstead Road - Fenchurch Street passenger trains would have additional carriages coupled at the rear and these would be detached at the junction and worked forward to Stratford Bridge (later Stratford Market), calling at Stratford Low Level en route. Trains travelling in the opposite direction would have the coaches attached at the junction, but the method of working was not ideal.

In 1856, the NLR constructed a station west of the junction and named it Victoria Park, although for its first three years it appeared in timetables as Victoria Park, Hackney Wick. It stood on the north side of Wick Lane (now Wick Road) and was entered by means of a substantial brick building at street level. From here passengers ascended to the two short platforms, built on embankment and initially devoid of shelter.

The station was brought into use on 29th May 1856 to serve an event which was being held in the park to celebrate the end of the Crimean War, although it was still unfinished at the time. Work soon resumed however and it was opened to regular traffic the following month.

The practice of detaching and attaching coaches remained as before, but this continued to cause problems so it ceased at the end of 1859 and from 1st January 1860, NLR passengers for Stratford had to change at Victoria Park.

After a few years it was decided to relocate the station to the junction itself and provide it with three platform faces. Two of these would be on the NLR Poplar branch, whilst the other would serve the Stratford line.

The replacement station stood on the north side of Cadogan Terrace and set back behind a small forecourt, fronted by iron railings and gates. The main building rose to a height of three storeys and was of a fairly utilitarian design. It opened on 1st March 1866, when the original closed. The earlier offices at street level were retained and in the following month it was decided that the redundant building should be converted into a pair of cottages.

The remains of the Poplar line platforms at Victoria Park station looking towards Bow in early 1966.

At the same time, the company agreed that an additional platform should be added on the Stratford side and this was quickly put in hand.

Victoria Park now had four platform faces, with two on each line, but the passenger subway only served the original three so the fourth had to be accessed by means of a boarded crossing.

The North London had operated a local service to Stratford Bridge but this was withdrawn on 1st September 1866 and replaced by through trains linking Chalk Farm with Barking. These used the fourth platform at Victoria Park, but ceased operation two months after they started. From then on, the passenger workings over the link were operated by the Great Eastern Railway and these shuttled back and forth between Stratford Bridge and Victoria Park. As they only needed one platform for both arriving and departing, the fourth face quickly proved superfluous and became very little used.

A footbridge was added in February 1891, but this only connected the three regularly used platforms and did not span above the GER tracks. Eventually the fourth platform was officially declared redundant and by 15th August 1895 its demolition had been completed.

From 1st October 1895 the GE trains were extended beyond Stratford Market to Canning Town, where they generally terminated in a bay platform on the down side. These ran at half-hourly intervals and some subsequently continued to North Woolwich.

From 1st February 1899, the NLR provided additional access from Riseholme Street and referred to this as the Hackney Wick entrance or, as it appeared on tickets, 'Victoria Park No 2'. It was a very basic affair, built of wood and protected when not open, by a pair of wooden gates. Above it was a large gaslamp and a board stating that trains ran *"every few minutes"* to various destinations which, for some unknown reason,

The former Victoria Park station exterior in 1968.

The junction, seen in 1968, with the Stratford lines to the left and Poplar branch on the right.

The remains of Victoria Park station in 1968, looking towards the junction from the Poplar line.

completely failed to mention stations on the Poplar line. Having entered the doors, passengers climbed the stairs to a covered passageway which led to the new ticket office adjoining the Broad Street-bound line, near the west end of the platforms.

Usage of this entrance must have dropped off during the early twentieth century as its opening hours were reduced from 11th July 1920.

A few years earlier, in 1917, the GE service was reduced to hourly and it was further reduced in 1921. The Sunday trains were taken off from 7th October 1923 and passenger workings were withdrawn completely from 1st November 1942.

The station does not seem to have suffered too badly in the Second World War, although an air raid on 20th March 1941 resulted in some of its buildings being damaged.

On 14th January 1943, a meeting was held at the station to discuss its total closure. This was attended by various officials from both the LMSR and the LNER, together with the station master from Hackney, who was also responsible for Victoria Park. Various reasons for closure were given, ranging from the general dilapidated condition of the buildings through to the decline in passenger receipts. With alternative facilities being available by road, it was clearly not worth keeping Victoria Park open and all those present agreed it should close. Therefore it ceased to function from 8th November 1943 and a waiting room on the Broad Street-bound platform was handed over as a meeting place for the local Home Guard.

The station survived relatively intact into the postwar era, but the footbridge had gone by 1950 and probably the Riseholme Street entrance as well. The upper floor of the main building became a private house, but the accommodation at track level lay derelict.

The building from the original 1856 station, now known simply as 339 and 339A Wick Road, survived as a pair of dwellings for many years, but finally succumbed to demolition in 1958.

Bit by bit, the second station disappeared, until by 1965 all that remained was the main building and some mounds where the platforms used to be. Even as late as this, a tatty paper sticker on one of the waiting room windows continued to show the station's name, whilst nearby a flight of stairs descended towards the subway but ended at a wall that had been added since closure. The end came in 1970, when everything was swept away to facilitate the construction of a new road and, at the time of writing, the only surviving remnant is the base of the final signal box, which had been opened in 1961 to replace an earlier cabin and had been largely demolished in the early 1990s.

Old Ford

Opened (North London Railway): 1st July 1867.
Service suspended (London Midland & Scottish Railway): 15th May 1944.
Officially closed (London Midland & Scottish Railway): 23rd April 1945.

Such was the success of the North London Railway in the 1860s that various new stations were added to existing lines, and one of these was at Old Ford. This was sited 33 chains north of Bow, on the Poplar branch and stood to the south of Old Ford Road.

It was designed by Thomas Matthews and built by the firm of G. J. Watts.

On 29th June 1867, the NLR informed the Board of Trade that Old Ford station was ready for use, and that they intended to open it on 1st July. As it was located on an existing line, they suggested an official inspection may not be necessary, but the BoT disagreed and assigned Lieutenant Colonel Hutchinson of the Royal Engineers to carry it out. He subsequently visited Old Ford and reported to the Board of Trade that *"The arrangements at this station are of a complete character and there is no reason why it should not be opened for passenger traffic."*

The street level building was a commodious affair, and was constructed largely of yellow stock brick. Its frontage featured a central arched doorway, with three matching round-topped windows positioned symmetrically either side. These were all detailed in stone and the finished results typified NLR stations of the period. The end walls were somewhat plainer, but both included a hard cement rendered panel, with the Company name incised in large sans-serif lettering. From the booking hall, a pair of covered stairways descended to the platforms, which included the usual facilities such as waiting rooms, staff rooms and toilets.

When viewed from Old Ford Road, the building appeared to consist of a single storey, but it actually comprised two. Its western end included living accommodation for the station master, with rooms on both floors. Access was by means of stairs which were situated behind a gate to the right of the frontage

The exterior of the disused Old Ford station seen from its western end a few years before demolition. Passengers entered into the booking hall through the doorway in the centre of the frontage, then descended stairs onto the platforms. The gate at right opened onto a flight of steps which led down to a door at lower level and into the former station master's living accommodation. Until the mid-1960s, the gate carried a sign showing the name "Station House".

and these led down to the ground floor, which was at platform level. Surviving drawings only seem to show the upper storey in detail, but it is known that the ground floor included a kitchen and it is assumed that the living rooms were at the same level. A curving staircase rose from the lower living accommodation to serve a pair of bedrooms which adjoined the booking hall, but these were walled off from it and therefore could only be accessed from below.

The ticket office was at the eastern end of the building and took up much of its width. Having purchased their tickets, passengers would make their way to the barrier, which was located immediately opposite the station entrance, and then turn either left if they were travelling towards Poplar, or right if they wanted the Broad Street direction. As well as leading to and from the booking hall, the top of the Poplar-bound stairway also included a further means of street access, and although not indicated as such on an 1860s drawing, this is believed to have been used as an exit, probably at busy times. This was separated from the pavement by a pair of gates, which according to the drawing, had a combined width of 6ft.

Old Ford signal box was located in an elevated position, north of the bridge carrying Old Ford Road and remained in use until being replaced by a new cabin near the south end of the down platform in 1874.

The minutes of the NLR Permanent Way, Works and Estate Committee meeting of 4th March 1896 recorded that it was agreed to convert *"the late Station Master's residence at Old Ford into dwellings for two inspectors"*, but apart from this, no other alterations appear to have been carried out until 1st July 1900, when a new signal box was built next to its 1874 predecessor. At the same time various signalling alterations were carried out and the earlier box was demolished.

The first decade of the twentieth century saw the fortunes of the Poplar branch decline as passengers turned away in favour of other forms of transport. The competition came largely in the form of electric tramways, which began serving parts of the district from 1906 onwards. In addition, there was the new sub-surface Whitechapel & Bow Joint Railway, which opened in 1902 and provided a more direct link between Bow and central London. It was popular from the start, but became even more so after 1905, when it was electrified.

Soon after becoming part of the London Midland & Scottish Railway, it seems that the platform buildings were being under-used, as in July 1923, the North Poplar Scout Group gave its address as *"The Waiting Room, Old Ford Railway Station, E3"*. The group was newly formed at the time and remained there until 1935.

On the morning of 2nd January 1929, a station inspector, noticed *"a crack or fissure in the wall underneath the bridge on which were the booking hall and other offices."* He immediately contacted headquarters and engineers were soon on site to assess the problem. According to a *Daily News* report *"They found that the damage was serious. One of the main girders* (supporting) *the bridge had been cracked. The engineers took steps to block the line and prop up the bridge."* The temporary supports were erected on the City bound track and single line working was introduced between Victoria Park and Bow. A further report stated *"the whole of the services on the Poplar to Broad-street section were thrown out of gear. In many cases people hurrying to business found other means of making their journey"*.

The incident was subsequently reported to the LMSR Works Committee on 27th February 1929. The minutes of the meeting recorded that the crack had been discovered in one of the girders of Bridge No 235, which carried Old Ford Road and the station street level building over the line. It was also recorded that, as a result, the girder was propped up pending replacement, whilst the work *"necessitated the removal of a portion of the booking office wall"* and that a temporary booking office had to be provided.

The incident was doubtlessly responsible for a complete rear section of building above the tracks being reduced in width to alleviate weight on the supporting girders, but no details of the reconstruction work have yet come to light.

During the 1930s, Old Ford was provided with 'hawkseye' style nameboards which were employed by the LMSR on stations throughout its system, but seemingly at no other location on the Poplar branch. The design of these boards was reminiscent to that used by the Southern Railway for its 'target' lamp tablets and displayed the station name in black lettering against a golden yellow background.

As is well known, the Poplar line suffered badly from enemy action during the Second World War and train services were suspended from 15th May 1944. The station booking offices were kept open for nearly a year to issue tickets valid on 'buses, but this arrangement ceased on 23rd April 1945 and the line was officially closed to passengers.

Old Ford stayed more or less intact for the best part of two decades and even retained one of its hawkseye nameboards beneath the up side awning. The end for the platform buildings came during June 1964, when they were all demolished along with most of those at Bow.

The former stationmaster's residence was subsequently vacated and some of the street level building windows were boarded up. It continued to stand until October 1967, when it was demolished. It was a very fine example of Thomas Matthews' work and a great loss to the architectural heritage of London's railways. After this disappeared all that survived were the overgrown platform remains and the crumbling vestiges of the stairways.

The construction of a new road cut through the east end of Old Ford Road, resulting in it stopping just

The eastern end of the building in 1966, showing how it had been affected by the girder failure in 1929. On first glance the incised lettering in the name panel appears to read "N London Railway", but the legend was actually "North London Railway" with the first four letters missing.

short of the former station site. From here, it petered out into a footbridge, which took pedestrians over both the old line and the new road. It is understood that the points at Victoria Park Junction were removed on 5th May 1984 and the trackwork between there and Poplar was subsequently removed. The section south of Bow was later restored as part of the Docklands Light Railway, but the stretch through Old Ford remained derelict.

Standing on the Old Ford Road footbridge, looking south, it is now impossible to imagine that at one time a thriving railway passed underneath.

The remains of the City-bound (towards Dalston Junction) platform in early 1966, with the 1900 signal box prominent in the foreground. The rear of the street level building can be seen in the distance, with the section above the tracks reduced in width following the changes of 1929.

Bow

Opened (East & West India Docks & Birmingham Junction Railway): 26th September 1850.
Service suspended (London Midland & Scottish Railway): 15th May 1944.
Officially closed (London Midland & Scottish Railway): 23rd April 1945.

Bow was one of the original stations on the East & West India Docks & Birmingham Junction Railway and opened with the initial section of line on 26th September 1850. It originally comprised two platforms and was entered by way of a street level building above the tracks on the north side of Bow Road, adjoining the corner of Avenue Road (now Kitcat Terrace).

In the mid 1860s, it was proposed to build a curve linking Bow on the North London with the London Tilbury & Southend Railway at Bromley. A Bill was presented to Parliament and the Act allowing the work to take place was passed on 17th June 1867.

It was logical to site the new junction south of the station, but this would have resulted in part of the NLR Bow Works complex being demolished. Therefore the decision was made to place it to the north and rebuild the station so it could serve four tracks. It was clearly going to be a major project and the architect Edwin Henry Horne was appointed to design the new main building. This was to be a very impressive affair and turned out to be one of Mr Horne's finest achievements.

The double-track connecting curve, which lay on the east side of the station, was opened for excursion traffic on 17th May 1869 and for regular services the following day.

The station facilities remained incomplete at that time however, and passengers had to access the platforms by way of a temporary entrance in Avenue Road. Work continued to progress and the new building was opened for public use on 26th March 1870. It included a booking hall and refreshment room at street level, together with a couple of railway offices. Above these rose a further floor which accommodated the Bow & Bromley Institute. This was used for lectures and also as a place of entertainment. *Herapath's Journal* clearly approved and the edition of 2nd April 1870 referred to the Institute as *"a handsome hall reaching the whole length and breadth of the station, 100 feet in length, 40 feet in width, and 45 feet in height. It* (was) *illuminated by two brilliant sun burners in the pointed roof, which* (was) *supported by ornamental iron girders and supports."*

Passengers entering the station did so by means of a double doorway in the centre of the frontage, then continued to the booking hall which was located on the left. Having purchased their tickets, they would pass through another pair of doors at the rear of the building and access a gallery, which in turn led to the stairways. Down below there were two side platforms and a central island. The two faces on the west side of the formation were used by Broad Street, Poplar and Fenchurch Street services whilst the pair on the east side accommodated trains operating to and from stations on the LTSR.

Local services over the curve originally operated between Chalk Farm and Plaistow. The western end of the route was subsequently amended a couple of times, but from February 1879 it permanently became a shuttle linking Plaistow with Bow. In connection with these workings, a run-round siding for locomotives was provided to the north of the station, along with watering facilities. At times, longer distance trains also operated by way of the connection, serving destinations on the LTSR including Southend and Tilbury.

In October 1872, the 'Match Tax Testimonial Fountain' was erected on the station forecourt. This was dedicated to the local firm of Bryant & May who were instrumental in defeating a tax on matches which had been proposed by Robert Lowe, the Chancellor of the Exchequer. It was designed in the gothic style by Rowland Plumbe who seems to have been a friend, or at least acquaintance of Edwin Horne as, in 1875, he proposed that the station's designer should be admitted to the Royal Institute of British Architects.

Apart from this, Bow station remained largely unaltered after rebuilding, until a footbridge was erected towards its northern end in 1892 to serve a newly created interchange with the Great Eastern Railway. Since 1869 the GER had operated a service between Bow NLR and Fenchurch Street by way of the original 1850 link at Gas Factory Junction, but with rising costs they decided to resite their existing Bow Road station and connect it with the North London by way of a covered footway. The replacement Great Eastern station opened on 4th April 1892 (see page 140) and the unremunerative Bow - Fenchurch Street shuttle service was withdrawn from the same date. As mentioned in the chapter on Bow Road GER, the interchange facility included an additional booking office which issued both companies' tickets, with those for the NLR showing the station of origin as 'Bow No 2'.

In December 1906 it was decided to convert the station master's house into residential accommodation for two inspectors and their families. The building faced onto the Broad Street-bound Poplar line platform and was entered from Avenue Road.

Further economies came as a result of the First World War, with the Bow–Plaistow shuttle service being withdrawn from 1st January 1916 and the footway connection with Bow Road GER closing the following

The frontage of Bow station taken from a coloured postcard of the early twentieth century, with part of the Match Tax Testimonial Fountain just visible on the extreme right. The Bow & Bromley Institute is prominent at upper floor level, with its exit doors located within the porch. A similar porch at the eastern end served as the Institute's entrance, but this is not visible here. The dome-like section just below roof level towards the left accommodated the Institute's organ, which dated from 1874 and was played during recitals in the hall.

year. The interchange facility never reopened, but through passenger trains returned to the Bow - Bromley spur between 1923 and 1935 to alleviate overcrowding at Fenchurch Street. Apart from these, the line was used by goods traffic and the occasional excursion.

The railway historian H.V. Borley once worked as a booking clerk at Bow and in a letter to the author dated 4th September 1981, he remembered the passengers who travelled on the through excursions: *"...the people were always poor but honest, even when hungry and the larder was empty. They would save for months to take the children to Southend, usually on a Sunday, and pay for the tickets in "small silver", always correct. Returning in the evening, joyful and a little noisy, but no damage was ever done to the carriages."*

The Second World War resulted in a great deal of air raid damage to the line between Dalston Junction and Poplar and passenger services were often severely interrupted as a result. There were a number of incidents reported in the vicinity of Bow, but the only one which directly affected the station occurred around 2am on 20th March 1941, when the premises were reported as being on fire. Poplar branch services were suspended from 15th May 1944, although official closure did not come until 23rd April 1945. During this period the booking office continued to handle parcels traffic and, along with some of the other stations affected, remained open to issue tickets valid on buses.

In March 1948 a reporter from the *News Chronicle* visited Bow and reported: *"Its clock has stopped at 9.26. The nameboards have been taken down, and the windows of its waiting rooms are grimy and broken. Even the Tyburn Sports Club which once made a waiting room its headquarters have gone... Bow Road* (sic) *Station formerly housed the Salvation Army but they left 13 years ago. Now a credit tailor has his office there, and another part is occupied by Bow Palais-de-Dance."*

The old Bow Institute led a rather chequered career, having become a branch of the East London Technical College in 1897. It closed in 1911 and was subsequently used by the Salvation Army and as the Embassy Billiard Hall. It later became 'The Bow Palais' and ended its days as the 'Emerald Ballroom'. A fire broke out on 15th October 1956 and the damage was serious enough for the upper storey and roof to be demolished. Edwin Horne's once magnificent building now presented a very sorry sight, having already lost the Match Tax Testimonial Fountain three years earlier.

The Bow - Bromley curve was the next to go, as it closed to all traffic from 13th September 1959 and was subsequently lifted

The platforms and associated buildings at Bow were largely removed during the summer of 1964, leaving just the former station master's house and the interchange footway still standing.

The main building, long-since shorn of its upper section, survived however and part of it continued in use as a parcels office until 1965. Around the back, the glazed wooden gallery, lay boarded up and derelict, but this was removed around the late 1960s, leaving just

Above: The remains of the station frontage at Bow in 1967, a little over a decade after the upper section had been removed following fire damage. The white-on-maroon nameboard on the wall fronting the old forecourt was for the parcels office which continued to function in the building until 1965.

Above right: A special train organised by the Railway Correspondence & Travel Society pauses at Bow on 21st October 1967 as the crew change ends before continuing into Fenchurch Street. The building to the left once had waiting rooms and toilets at platform level and living accommodation for the station master above.

the shell of the main building, which finally went in November 1975. At the same time, the former station master's house was also demolished, thereby leaving just the old footway and some meagre platform remains.

After lying derelict for a few years, the trackbed through the station was adapted to serve the Docklands Light Railway, where it climbs up from the old NLR formation to run alongside the Great Eastern main line en-route to Stratford.

At the time of writing, all that is left standing is a truncated porch column at street level, along with sections of wall which once supported the main building and a length of interchange footway. The railway side of these can be viewed from passing DLR trains, but otherwise the remains, albeit obscure, are best viewed from Bow Road or Kitcat Terrace. The exterior of the former footway, long since devoid of its roof, has two doorways, which are thought to be original and may have been used as staff access. Apart from these insignificant reminders however, the splendid station which doubtlessly helped Edwin Horne to join the prestigious Royal Institute of British Architects has vanished without trace.

The present DLR Bow Church station stands to the south of its predecessor, on the opposite side of the main road.

A 1966 view of the station, taken from the old London & Blackwall Extension Railway route, with the covered footway connection to Bow Road GER on the right. Its far end once led onto a footbridge connecting all platforms, but this disappeared a number of years earlier. The route of the lifted connection to Bromley (now Bromley-by-Bow) on the former LTSR line is clearly discernible on the left, whilst to its right are the tracks of the Poplar branch. In the middle distance is the rear of the street level building with its wooden gallery which once provided access to the stairways serving the platforms. Just in front of the gallery, to its right, is the building which had housed the station master.

South Bromley

Opened (North London Railway): 1st September 1884.
Service suspended (London Midland & Scottish Railway): 15th May 1944.
Officially closed (London Midland & Scottish Railway): 23rd April 1945.

South Bromley was located between Bow and Poplar East India Road stations and was opened by the North London Railway on 1st September 1884.

Being a later addition it had to be built on a restricted site, so consisted of a single island platform. Access was initially only available from the east side of the line, where two flights of stairs led from Railway Street to a brick booking hall building constructed above the Poplar-bound track. A further entrance was added at the tail end of 1890, when a stairway and footbridge was constructed to the west of the formation, with access from the east end of Rifle Street. This was tucked away alongside the premises of the Far Famed Cake Company and was described by the late Michael Robbins as *"the most inconspicuous station entrance in London"*. The railway historian H.V. Borley, who had worked on the NLR and knew the route well, referred to it simply as *"a hole in the wall"*.

The elevated booking office building was constructed in a recognisably 'North London' style, but lacked the architectural detailing of earlier stations. The full width of its south end was taken up by the ticket office, which had a panelled wooden screen, glazed at the top, and a pair of issuing windows.

From the north side of the booking hall, a stairway descended to the platform, where it ended in a wooden lobby section, glazed on either side by two pairs of windows. On the western side of this lobby stood the ticket collector's box, which had a window facing north and a built-in table or cupboard beneath. Beyond this were two further wooden buildings and all three were covered by a continuous awning, supported on cast iron columns.

The signal box comprised a wooden upper section on a brick base and was located between the tracks to the north of the platform.

In 1906 the London County Council erected a public footbridge over the formation, which linked Fawe Street with Clutton Street. This crossed above the station, north of the platform buildings, but was purely for pedestrian use and never provided a means of access.

In 1913 a fire broke out in the porters room which was located under the stairs leading to and from the booking hall. At the time it was rumoured to have been started by Suffragettes, but on investigation it seemed more likely to have been the result of a carelessly discarded match or cigarette. The fire gutted the porters' room and also damaged the stairway and a nearby stretch of awning.

The northernmost of the two stairways serving Railway Street seems to have fallen into disuse by the 1930s and became due for demolition. This did not take place however and it remained standing for the rest of the station's existence.

South Bromley closed along with the other Poplar branch stations when services were suspended in 1944, but by this time it was seemingly in a sorry state. The surrounding area suffered dreadfully from the effects of enemy action during the Second World War, although searches through the National Archive files at Kew have not revealed any mention of the station ever being the subject of a direct or nearby hit. However, in a 1980 letter to the author, H.V. Borley stated that the booking office along with its adjoining bridge was badly damaged in an air raid and declared unfit for use. This resulted in intending passengers having to be led across the track by a flagman to a *"waiting room"* which had

South Bromley station in May 1946. The booking office building can be seen above the island platform, with the bridge providing access from Rifle Street to its left and the Railway Street stairs to its right. The northern staircase seems to have lost its roofing, but was otherwise standing, as were the platform buildings. The former booking office seems to have lost its windows, although it's difficult to say from the photograph. Its roof appears to have been intact though, so the air raid damage referred to by H V Borley may not have been as serious as described. The Fawe Street public footbridge is seen to the right of the view, with the signal box just beyond the platform end.

been fitted out for the issue of tickets. This description however does not tally with some early postwar aerial photographs which seem to show that the station had sustained very little damage.

Nevertheless, no time was wasted in demolishing the buildings after closure, as a photograph taken in July 1948 shows just a bare empty platform, the lower section of the booking hall and the footbridge link with Rifle Street. An actual date of demolition has not been traced, but a typed note in a file now held at the Tower Hamlets Local Studies Library, Bancroft Road, states that the war damaged remains of Poplar station were demolished in March 1947. Given that Poplar was the next station along the line and that South Bromley had lost its buildings by the summer of 1948 it seems likely that they both went around the same time.

The signal box closed on 25th September 1954 and was subsequently removed, as was the lower section of booking hall and the Rifle Street footbridge. The derelict platform lingered on however, becoming more overgrown with the passage of time, until it was finally swept away when the trackbed was being prepared for reopening as part of the Docklands Light Railway. Today, only the much-rebuilt pedestrian council footbridge of 1906 remains to provide an indication of where South Bromley once stood, whilst a little closer to Poplar, the DLR station at Langdon Park now serves the same area as its predecessor.

Left: A view taken from the Fawe Street public footbridge in the summer of 1969, with the north end of the former South Bromley station platform on the left and the Spratt's factory behind. The remains of the lamp in the right foreground belonged to the bridge and probably dated from its erection in 1906.

Below: A later view of the station remains, looking towards Bow, with the Fawe Street footbridge to the right. The rendered areas with incised lettering on the left promoted The Far Famed Cake Company who owned the factory. The cable run stretching the length of the platform was added in the 1950s, but subsequently fell into disuse.

Poplar East India Road

Opened (North London Railway): 1st August 1866.
Service suspended (London Midland & Scottish Railway): 15th May 1944.
Officially closed (London Midland & Scottish Railway): 23rd April 1945.

The exterior of Poplar East India Road station during pre-grouping days. In the LMSR period, the frontage was partially obscured by advertisement hoardings, which completely covered the two windows either side of the doorways and also blocked the lower part of the window in the centre. The entrance to the Docklands Light Railway station at All Saint's Chrisp Street Market now occupies part of the site.

When the East & West India Docks & Birmingham Junction Railway extended its tracks south of Bow Junction, they constructed a station in Poplar High Street, but it never opened.

In 1865 however, the NLR had a change of heart and decided to introduce passenger traffic over this stretch of line. The replacement station was to be located on a new site, a little to the north of the original and Thomas Matthews was requested to prepare the necessary plans.

These were soon accepted and work commenced. The station was completed by the summer of the following year and opened on 1st August 1866.

The main building stood on the south side of East India Dock Road and was designed in a similar, but less flamboyant style to the those on the City Extension which had opened in the previous November.

It was largely built of London stock brick, but also included a small amount of Portland stone detailing. It bore a strong similarity to the slightly later building at Old Ford, but had two doorways instead of one and the window layout was different. Above the entrance were two incised panels with that at the top reading "North London Railway" and the one below "Poplar Station". These may have been fabricated from Portland stone, but were more likely to have been of hard cement render.

On entering the station, passengers found themselves in the ticket hall, with a parcels office on the right and booking office to the left. Having purchased their tickets, they would make their way towards the Broad Street-bound platform and descend the stairs on the right. Just beyond the foot of the stairs lay the platform building, which housed various facilities, including a station master's office and a ladies' toilet. At the south end of this platform stood East India Road Junction signal box, whilst behind it lay two sidings, used for stabling stock. Beneath the stairs was a gentlemen's toilet with six stalls and two water closets. To the right of this, beneath the street level parcels office was a room for the station inspector, but the rest of the 'ground floor' is thought to have been taken up by residential accommodation for the station master and his family.

The other platform was used by services arriving from Broad Street and, as passengers were expected to be alighting from incoming trains, the only facility included was a gentlemen's toilet. This was of a similar size to that already described, but was clear of the stairs and backed onto the brick retaining wall. Both stairways were covered and the platforms were protected for part of their length by awnings.

The North London station was always known

officially as "Poplar, East India Road', but whether this was to avoid confusion with Poplar on the LBR, or the unopened 1851 High Street premises is not known.

It had long been the intention of the NLR to extend its passenger services to Blackwall and this finally happened on 1st September 1870, after the connection between the two lines at Poplar had been re-modelled to allow through running.

The station was provided with two signal boxes. East India Road has already been mentioned, but there was also High Street Junction to the south. In time however it was decided to replace these by a single cabin called Poplar Central and this was brought into use on 9th September 1888, when the earlier pair were closed.

Two years later, it was decided to withdraw the passenger service between Poplar, East India Road, and Blackwall, and the short spur linking the two lines was closed from 1st July 1890. The points at the eastern end were removed and the former curve was converted into a carriage siding, reached from the NLR end.

Despite these changes, Poplar East India Road itself remained little altered throughout its life, although the former station master's residential accommodation was converted into dwellings for two station inspectors in August 1901.

Three years later, the East India Dock Road bridge was reconstructed in connection with tramway electrification, but this did not affect the station building which faced its southern side. However, the trams themselves certainly wooed away many potential passengers and patronage began to decline.

Poplar suffered dreadfully from the onset of the Blitz in September 1940 and much of the local railway infrastructure was subsequently left in ruins. Poplar, East India Road station was first hit on 20th March 1941, when the buildings and tracks were damaged, then the platforms and signal box met a similar fate nearly two months later on 10th and 11th May. Further devastation came on 29th January 1944, when a high explosive bomb struck the station and also damaged a couple of local signal boxes.

No photographs have been located of the damage, but the station must have been reduced to a total mess. By January 1944, the street level facilities were all out of use, although the building was still available as a means of accessing the two stairways. Passengers requiring

The north end of Poplar East India Road in 1969. The street level section of the main building had been demolished in 1947, but the lower part, which once included an inspector's office and residential occupation for the station master can be seen to the left.

Left: The remains of the station frontage in 1970, with the window ledges visible below the advertisement hoardings. The gateway used by railwaymen to reach Poplar Central signal box is on the left.

tickets now had to buy them from a makeshift booking office on the Broad Street-bound platform, which had been adapted from one of the existing rooms.

With such devastating damage, it's not surprising that the LMSR took the decision to suspend the passenger services and this took place from 15th May 1944. The final death blow for the station came at around 1am on 16th June, when a high explosive bomb struck the rear of the building, causing masonry to crash onto the track and blocking all lines. Any hope that Poplar East India Road would ever reopen must have quickly evaporated and it was only a matter of time before the ruin would be swept away.

Official closure came from 23rd April 1945 and the handful of staff still employed to deal with parcels and issue tickets were transferred elsewhere. Although it is known that some of the station buildings on the line indeed continued to be staffed until then, it seems unlikely that anybody remained at Poplar as it was so badly damaged.

The upper section of the main building was demolished in March 1947, although the lower part of this remained standing. The stairway at the north end of the old Blackwall-bound platform was retained and tidied up to provide staff access from East India Dock Road to the signal box at Poplar Central. The southern end of the platforms were stripped of their coping, but otherwise were left untouched.

The surviving stairway was subsequently removed and replaced by a less-substantial wooden affair. The date of this alteration is not known, but it was probably in the later 1950s. Access to the stairs was by means of a gate at the eastern end of the old street level building, of which, the lower section of frontage had been retained as a boundary wall alongside the pavement. Part of this was used to support advertisement hoardings, but the 6 or 7 feet which remained visible below, still exhibited the stone windowsills, whilst newer brickwork indicated where the entrance doors had been.

From then on little changed, although by the mid-1960s the surviving coping had been removed and the platform surfaces had deteriorated, resulting in the spread of weeds.

Poplar Central box remained open, but not for much longer as it was officially closed on 22nd November 1970, when its points were converted to hand operation. Whether the box indeed survived until this date is uncertain however, as a visitor to the station in December 1969 recorded that it had already been demolished!

The platforms continued to linger however, becoming more and more overgrown with the passage of time. The goods traffic, which had once been so important to the line dwindled as a result of road competition, but the trains still ran, albeit less frequently and with fewer wagons. Eventually in 1984, the line between Victoria Park and Poplar fell into complete disuse.

This was not the end however, because the route between Bow and Poplar was subsequently incorporated into the Docklands Light Railway, which opened to the public on Monday 31st August 1987. The scheme included the construction of a new station on the site of Poplar East India Road and this was given the name All Saints, Chrisp Street Market.

Thomas Matthews' station of 1866 retained a presence of sorts however, as a fragment of its frontage survived alongside the DLR entrance for a time after opening, but this has now gone.

The Docklands Light Railway has of course been a great success story and its trains are well patronised. It has brought new life to part of a route which seemed to be a long time dying and one where revival once seemed impossible.